ORDER
FOR THE
EUCHARIST
AND FOR
MORNING AND EVENING PRAYER
ACCORDING TO THE
ANGLICAN AND ROMAN RITES
2008

With seasonal notes,
information about recent
changes, and guidance from
the Orthodox tradition.

ORDO MISSAE CELEBRANDAE
ET DIVINI OFFICII PERSOLVENDI
PRO ANNO LITURGICO
2007–2008

☐ Roman provisions are given and are clearly distinguished ☐

☐ where they do not coincide with Anglican usage. ☐

ISBN 978–1–85311–796–1

ACKNOWLEDGMENTS

The *Revised Common Lectionary* is © the Consultation on Common Texts, 1992 and is reproduced with permission. *The Christian Year: Calendar, Lectionary and Collects* (1997), which includes the Church of England's adapted form of the Revised Common Lectionary (published as the Principal Service Lectionary), the Second and Third Service Lectionaries and the *Common Worship* Calendar, and the Weekday Lectionary are © The Archbishops' Council 2002.

The Calendar and Lectionaries in *The Alternative Service Book 1980* are © The Archbishops' Council 1999; the Daily Eucharistic Lectionary derives, with adaptions, from the *Ordo Lectionum Missae* of the Roman Catholic Church.

The Lectionary authorised by the Convocations in 1961 and the Lectionaries from *Lent, Holy Week and Easter* (1986) and *The Promise of His Glory* are copyright © The Archbishops' Council 1999.

Material from these Lectionaries and Calendars is reproduced with permission.

Typeset by Rowland Phototypesetting Ltd, Bury St Edmunds, Suffolk
Printed in Great Britain by William Clowes Ltd, Beccles, Suffolk

PRAENOTANDA

● PLEASE WRITE TO THE COMPILER with comments, questions, suggestions. He may to be able to supply new propers and other materials mentioned on various pages of the ORDO: but PLEASE say what you need and don't just say 'send everything'. Because of the exigencies resulting from early retirement he must insist on a stamped and addressed envelope and IN ADDITION *at least* one loose FIRST CLASS STAMP. Clergy who desire several items and who have discretionary funds . . .

Fr John Hunwicke SSC
Lewdown Rectory
Devon EX20 4DN

● 2008 is a remarkable year in that **Easter** comes earlier than it has since 1913. It will not again come so early during this century. This has a spin-off in terms of the relationship between Christian Holy Days and secular holidays. It has also caught poor old *Common Worship* (CW) on the hop; its weekday lectionary contains no provision for the week after Trinity 23, so that what your *Ordo* and other calendars provide is – horror of horrors – not synodically authorised.

● It also means that (CW) the **Annunciation** and **S Joseph** queue up to be observed after Low Sunday. Rome (CDW) spotted this and decided that S Joseph be transferred to the Saturday before Palm Sunday, leaving just Lady Day for the Monday after Low Sunday. You will have to decide which of these august authorities to follow.

● BCP, following the Tridentine rule, provides for the missing Sunday masses in November, as follows:

The Sunday falling on	is numbered	but we use the proper called
November 9	Trinity 25	Epiphany 5
November 16	Trinity 26	Epiphany 6
November 23 (Christ the King)	Trinity 27 (Next before Advent)	Trinity 25

● CW has another problem this year. That is because of its dotty, blinkered and novel determination to create an '**Epiphany season**' *exactly* modeled on Eastertide, with Sundays '*of* Epiphany' rather than '*after* Epiphany'. This means that when January 6 is a Sunday, that day is both 'Epiphany' and the 'First Sunday of Epiphany', with the result that displacement of subsequent lectionary provision would leave the C of E out of sync' with both the Roman lectionary and the International Common Lectionary. When this was eventually noticed, complex amending legislation had to be passed and you will find a simple explanation of the exotic results on the appropriate page in the *Ordo* (page 7).

● Reverend and Right Reverend users will be aware that the *English* Roman Catholic Church has secured permission from Rome to transfer the **Ascension** and **Corpus Christi** to the following Sundays. This is *not* a universal change and does *not* affect the whole Western Church or the *editiones typicae* of its liturgical books; and your Compiler questions whether a provision granted specifically to the *Westminster* hierarchy needs to be regarded as normative in the provinces of Canterbury and York. Willingness to allow an obligation of public worship to be driven, by the encroachment of secularism, out of weekdays, seems to him to run contrary to the admirable ideology of the Instruction *Liturgiam authenticam*, in which Rome robustly urged that our Christian liturgical culture should engage vigorously and aggressively with the circumambient culture, rather than timidly retreating. But your *Ordo* now provides for both options.

● See the Introduction, paragraph 25, for a minor change with regard to **Ember Days**.

S JOSEPH, HUSBAND OF THE BVM (transferred)

	1 EP of foll		Isa 11:1–10	◁
		Ps: 25, 147:1–12	Mt 13:54–58	◁
W	MP	Ps: 20, 122	Exod 5:1 – 6:1	◁
			I Cor 14:1–19	◁
	Mass	*Gl; Cr; R: Proper Pref; CW, of a Saint*		
		CW: II Sam 7:4–16; Ps 89:27–36; Rom 4:13–18; Mt 1:18–25		
		R: II Sam 7:4–5a & 12–14a & 16; Ps 89; Rom 4:13 & 16–18 & 22;		
		Mt 1:16 & 18–21 & 24a or Lk 2:41–51a		
	2 EP		Gen 50:22–26	◁
		Ps: 1, 112	Mt 2:13–23	◁

If S Joseph is kept (Rome) on the Saturday before Psalm Sunday, he has 1 EP, MP, Mass, but not 2 EP. If (CW) he is kept on the Tuesday after Low Sunday, he has MP, Mass, EP, but no 1 EP.

THE FESTUM OF A SAINT ON SUNDAY

may not be observed even on a 'Green' Sunday according to the Roman Rite, unless, being of a patron, it becomes a Solemnity. Festa of Saints on 'Green' Sundays are suppressed by Rome; CW allows them EITHER to displace a 'Green' Sunday OR to be transferred to Monday OR 'at the discretion of the minister, to the next suitable weekday.' This year, two festivals are affected: August 24 and September 21. We give here their propers for insertion according to local decision.

S Bartholomew, Apostle

R	MP	Ps: 86, 117	Gen 28:10–17	Deut 18:15–19
			Jn 1:43–51	Mt 10:1–15
	Mass	*Gl; R: Pref of Apostles; CW, of Saints*		
		CW: (Isa 43:8–13); Ps 145:1–7; Acts 5:12–16 (I Cor 4:9–15); Lk 22:24–30		
		R: Rev 21:9–14; Jn 1:45–51		
	EP		Ecclus 39:1–10 or Deut 18:15–19	Isa 49:1–13
		Ps: 91, 116	Mt 10:1–22	Mt 10:16–22

S Matthew, Apostle

R	MP	Ps: 49, 117	I Kgs 19:15–21	Prov 3:1–17
			II Tim 3:14–17	Mt 19:16–end
	Mass	*Gl; R: Pref of Apostles; CW, of Saints CRP*		
		CW: Prov 3:13–18; Ps 119:65–72; II Cor 4:1–6; Mt 9:9–13		
		R: Eph 4:1–7 & 11–13; Ps 19; Mt 9:9–13		
	EP		Eccles 5:4–12	I Chron 29:9–18
		Ps: 119:33–40 & 89–96	Mt 19:16–30	I Tim 6:6–19

HOW TO USE THIS ORDO

FOR EXAMPLE

The Liturgical Colour			Matins and Evensong readings CW			Matins and Evensong readings (1922/1961) for use with BCP	
↓			↓	↓	↓	↓	↓ ↓
MONDAY			Feria (☐ S Jane Frances de Chantal, Rel)				
12 P (or W)		MP	Ps: 99, 100 (or 95), 101	Isa 44:24–end I Thess 4:13 – 5:11		Isa 17 Mk 4:21–end	
		Mass	*of Advent 2; no Gl or Cr; Pref of Advent (1) (or of the Saint)* *Isa 35; Ps: 85:7–end; Lk 5:17–26*				
		EP	Ps: 102	Isa 6 Mt 15:21–28		Isa 18 Rev 12	

Monday is an ordinary weekday, or 'Feria'.

MP: Two lines in Roman type give Psalms and readings for Matins. EP: ditto.

Mass: Lines of italic give directions for the Eucharist; the second of these lines gives the Roman readings ('The Weekday Lectionary') which are permitted by CW. These form a continuous course of readings, and so are suitable where mass is said (almost) daily. Where mass is not said so often, the mass of last Sunday is more suitable.

Instead, the minister has the discretion to observe the (Colour, Hymns, Collect of the) 'Optional Memorial' of S Jane. ☐ shows that the Saint is 'unAnglican'; in fact, S Jane is from the Roman Kalendar.

TUESDAY			S Lucy, V & M (Ember Day)				
13 R		MP	Ps: 105:1–22	Isa 45:15–end II Thess 1		Isa 21:1–12 Mk 5:21–end	
		Mass	*of the Saint (**Charles Simeon**)* *Isa 40:25–end; Ps: 103:8–13; Mt 11:28–end*				
		EP	Ps: 105:23–end	Isa 8:16 – 9:7 Mt 16:1–12		Isa 22:1–14 Rev 14	

Tuesday is a 'Memorial for General Use', and so S Lucy (Colour, Hymns, Collect) displaces, compulsorily, the Feria. The readings given for mass, however, are still the weekday ones, since those saying mass often will probably take advantage of the permission to keep this continuous course of readings as unbroken as possible by using them even on memorials. If preferred, readings for the appropriate class of Saint can be used, and are more suitable where mass is not said daily. The 'Weekday Missal', in its more recent Editions, suggests appropriate readings for most Saints; and so does CW. See Introduction, pages xxvi and following. V & M: abbreviations inside front cover.

(**Charles Simeon**) in the Mass line: see Introduction paragraph 3.

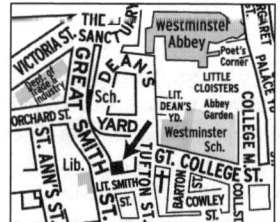

ORDER FORM

 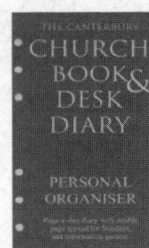  

Advance order for the 2009 editions

Avoid disappointment by ordering the 2009 editions now !   *(All to be published in May 2008)*   *quantity*

CANTERBURY CHURCH BOOK & DESK DIARY 2009 - *Cased*.................... £16.99 + p&p* ....

CANTERBURY CHURCH BOOK & DESK DIARY 2009 - *Personal Organiser*...£17.99 + p&p* ....

CANTERBURY PREACHERS COMPANION 2009....................................... £16.99 + p&p* ....

ORDER FOR THE EUCHARIST 2009.. £7.99 + p&p* ....

Order a complete set of CANTERBURY CHURCH BOOK AND DESK DIARY *(either cased or personal organiser edition)*, CANTERBURY PREACHERS COMPANION and ORDER FOR THE EUCHARIST at the combined **advance order price of £34.00** + p&p*

Order additional copies of the 2008 editions
Subject to stock availability

Desk Diary £16.99*.........   Organiser £17.99*.........   Preacher's Companion £16.99*.........   Order for the Eucharist £7.99*.........

Ask for details of discounted prices for bulk orders of 6+ copies of any individual title when ordered direct from the Publisher.

Sub-total: £............

*Plus **£2.50** per order to cover post and packing (UK only): £............

All orders over £50 are sent POST FREE to any UK address.
Contact the Publishers office for details of overseas carriage.

TOTAL AMOUNT TO PAY: £............

I wish to pay by…

…**CHEQUE** for £...................... made payable to **SCM-Canterbury Press Ltd**

…**CREDIT CARD**   Visa, Delta, MasterCard and Switch accepted (please delete as appropriate)
Your credit card will not be debited until the books are despatched.

Card number:...   Expiry: ___/ ____

Switch Issue No: ....   Valid from: ____/ ____

Signature of
cardholder:...   Security code: ....
Last three digits on signature panel

Please **PRINT** all details below.

Title:................ Name:...

Delivery address: ....

....

....

....

....

....   Post Code:.....................

Telephone:...   Date:...............................

Return this order form - with details of payment - to
Canterbury Press Norwich, St Mary's Works, St Mary's Plain, Norwich NR3 3BH, UK

Telephone: 01603 612914   Fax: 01603 624483   Website: www.scm-canterburypress.co.uk

Starvation
Exploitation
Poverty
Drought

Who cares?

You do.
And you're not alone.

Twenty-two thousand churches support Christian Aid's work to eradicate poverty. Why? Because we believe in a God of love and justice.

We're here to help you make an impact on poverty in communities all over the world.

To find out more, call 020 7523 2014.
www.christianaid.org.uk

 **christian aid**   We believe in life before death

UK registered charity number 1105851 Company number 5171525 Republic of Ireland charity number CHY 6998

CONTENTS

your advertisement

in front of over 250,000 Anglicans — 'the people in the pews'

That's right: you could be advertising to more than 250,000 readers of these two much-loved and long-established parish magazine insets.

The Sign has been in publication for nearly a hundred years. *Home Words* even longer. Together, but independently of each other, they help parishes to improve the look and content of their own local magazines.

So, once a month you have the chance to advertise nationally, but in a local publication. All the benefits that come through local, trustworthy and sought-after parish magazines are transferred to you and your advertisement.

Both magazine insets accept advertising from anyone, from individuals to large businesses and charities. You can advertise a holiday letting, or make a charity appeal — anything that is relevant to parishioners.

Want to know more? Simply make contact:

Stephen Dutton, The Sign & Home Words, c/o Church Times
33 Upper Street, London N1 0PN

Tel. 020 7359 4570   Fax 020 7359 8132
email: stephen@churchtimes.co.uk

INTRODUCTION

1   **THE purpose** of this ORDO is to serve worship needs of Anglicans and Roman Catholics. For the former, it provides for the recitation of Morning and Evening Prayer and the celebration of the Holy Communion in accordance with modern forms authorised or encouraged in the **Provinces of Canterbury and York**. These forms are *selected, arranged* and *interpreted* in the spirit of what has become generally customary in Western Christendom since the Second Vatican Council; but notes draw attention also to **Orthodox** insights.

It also provides a full Calendar according to the **Modern Roman Rite**, together with explanatory and catechetical notes. For the convenience of Anglicans, such Roman material as is not also authorised by General Synod, is given clearly distinguished for use by those who desire it. The use of this material is covered by Canon B.5.1.

Anglicans who prefer forms of Liturgy based on the *Book of Common Prayer* will find a Lectionary designed for use with the BCP printed in the far right hand column of each page.

Calendar

2   ☐ Indicates observances for which there is no Anglican Synodical authority.

✠ Sundays and Holy Days of Obligation ('Principal Feast'; 'Principal Holy Day' CW).

SOLEMNITY: A major 'Red Letter' day or 'Festival' (CW); a Sunday. Those days normally have a First Evening Prayer.

Festum: A lesser 'Red Letter' day; 'Feast' (Roman); 'Festival' (CW).

Memorial: A 'Black Letter Day' to be generally kept; a 'Lesser Festival' (CW).

Feria: An ordinary weekday.

Feria (. . . . . .): An ordinary weekday (with Optional alternative Memorials).

This ORDO gives a majority of Saints as Optional Memorials (CW says they '*may*' be used). Rome prefers not to compel 'serious incursion on the weekday cycle' and desires 'to expand the number of celebrations while reducing the extent of obligation, i.e. to maximise choice and flexibility'; and CW urges the minister to 'remember the need not to lose the spirit of the season, especially of Advent and Lent, by too many celebrations that detract from its character'.

(*Memorials for Optional Use*) are from CW, or ASB, or Rome, or 1662, or 1928; or the New Roman Calendar for England.

Local, and other commemorations may be added, especially Dedication and Patronal Festivals (see Appendix 2). Those authorised by the Diocesan are *Optional* (Canon B.6.5).

Scottish, Welsh, and Irish Solemnities, Festa, and Memorials for *General* Use are included. (Memorials in the Scottish Calendar of 1991 marked '5' or '6' are *Optional*. Memorials in the Welsh Calendar of 1993 marked 'iv' or 'v' are *Optional*. This Order does not print them. Nor is the new Church of Ireland list of Diocesan Saints given.)

Rome and CW allow, on a 'green' Feria, the observance, for a good reason, of *any* Saint listed for that day on an authorised list.

3   **COMMEMORATIONS.** This ORDO follows a CW suggestion by including, in the line starting '*Mass*', names of uncanonised people who appear in CW as 'lesser festivals', urging that those who are unhappy to observe them liturgically may nevertheless

incorporate them into the Intercession. Pope John Paul II particularly urged 'local Churches' 'to ensure that the memory of those who have suffered martyrdom should be safeguarded' and calls this 'the most convincing form of Ecumenism'.

4 ✠ DAYS OF EUCHARISTIC OBLIGATION

CANTERBURY & YORK		ORDO	ROMAN []= not in England
Every Sunday	Byz	✠	Every Sunday
			[January 1]
January 6*	Byz	✠	January 6*
February 2*	Byz		
March 25	Byz	(✠)	
			[March 19]
[Ash Wednesday]		(✠)	
[Maundy Thursday]		(✠)	
Ascension	Byz	✠	Ascension*
		✠	Corpus Christi*
	Byz	✠	June 29
	Byz	✠	August 15
November 1*		✠	November 1
			[December 8]
December 25	Byz	✠	December 25

'Byz' indicates days which, being among the Twelve Great Festivals of the Byzantine Rites, may be said to have Ecumenical Status. (Byz adds June 24; Aug 6 and 29; Sept 8 and 14; Nov 21)

EAD includes on its list June 29 and August 15, but allows them on the nearest Sunday, as it does the Ascension and Corpus Christi. It omits March 25.

**CW* envisages Jan 6, Feb 2, Nov 1 being transferred to a Sunday: see Paragraph 5(C). Parish Priests decide.

**R:* envisages Jan 6, Ascension, Corpus Christi being transferred to a Sunday: see Paragraph 5(C). Local hierarchies decide.

**R:* envisages Holy Days of Obligation falling on a Saturday or Monday being transferred to a Sunday: see Paragraph 5(B). Local hierarchies decide.

In the Church of England (Canons B6, B14, and C26) Mass is to be celebrated in every Parish Church and (except on Ash Wednesday and Maundy Thursday) every Bishop Priest and Deacon is to celebrate or to be present at Mass.

Good Friday (Canon B.6.4) is "ever to be observed . . . by attendance at Divine Worship." CW added February 2 to the list of Principal Festivals, but, since CW is optional, it is unclear how far this creates obligations under Canon.

The Roman Catholic Church, less clericalist than Anglicanism, expects the participation of *all* God's Holy People.

5 TRANSFER? OMIT?

(A) *External Solemnity.*

When a Solemnity, or a *Festum of Our Lord*, falls in the week after a Sunday in Ordinary Time ('Green'), the Roman Rite allows all the masses and the entire office (including 1 EP) of the Day on the Sunday, *the Holy Day itself also* being celebrated on its proper day.

Transference

(B) Holy Days of Obligation, among English R.C.s, are transferred to the adjacent Sunday when they fall on Saturday or Monday.

(C) A 'Principal Feast' (CW) or 'Solemnity' (R:) supersedes an ordinary ('Green') Sunday 'per annum'. But other 'Festivals' (CW) or 'Feasts' (R:) falling on such a Sunday are, according to R:, omitted that year. According to CW, they must be observed: this may be on the Sunday or the first available day thereafter: see (D) below.

(1) *Epiphany*, in the English Roman Catholic Church and in *some* other countries, is celebrated on the Sunday between January 2 and 8. According to CW, the Epiphany may be transferred to a Sunday between January 2 and 8 'for pastoral reasons'.

(2) *Presentation*, according to CW, may be celebrated *either* on February 2 *or* on the Sunday falling between January 28 and February 3. (According to R:, it could have an External Solemnity on the Sunday *before* but is *still* celebrated on February 2.)

(3) *Ascension*, in the English Roman Catholic Church and in *some* other countries, is celebrated on the Sunday after the appropriate Thursday. There is no General Synod encouragement for this, but EAD permits it.

(4) *Corpus Christi*, in the English Roman Catholic Church and in *some* other countries, is celebrated on the Sunday after the appropriate Thursday. There is no C of E encouragement for this, but Lectionary note 6 would cover it and EAD permits it.

(5) *All Saints*, according to CW, is celebrated on *either* November 1 *or* the Sunday between October 31 and November 6 *or* both. (According to R:, it could have an External Solemnity on the Sunday *before* but is *still* celebrated on November 1. R: also allows local hierarchies to transfer the day.)

(D) *Call it a Votive?* Anglican custom 1928–1980 made a Festum which fell on a 'Green' Sunday supersede that Sunday: CW (C above) allows either observance on the Sunday or transference. Roman rubrics dislike displacing the Sunday because they emphasise the priority of Sunday as the weekly memorial of the Lord's Resurrection. But the older Anglican custom can be harmonised with Roman regulations by regarding the mass of the Festum as a (First Class) Votive 'by command or permission of the Ordinary because of pastoral usefulness' (and *Liturgy of the Hours* permits votive offices). In EAD Ss John Baptist and Peter and Paul; the Assumption; All Saints; the Sacred Heart; Titles; and Dedications; 'may be observed on the nearest Sunday'. But this would not eliminate the observance on the proper day.

6 **EVES.** CW and recent Vatican reforms prefer the Liturgical Day to last from midnight to midnight. However, modern Western usage preserves the ancient custom of considering *Sunday* to begin on the evening of Saturday. So the Collect of each Sunday is used on the Saturday evening before it, and the practice is spreading of celebrating a Sunday mass on the Saturday evening: attendance at this fulfils obligations of Sunday worship. [Do NOT use the CW 'extended preface' for ordinary Sundays at Vigil Masses.]

Solemnities also have a First Evening Prayer. Here, again, obligations of worship can be fulfilled the previous evening. The Roman Missal provides 'Vigil Masses' for Christmas, Pentecost, S John Baptist, SS Peter and Paul, and the Assumption. These masses are said with *Gloria*, *Creed*, and the colour of the Solemnity, either before or after the First Evening Prayer. The collect of a Vigil Mass is also used at the First Evening Prayer.

Festa do not have a First Evening Prayer. But in years when a Festum displaces a Sunday office, or places where a Festum becomes a Solemnity because it is a Patronal Festival, it acquires a First Evening Prayer.

7 **COLOURS.** The capital letter under the day indicates the colour of the Office. This applies throughout the day, unless another colour appears for Mass and Evening Prayer. The colours suggested in the ORDO are 'traditional', (CW; CW itself suggests, without

being 'mandatory', the use of white up to the Presentation; of red between All Saints and Advent; of red on the Monday, Tuesday, and Wednesday of Holy Week.)

On very solemn days one can use 'festival', or more 'noble' vestments, even if they are not of the colour of the day.

In some churches a 'Lent array' of unbleached linen is used as an alternative to purple during Lent.

Votive Masses may be celebrated in the colour which best suits the character of the chosen Mass, but it is permitted to use instead the colour of the day or season.

Ember and Rogation Masses are said in the seasonal colour. Purple or Black is used at Requiems. In America, Rome allows White.

8 **SELF DENIAL etc.**

	A	B	C
Roman	PENANCE	ABSTINENCE	FASTING
Canons		Ash Wednesday	Ash Wednesday
1250–1253	Fridays	Fridays EXCEPT	Good Friday
	Lent	Solemnities	
Canterbury	DISCIPLINE AND		
& York (CW)	SELF DENIAL		
	Fridays EXCEPT Solemnities and Festivals outside Lent; and EXCEPT during Eastertide. Weekdays in Lent		

'A' and 'C' are not legally defined in the Universal Canon Law.

Local Episcopates may regulate 'B' and 'C' in detail, substituting charitable works or pious exercises, in whole or in part, for both Abstinence and Fasting.

Abstinence is abstaining from meat. (English Roman Catholics are allowed to substitute some other form of abstinence, or perform some act of piety or charity.) Abstinence binds those above 14 years.

Fasting is defined for English Roman Catholics as 'the amount of food we eat is considerably reduced.' It binds those who are more than eighteen until the beginning of their sixtieth year. It is *recommended* also on Easter Eve up to the Vigil.

9 **'EPIPHANY SEASON'.** The main CW innovation is the suggestion of an Epiphany season modelled on Eastertide: starting on Epiphany and ending on the Presentation. *Arguments in favour* include: it cheers up January and helps to rescue Epiphany and Presentation from oblivion. *Arguments against*: it introduces a new divergence from Roman and Orthodox practice (despite the 1968 pre-ARCIC agreement that we would 'not undertake any significant changes in the seasons') and it mars the (primitive and ecumenical) uniqueness of Easter, the Lord's 50-day-long Great Day of Festival.

If one wishes to follow this CW suggestion, one stays in white vestments and uses Epiphany Office Hymns and an Epiphany Preface until the Presentation; one calls the Sundays 'of' (not 'after') Epiphany; one treats the Presentation as a Solemnity (with 1 EP; Creed at Mass) and as a Day of Obligation. Saturday votives of the Immaculate Heart of Mary (see p. 39) will be particularly appropriate.

Epiphany Hymns: MP 40 (NEH 48) EP 38 (NEH 46).

9A **BIBLICAL TRANSLATIONS** The Vatican now insists on faithfulness to the inspired originals in matters such as grammatical genders and the preservation of as many as possible of the layers of meaning in the original texts, even when these may not be politically correct. 'For example, where the New Testament or the Church's tradition have interpreted certain texts of the Old Testament in a Christological fashion, special care should be observed in the translation of these texts so that a Christological meaning is not precluded ... the word "man" in English should as a rule translate "adam" and "anthropos", since there is no one synonym which effectively conveys the play between the individual, the collectivity and the unity of the human family so important, for example, to expression of Christian doctrine and anthropology.' Among modern translations, such faithfulness can be secured by use of the RSV but NOT the NRSV. Psalter: See Para 29.

Mass

10 **THE LEGALITY OF 'VARIATIONS'.** LHWE and PHG provided forms for 'occasions for which no provision is made' in BCP or ASB. (Such forms of service can be legal if authorised by the Convocations [Canon B:4:1] Archbishop [B:4:2] Ordinary [B:4:3] or Minister having the cure of souls [B:5:2].) *But* LHWE and PHG *also* provided *many* 'variations' in areas where ASB *did* already make *full* and *compulsory* provision; these 'variations' were 'commended by the House of Bishops'; the only legal basis for which can be the words in Canon B:5: 'the minister who is to conduct the service may in his discretion make and use variations which are not of substantial importance'.

Most of the useful material in LHWE and PHG has been superseded by the recently authorised materials. But LHWE and PHG established useful precedents concerning what is a 'variation not of substantial importance' within 'the discretion of the minister who is to conduct the service.' This formula – according to the House of Bishops in 1984 and 1990 – includes **unauthorised Greetings; unauthorised Confessions; unauthorised Collects; unauthorised Readings; unauthorised Prefaces; unauthorised Invitations to Communion.** The fact that some of this material was *subsequently* incorporated in and thus authorised by CW does not change the fact that it was totally unauthorised when the Bishops said it came under the umbrella of Canon B:5:1. So unless the Bishops were wrong in 1984 and 1990, it remains true that Canon B:5:1 still covers the use, at the discretion of the Minister who is to conduct the service, of **unauthorised Greetings; unauthorised Confessions; unauthorised Collects; unauthorised Readings; unauthorised Prefaces; and unauthorised Invitations to Communion. But his discretion is not confined to these areas: see Para 19 below.**

It is to be noted that the Bishops, either collectively or individually, have *no* canonical right to order, *or even allow, any* 'variations' to authorised services. The only right to 'make and use' such 'variations' is that of the 'minister who is to conduct the service' by virtue of Canon B.5.1.. The use of this canon by the Bishops in promoting LHWE and PHG was a creative use of canon law to loosen the straightjacket which otherwise surrounds the law of public worship. And they are still at it: see Para 18 below. But what is sauce for geese ...

Dix (*Shape* pp. 587–9 and 716–7) wisely sets concepts of 'Liturgical Authority' against their historical background.

11 **CW 'SEASONAL PROVISIONS':** Sentences before the Confession and the Peace; Alleluia before the Gospel; and Proper Prefaces, of different lengths, for some but not all Eucharistic Prayers, appear ('*may* be used') all to be optional. CW does not itself provide, but invites the use of, Entrance and Communion Sentences.

12 **CONFESSION AND KYRIES:** both may be combined into the form of Penitential Rite now popular among Roman Catholics. The sentences prefixed * in the version given below may be varied according to the season. (CW gives three examples, and there are more in PHG and R:.)

The priest invites the people to call to mind their sins, and a pause for silent reflection follows.

Minister:	*You raise the dead to life in the Spirit: Lord, have mercy.	*Priest:*	May almighty God have mercy on us, forgive us our sins,
People:	**Lord, have mercy.**		and bring us to everlasting life.
Minister:	*You bring pardon and peace to the sinner: Christ, have mercy.	*All:*	Amen.
People:	**Christ, have mercy.**		
Minister:	*You bring light to those in darkness: Lord, have mercy.		
People:	**Lord, have mercy.**		

PHG also reminds us of the Asperges (the people are sprinkled with holy water to recall them to their Baptismal commitment; this rite also replaces both the Confession and Kyries and is particularly suitable in Easter Time), giving on p. 249 an abbreviated version of the Roman texts, and on p. 229 versions of the traditional anthems. Or one could 'mine' the materials at CW pp. 48–9. PPL and PHG urge this rite on the Lord's Baptism.

13 **GLORIA IN EXCELSIS** is used on Sundays outside Advent and Lent; Solemnities; Festa; and during Christmas week and Easter week; but not on weekdays and memorials. *Gloria* may be used at special more solemn celebrations.

14 **COLLECTS.** No more than one Collect is ever said at Mass. On Ferias CW orders the collect of the previous Sunday to be used; the Roman usage permits, during the 'green' seasons, any 'green' Sunday Collect to be selected.

On the Sundays between Trinity and All Saints, the Collect to accompany CW readings *will differ from year to year*. While the *readings* come from the 'Sunday of the Year', described by CW as 'Proper number x', the *Collects* are 'after Trinity'.

This new series of CW collects includes a number of the BCP collects from the ancient Roman Sacramentaries, given for use on the same Sunday as in BCP, and very lightly modernised in language (the BCP originals may be used). This welcome development will still leave us using fewer such collects than does the current Roman Rite. Dix (SL p. 367) describes these collects as 'both ancient and beautiful . . . lovely things, grave, melodious and thoughtful, and compact with evangelical doctrine – characteristic products of the liturgical genius of Rome in the fifth and sixth centuries. Cranmer's reputation as a writer of English prose largely rests on his translations . . . and rightly so, for they are among the very best translations ever made . . .'. There is nothing to stop a celebrant using the original, or lightly modernised, versions of those remaining BCP After Trinity collects which CW ignores.

For each weekday in Advent, Christmas, Lent and Easter, Rome provides a separate and seasonally appropriate collect (printed with the readings in the Weekday Missal).

Collects end thus (CW):

Longer Ending (for the Collect itself):

'Through Jesus Christ your Son our Lord, who is alive and reigns with you in the unity of the Holy Spirit, one God, now and for ever'. [But if the Son is addressed: 'for you are alive and reign with the Father in the unity of the Holy Spirit, one God, now and for ever'.]

Shorter Ending (for the prayers Over the Offerings and Post-Communion): 'Through (Jesus) Christ our Lord'. [But if the Son is addressed: 'for you are alive and reign, now and for ever'.]

15 **EUCHARISTIC READINGS: SUNDAYS AND HOLY DAYS** are all in italics.

The *first* line of readings is CW (see paragraph 36 below). This Lectionary was based on the Roman Lectionary in which, S John's Gospel being used particularly in Eastertide, the three Synoptic Gospels take it in turn to dominate the Sundays of the Year (Year A, Matthew; B, Mark; C, Luke). The Roman original has been 'improved' several times by Anglican committees. **Where it is desired to abbreviate a CW reading, R: might be helpful (see below).**

This ORDO assumes that users will prefer the OT readings which will relate thematically to the Sunday Gospel (CW repeats them from R:) rather than the alternative 'continuous' OT readings. 'Typology' is the Bible's own way of using itself intertextually (I Cor 10:1–5; I Pet 3:20, etc.).

The *second* line is the original Roman provision, preceded *R:* (the psalm provision gives the psalm number according to the Anglican system of numbering psalms, but does not specify the detailed uses and combinations of verses).

Advantages in using the Roman version: (a) it will be practical to use books, of R.C. origin, in which the lessons are printed in full; (b) the R: readings generally represent a tighter selection of verses. Whether the differences between CW and R: are slight or greater, the use of R: will constitute a variation 'not of substantial importance' in terms of Canon B.5; and CW itself allows 'the minister' to 'depart from the Lectionary provision for pastoral reasons or preaching or teaching purposes' during 'Ordinary Time', after 'due consultation with the PCC'. (PCCs could pass a resolution 'that this Council has received such due consultation as may be necessary for the Incumbent at his discretion to depart from authorised lectionary provision.')

In the Roman rite, Solemnities have *two* readings before the Gospel; Festa only *one*. Where this ORDO prints two, it is because Rome offers them as alternatives. CW, on the other hand, offers *two* readings even for some 'Lesser Festivals'; i.e. Memorials.

16 **EUCHARISTIC READINGS: WEEKDAY LECTIONARY.** CW continues the authorisation ASB gave to the Roman weekday Eucharistic lectionary; its readings may be used both on Ferias *and* on Memorials. They are printed in full, in italics, although those who wish to use these readings daily at mass will find it simpler to follow the Liturgical Commission's advice and use copies of the small, cheap Roman 'Weekday Missal', containing these readings, than to have to mark up lessons in a Bible each day. See page i for further advice. Psalms follow the CW verse numbers.

Roman Psalms: the complexity of juggling the different versification systems in the Vulgate, King James, BCP and CW Psalters is too much for your compiler. Accordingly, just the psalm number (BCP numeration) is given for the Roman Psalms: which verses are used, how they are combined, and when the Response comes, will have to be discovered from liturgical books.

17 **THE CREED** is to be used on Sundays and Solemnities and *may* be used at special more solemn occasions. The 'Apostles' Creed', the ancient baptismal confession of the Apostolic Roman See (which , together with Quicunque Vult, is also allowed by CW), is particularly recommended by Rome during the baptismal seasons of Lent and Easter and when there are many children present. When it is used, Rome insists that *Carnis Resurrectionem* must be translated *Resurrection of the Flesh* (compare our Article IV). CW institutionalizes an *ad hoc* Vatican custom of omitting *Filioque* when ecumenical considerations urge this.

18 **PREFACES.** ASB and PHG moved, with Rome, in the direction of a generous supply of prefaces; CW only gives a minimum. Rome offers 'extended prefaces' and

others may be found in ASB and books 'commended' by the Bishops (but which have no synodical force). See paragraph 10 above for what is 'legal'.

On Memorials which lack a proper preface, the Common Preface is used (in Advent and Easter, the Seasonal Preface) *or* the appropriate Preface of the Saint.

19 **POST SANCTUS.** Before the 1960s, in both the Roman and Anglican rites, there was but one unchanging 'Consecration Prayer' or 'Canon', so that this part of the service constituted a moment of familiarity, commonality, and invariability deeply sanctified by Tradition. But since CW follows Rome in now offering a dozen or so alternative EuPrs, the authorities in both communions have in effect abrogated this tradition, and transferred discretion to the officiating presbyter.

Does this discretion, combined with the canonical discretion to 'make and use variations' (see Para 10 above), entitle him to use EuPrs not authorised by General Synod or to improve CW EuPrs by introducing ancient, ecumenical and ARCIC verbs such as 'become' and 'offer'? Canons B.5.1, B.5.5 and B.1.3.iii make clear that the celebrant's 'discretion' (see para 10 above) *does* extend to the whole Eucharistic Prayer.

On 26 i 1988, the House of Bishops expressed the view that the use of Eucharistic rites which were once 'canonically authorised' but whose 'authorisation' had 'lapsed' would be a variation 'not of substantial importance' and therefore, in their pastoral judgement, legal. While the Bishops clearly only had in mind some of the temporary rites briefly authorised since 1965, this principle obviously and *a fortiori* also covers 'where well established' the first of the four Roman Eucharistic Prayers, which was frequently used in the Church of England between 597 and 1559. Roman rubrics strongly urge the use of this EuPr on all Sundays; the Octaves of Christmas and Easter; the Apostles and Saints listed in it; the Epiphany and Ascension; and Ritual masses. The Tudor English translation authorised by Rome may be sought from the Compiler. In the judgement of liturgical experts, if this venerable prayer, brought by S Augustine to Canterbury in 597, lacks Twentieth Century Synodical 'legality', it has the 'authority' of nearly a millennium of Anglican use. There are clearly no theological objections to the contents of this Prayer since the House of Bishops (GS Misc 632) has spoken of Anglicans finding 'that they can, with good conscience, say a heartfelt Amen at the end of the [Roman] Eucharistic Prayer.'

The 1988 'statement', so one Bishop points out, also covers ASB EuPrIII, which has a more satisfactory *oblatio* that CW'B', its successor.

It has been suggested that CW EuPr G should not be ignored by Catholics. It breaks new ground in providing a post-consecration intercession into which episcopal names (see para 21) could be inserted. This intercession could be popped into other CW EuPrs.

20 **SAINTS IN THE EUCHARISTIC PRAYER.** The CW Eucharistic Prayers B, E, F, G invite mention by name of Saints, and they are easily inserted into the other Prayers. Rome and Orthodoxy agree that diachronic 'permanence through history' is 'brought into focus' by the mention of the Saints in the Canon. The Ecumenical (Roman and Orthodox) custom since early centuries has been at every mass to name our Lady, and always to do so using her ecumenically agreed official doctrinal title **Mother of God** (*Theotokos*, Ephesus, 431, and Chalcedon, 451; some may be attracted by the ARCIC suggestion of translating this 'Mother of God Incarnate'). The older Byzantine and Latin prayers add another official ecumenical title: **and Ever-Virgin** (*aeiparthenos*, Chalcedon, 451, and Constantinople, 553). Mention of others, in addition to our Lady, (e.g. the Forerunner; Apostles; Patrons; Saints of the Day) varies from rite to rite.

21 **THE BISHOP.** The fundamental sacramental unit of Christ's Church is neither a 'National' Church or Province or 'Communion', nor a parish, but a unity of Bishop,

Presbyterium, and People. So, when a priest offers mass apart from his Bishop, he does so as the Bishop's representative. The Orthodox and Roman Churches agree that it is 'essential' to show this by including his name in the Eucharistic Prayer. This is not merely a prayer *for* the Bishop but an expression of full ecclesial communion *with* him. Where CW formulae are used, at appropriate points after the Consecration the following (see Prayer G) can be interpolated: **Remember, Lord, your Church in every land. Reveal her unity, guard her faith, and preserve her in peace: together with . . .**

A priest says: **. . . our bishop (or whatever) N** adding, if appropriate, **and his assistant bishop N** or, if there are several of them, **and his assistant bishops**.

22 **COMMUNION:** LHWE and PHG print Roman introductions to the Our Father; and the Embolism ('Deliver us, Lord . . .') after the Our Father, as in the Roman rite, is printed in PHG. CW permits the Peace after the Our Father, as in the Roman rite. The (nonR:) CW formulae at the Fraction are only mandatory on Sundays and Principal Holy Days: could this be the moment quietly to dump them? The ASB/CW Zwinglianization of *ECCE Agnus Dei* could be got round in parish leaflets thus: "The priest invites the faithful to receive Jesus, the Lamb of God; they reply . . ."

23 **POSTCOMMUNION.** CW provides, together with the Collects referred to in paragraph 14, post-Communion collects, many of which will be found either eloquent or verbose according to differing tastes. Not one of them is a post-Communion in those same early sacramentaries which provided so many of Cranmer's collects. CW, however, envisages the use of 'another suitable prayer'; which could be found in the Roman selection, or the old one in the 'English Missal'. They replace, *or* are in addition to, '. . . send us out into the world . . .'.

24 **CONCLUSION OF THE MASS.** (i) On Solemnities and Festa outside Lent, and at Requiems, a solemn blessing is encouraged. The deacon or priest says: **Bow your heads and pray for God's blessing**; the blessing follows; and then the dismissal.

(ii) On Sundays and Weekdays in Lent, Prayers Over The People have been optionally restored in the Roman Rite. They are available for 'Green' Sundays. The deacon or priest says: **Bow your heads for God's blessing**; the Prayer is said, followed immediately by **'. . . and the blessing . . .'**; then the dismissal. The new latin Missal provides new texts; until translations are available, the English Missal could be used.

(iii) Otherwise, Mass ends with *The Lord be with you* and its response, the Blessing, and the Dismissal with its response. This applies to Requiems. When a liturgical function immediately follows the Mass, this Conclusion is omitted.

25 **EMBERS & ROGATIONS.** Embers were originally pagan Roman harvest festivals, christianized by being made fasts! Because of the fast, they attracted ordinations. (The Weekday Missal has Votives For Productive Land and the Blessing of Man's Labour.) We indicate the Ember Weeks as given, according to ancient tradition, in BCP and the Roman Tridentine Calendars (the information given in CW being erroneous). But CW allows bishops to transfer them, so that they precede Diocesan Ordinations.

Ember and Rogation Masses may be said on Ferias and Optional Memorials; on Solemnities, Festivals, and General Memorials the expression of Ember and Rogation themes is confined to the Intercession, unless they are Class 1 or Class 2 Votives (see table).

The seasonal colour is used at Ember and Rogation Masses.

26 **RITUAL MASSES, REQUIEMS, VOTIVES.** The table opposite indicates when these may and may not be said.

(a) When a Wedding includes a **Nuptial Mass:** On Sundays and Solemnities, the Mass of the Day is said. But one of the Wedding readings may be included, except from Maundy Thursday to Easter Sunday and on Solemnities of Obligation. If the Parochial community is not present at a Wedding on a 'Green' Sunday or a Sunday after Christmas, the entire Nuptial Mass may be said. The ancient 'Nuptial Blessing' is traditionally said over the newly-weds immediately after the Our Father of the Wedding Mass. Consigned now by CW to oblivion for Political Incorrectness, versions of it will be found in R: and BCP (*O God who by thy mighty power . . .*) and ASB (Additional Prayer 35, on page 299.)

(b) **Our Lady on Saturday** (*in Sabbato*): (i) since at least the Eighth Century liturgical reforms associated with the name of Alcuin of York, our Lady has in the West been particularly commemorated on Saturday (on the Sabbath God the Creator rests from His labour in Mary's womb before His Great New Deed of Creation on His Eighth Day; Mary is the faithful Daughter of Zion, whose Faith begins the New – as Abraham's did the Old – Covenant; in her own Eschatological Rest she prefigures the Sabbath Rest to which God's Pilgrim people is journeying). Post Vatican II legislation confined this usage to when, after Epiphany and Trinity, there is no Solemnity, Festum, or Memorial for General Use. But since IGMR now 'commends' the observance *peculiari modo*, it should be the norm on free Saturdays after Epiphany and Trinity. (As a Class 2 votive – see page xxi – it may be used until December 16, after January 1, and after Low Sunday in Eastertide, and on Memorials for General Use.) (see p. 38 for the **Immaculate Heart**.)

(ii) Variety may be secured by using the **"Collection of Masses of the BVM"**, issued by Rome particularly for use in Marian shrines (where, during pilgrimages, votives from the Collection may also be said on any weekday of Advent, Christmas after January 1, and Lent) and on Saturday. The Compiler (front of volume) can supply a sample mass. *Invariability may be secured from CW pp. 511–2 & 310–1.*

(iii) But, of course, the Feria, or an occuring optional Memorial, may be observed.

(c) **The Sacred Heart on Friday:** see p. 38.

(d) **Votive Masses** may be of the mysteries of the Lord or in honour of the BVM, Angels, any Saint, All Saints; and may be said on any feria when there is not a Memorial for General Use (with the exception of the Immaculate Conception, masses referring to events in the lives of the Lord and His Mother may not be used as votives). *Votive offices*, for a public cause or out of devotion, may be used on *any* day except Solemnities; Sundays of Advent, Lent, or Easter; Ash Wednesday; Palm Sunday to Low Sunday; and 2 November.

MASSES 'FOR VARIOUS OCCASIONS', & VOTIVES / REQUIEMS

	MASSES 'FOR VARIOUS OCCASIONS', & VOTIVES			REQUIEMS		
	CLASS 1 — Permitted or ordered by the Bishop when they have an unusually serious pastoral need or use; and also **RITUAL MASSES:** e.g. at Baptism, Confirmation or Ordination.	**CLASS 2** — When they have a real pastoral need or use; e.g., a First Friday; the Sacred Heart; Rogations. BVM on Saturday	**CLASS 3** — Chosen by the Celebrant for the Devotion of the people.	**CLASS 1** — at Funerals	**CLASS 2** — After hearing the news of a death, on the occasion of the final burial, and on the first Anniversary	**CLASS 3** — 'Daily' masses for the Dead.
Solemnities 'of obligation'; Sundays of Advent; Sundays of Lent; Sundays from Easter to Trinity Sunday inclusive; Maundy Thursday to Easter.	NO	NO	NO	NO	NO	NO
Solemnities NOT 'of obligation'; Ash Wednesday; Monday, Tuesday and Wednesday in Holy Week; Easter Week All Souls' Day.	NO	NO	NO	YES	NO	NO
Ordinary (green) Sundays; Sundays of Christmas; Epiphany Sundays; Festa.	YES	NO	NO	YES	NO	NO
Weekdays December 17–24; the Octave of Christmas; Weekdays of Lent.	YES	NO but see para 26b ii	NO	YES	YES	NO
Memorials for General Use; Weekdays of Advent up to December 16; Weekdays of Christmas after January 1; Weekdays of the Easter Season after Low Sunday.	YES	YES	NO	YES	YES	NO
Ordinary (green) weekdays of the year; Epiphany weekdays; and Memorials for Optional Use.	YES	YES	YES	YES	YES	YES

Divine Office

This ORDO is arranged on the assumption that clergy will 'say daily the Morning *and* Evening Prayer [at least!] either privately or openly' (1662); 'Bishops, priests and deacons . . . must give due importance to Morning and Evening Prayer . . . and be careful not to omit them except for a grave cause' (Liturgy of the Hours).

27   Versions of the Opus Dei formally prescribed or permitted by Synod in England:

(1) Sarum (1542);

(2) BCP (1662);

(3) 'A Service of the Word' structured in conformity with CW pp. 24–27. These regulations were authorised so that (GS 1342 p. 3) their 'provisions would now give legal "cover" to the use of forms of Daily Office' such as the Roman Breviary ('Liturgy of the Hours') and 'Celebrating Common Prayer'; except that on Sundays and Principal Holy Days when such an Office is the principal service (i.e. in Churches where mass is not said), an Act of Penance, a sermon, and a Creed need to be added to a form which does not already possess them. IT MUST BE CLEARLY NOTED that the forms given in CW pp. 30–45 are purely '*examples* of forms which comply'; they are not mandatory *or even recommended* and take *no* priority over forms which the minister may borrow from elsewhere or devise himself.

Similarly (as one of the Bishops who sat on the Liturgical Commission and helped to write it has explained) *Common Worship: Daily Prayer* is no more than an 'outworking' of 'A Service of the Word' – as is the RC Divine Office.

28   **OFFICE HYMNS**, at Morning and Evening Prayer, are an ancient and integral part of the Divine Office. They now *precede the variable psalms* and state the theme of the Office.

This ORDO provides traditional Office Hymns from the old English Sarum Breviary and the current Latin Office Book, with a very little supplementation, according to the English Hymnal, which covers most needs. *We also give New English Hymnal numbers. But the NEH gives a much poorer selection than EH; we do the best we can with it while recommending EH for those who desire to use the traditional hymns in their daily office.*

Hymns for the 'Green' seasons and the Commons are in the table on page xxiii. Hymns for Advent, Christmas, Lent and Easter are indicated in the *Notes before those Seasons*.

Hymns for some other days are in the body of the ORDO; H: 5 (NEH 6) means that 5 is the English Hymnal number; 6 the New English Hymnal number. If no provision is made for Morning Prayer, the evening hymn is to be used; and vice versa.

29   **PSALMS:** arranged as given in GS 1520A. We follow the permission there to use 'Ordinary Time' psalms throughout nearly all the year, as Rome does. We assume also the traditional use of substantial psalmody. But any arrangement of the psalms is equally lawful. CW includes a psalter; but it was not passed by General Synod and has no more authority than any other translation. Nevertheless the Compiler has tried consistently to give verse numbers according to CW. 'The Revised Psalter' of 1964 (BCP sensitively adjusted by biblical scholars in collaboration with T.S. Eliot and C.S. Lewis) is considered by many the best English version.

Office Hymns

PER ANNUM (The 'Green' Seasons after Epiphany and Pentecost)

	Morning Prayer		Evening Prayer	
	EH	NEH	EH*	NEH
Sunday	50	53 or 149	51/164	150 or 54
Monday	52 or 632		58/81	61,
Tuesday	165	149	59/264	241,
Wednesday	54	or	60/262	248,
Thursday	55, 53 or 254	151	61/269	or
Friday	56		62/265	152
Saturday	57		49/280	
BVM on Saturday	213, 214, or 215	180, 181 or 183		

COMMONS for the entire year.

N.B. On days which are memorials, R: allows *either* the weekday hymns (according to season), *or* these hymns from the Commons.

BVM	214&215	181&183	213	180
Apostles, Evangelists	174 (R: Proper)	‡	176	214
in Eastertide	124 pt 2	‡	123 pt 2	100 vv4–end
Several Martyrs	175† or 183	213†	182	218
One Martyr	180 or 185	217	181	218
A Virgin Martyr	180 or 185	‡	191	222
A Virgin	‡	‡	192	222
A Holy Man	‡	‡	189	223
A Holy Woman	‡	‡	193	222
[Group Commem]	‡	‡	[253: 1&7–13]	[223]

* The first hymn is from the Seventh Century Weekly Cycle celebrating the Days of Creation; the second is a suggested alternative.
† *Correct to* The Martyrs' glorious deeds . . .
‡ Use the Evening Hymn.

(None of the Roman hymns for 'Pastors' is to be found in Anglican hymnals. EH 188(NEH 220), the traditional hymn for 'Confessors', is now confined to S Martin, for whom it was composed.)

VOTIVE OFFICES: as on the day. See paragraph 26 (d).

Those who feel like spending $30 (Canadian) on a volume containing all the traditional Office Hymns – mainly translated by J. M. Neale – should contact:
The Parish of St John the Evangelist
990 Falmouth Road
Victoria, BC
Canada V8X 3A3

The Church does not use the psalms in an individualistic way, or academically as pieces of historical Hebrew poetry; but corporately and Christologically according to the *sensus messianicus* (cf. Mt 22: 41–46; Lk 24: 44; Acts 2: 25–28 & 34–35; Hebrews passim). The Fathers received and explained the Psalter as a prophecy of Christ and the Church, and in the psalms, heard Christ crying to the Father, or the Father speaking with the Son, or the voice of the Church ('Christ prays for us as our Priest; in us as our Head; He is prayed to as our God'). Thus, in praying the psalms, the Body of Christ enters into the relationship between Son and Father.

So it is irrelevant whether the 'mood' of a psalm suits that of a particular worshipper at a particular moment. Nevertheless, the modern Roman Office, no less than Anglican equivalents, avoids some 'bloodthirsty' places because of their 'psychological difficulty'.

30 **OFFICE READINGS.** From Advent 3 to the Baptism, and from Palm Sunday to Trinity, CW expects 'authorised' readings to be used. Otherwise . . .

In the middle column the readings of the text are based on CW. ('Second Service' provides the 2 EP, and 'Third Service' the MP, on Sundays; on weekdays we use the lectionary contained in GS 1520A/B. *In the third column* the readings are in the tradition of the 1922 (still legal) and 1961 lectionaries, designed to accompany the BCP.

Technically, CW covers interchanging readings between MP, EP, and Mass, but the distribution of readings as given in this ORDO is to be recommended.

When a reading begins with a personal pronoun the reader may substitute the appropriate noun.

Verses printed within (parentheses) are permitted additions to the appointed passages. Verse numbers followed by 'a' or 'b' indicate the first or second part of the verse. Verse numberings generally follow the *(New) Revised Standard Version*. When other versions are used, such adaptations may be made as are necessary.

31 **CANTICLES & FINAL ANTHEMS.** The ancient Canticles of the Western Church (R: and BCP) are: MP *Benedictus* EP *Magnificat* and *Nunc Dimittis*. MP includes the *Te Deum* on all Sundays outside Lent, and on Solemnities and Festa. By long custom encouraged by an Archbishop of Canterbury, this Office concludes with an anthem to our Lady (Celebrating Common Prayer pp. 265–7).

32 **RITUAL.** Rome still anticipates the Sign of the Cross at *O God make speed* . . . , and the beginnings of the Gospel Canticles; the Cross on the mouth at *O Lord open* . . . ; and, **together with Byzantium expects the congregation to be standing for the proclamation of a Gospel reading!** PHG encourages a service of Light before EP, the ancient *Lucernarium*. It is not always realised that, since MP and EP occupy the time of the Temple morning and evening offerings of incense, its traditional use at the *Benedictus* and *Magnificat* is more than just a piece of highchurchery. EAD urges consideration also of 'a proper focus on the Blessed Sacrament, exposed for adoration.' Elliot (Int P38) tells you how to do it.

Resources

33 **'TRADITIONAL LANGUAGE' LITURGY.** While the Prayer Book Communion may be used as it is printed, for many years it was universally modified (e.g. omission of long exhortations). Nearly all the customary modifications of the 1662 eucharistic rite, including the 'Interim Rite', have now been given legal 'cover' by recent legislation.

With this rite one may add to the BCP propers the bulk of the additional *collects and propers from the 1928 Prayer Book* (and Old Testament readings from the old Series I), which were authorised by General Synod in 2000.

As far as *Series One and Two* are concerned, on 26 i 1988 the House of Bishops 'agreed in regarding the continued use, where well established, of any form of service which has, at any time since 1965, been canonically authorised (notwithstanding the fact that such authorisation was not renewed after it lapsed) as not being of 'substantial importance' within the meaning of Canon B5.4' . . . a creatively cheeky use of Canon Law.

34 **'LENT • HOLY WEEK • EASTER:** Services and Prayers', (LHWE) 'commended by the House of Bishops' provides forms of traditional liturgy for the period from Ash Wednesday to Pentecost. This may be used under the Diocesan's authority (Canon B4) or by decision of the Parish Priest (Canon B5). Since (LHWE) 'the Services . . . are set out so that they can be used as they stand. Alternatively, they may be used as source material . . . Every part of these services is optional . . .', it is clearly not illegal to borrow from other Churches and Rites.

Many priests have found the existence of LHWE an influential pastoral tool in recommending traditional Lenten and Holy Week rites to congregations unfamiliar with them. The texts provided for Holy Week are in fact the Roman texts with mostly insignificant alterations. Some of these changes slightly improve the Roman (ICEL) wording; unfortunately, LHWE lacks the detailed rubrical directions required (e.g.) for the traditional rites surrounding the Paschal Candle; and, for example, has seen fit to eliminate such memorable pieces of liturgical poetry as *O felix culpa*.

On Good Friday, the earlier tradition, preserved by the Roman rite, is for the intercessions to come between the Passion and the Veneration of the Cross; LHWE makes 'The Proclamation of the Cross' precede the Intercessions.

35 **'THE PROMISE OF HIS GLORY'** (PHG) contains a great deal of liturgical material beyond the scope of this ORDO. It provides Mass (R:) and Office for the Holy Family, and the (R:) Eucharistic readings for the Solemnities of Our Lady (Dec 8 and Jan 1); but in its movement towards the three-year Lectionary it has now been superseded by CW. This ORDO draws attention to such PHG material, from All Saints to the Presentation, as remains relevant.

36 **CALENDAR LECTIONARY AND COLLECTS 2000** finally sanctioned the three-year Roman Sunday and Festival Eucharistic Lectionary. This had already been 'improved', and the 'improved' version called the Revised Common Lectionary. Before General Synod promulgated it, it 'improved' it some more (although not as much as some pressure groups desired). There is NO *single* version of this Lectionary with readings printed out in full which is authorised by General Synod. *Any* translation of the Bible may be used. Mowbray/Cassell have published a version with NRSV texts; Hodder and Stoughton favour the NIV; etc; but none of these possesses any exclusive 'official' status.

CW accommodates Evangelical dislike of the Deuterocanonical books by providing alternatives to readings from them (a recent custom; 1549 and 1662 denied such alternatives). This ORDO assumes that users have no problems with those Deuterocanonical books which the C of E and the Roman Catholic Church both receive.

37 **SUNDAY MISSAL; WEEKDAY MISSAL.** The cheapest and simplest way of using the Roman Sunday readings (which are much the same as those now authorised in CW) is by purchasing a small Collins 'Sunday Missal'. The Collins 'Weekday Missal' prints in full the readings of the CW Daily Eucharistic Lectionary, propers for all the Saints in the Roman Universal Calendar, and a small Supplement of the main National Saints.

38 **CEREMONIES OF THE MODERN ROMAN RITE** by Msgr P.J. Elliot. This gives full, intelligent, and sensitive advice about the performance of Mass and Office in the Western tradition; it is modern, yet sensitive to the desire to do God's Work in a decent and orderly way not totally divorced from earlier traditions. It is the modern replacement for both 'Fortescue' and our own 'Ritual Notes'. It includes information about what to do with the Bishop! It costs £21.95 (+£2.20 p/p in the UK). It may be bought from Faith House Bookshop. (The same author's follow-up of 1998 is called "Liturgical Question Box", and another volume deals with the Seasons.)

39 **AKATHIST HYMN:** that great explosion of Byzantine wit and of Sixth Century devotion to our Lady is suitable, as the late Fr Colin Stephenson of Walsingham used to urge, for use in the Mary Month of May. PPL warmly encourages it. (During the Jubilee Year of 2000 it was used in Rome on October 1 and December 8). Two English translations (by Bishop Kallistos Ware and Roger Green) are suitable. A limited number of copies is available from the Ecumenical Society of the BVM at £1.35 each including p&p (cheques to ESBVM).

40 **COLLECTION OF MASSES:** see paragraph 26b ii.

The following observance of the Principal Joys of Mary by daily votives has received strong episcopal encouragement in the Diocese of Exeter. The bracketed numbers are the Compiler's suggestions as to which votives in the 'Collection' (above) fit.

Sunday: Nativity of BVM (20)
Monday: Annunciation (2)
Tuesday: Nativity of the Lord (4, 5, 19)
Wednesday: Adoration of the Magi (6)
Thursday: Purification of BVM (7)
Friday: Compassion of BVM (11, 12)
Saturday: Assumption of BVM (29)

---

41 *A MANUAL OF ANGLO-CATHOLIC DEVOTION* by the Bishop of Ebbsfleet contains a wealth of traditional resources.

42 *THE DIRECTORY ON POPULAR PIETY AND THE LITURGY*, a Vatican production, offers 'principles' and takes us through the liturgical year. Fun.

Appendix 1: Particular days

JANUARY 1: The Vatican observes World Peace Day. Leo the Great pointed out that the association of Peace with Christmastime is based as much on dogma as on sentiment. The Old Covenant community, defined by Circumcision, is replaced by Christ, the Father's One New Creation, into whom we are incorporated by Baptism. All peoples are called to this Unity and Peace. See the readings at the Office for Mary, Mother of God.

JANUARY 18 (PHG) OR □ FEBRUARY 22 (R:)
The { Confession (PHG) / □ Chair (R:) } of S Peter, Apostle

W			
	MP		Ezek 34:11–16
		Ps: 30, 34	Jn 21:15–22
	Mass	Gl; R: Pref of Apostles; CW, of a Saint	
		Ps 23, I Pet 5:1–4; Mt 16:13–19	
	EP	H: 226 (NEH 171) vv 3&6	Ezek 3:4–11
		Ps: 71, 145	Acts 11:1–18 (= R:)

The *Week of Prayer for Christian Unity* began in 1908 (among Anglicans who sought unity around the See of Peter) as the *Chair of Unity Octave*. It linked the Feasts of S Peter's Chair (January 18) and S Paul's Conversion (January 25). In 1969 Rome suppressed the former feast because it duplicated the Fourth Century Feast of the Chair (i.e. 'Episcopal Consecration') of S Peter in February (which R: retains). PHG put S Peter back at the start of our annual Prayer for Unity and, despite the lack of interest of CW, he survives there in some Diocesan Calendars. Even those who prefer the more ancient date and title in February might like to begin the Week of Prayer with a votive mass and office of S Peter.

MP commemorates the Pastoral Charge to Peter; in the Gospel at mass Peter's Confession of Christ leads to the granting of the keys; and EP shows Peter unlocking the Church's doors to the Gentiles.

At mass, the texts in the Missal for February 22 may conveniently be used on either day. PHG suggests the ASB Collect on p. 780 (a more prolix version of the Roman).

SUNDAY IN THE CHAIR OF UNITY OCTAVE

PHG follows the old English R.C. practice in allowing a mass for Unity on this Sunday (in green vestments). The Missal has texts towards the end; PHG on pp. 246 ff with Collects on pp. 366 f.

> R: = CW = PHG Sunday Mass: *Gl; Cr; Pref of Unity, PHG p. 257 (= R:)*
> *Ps 100, 122; Zeph 3:16–end; Eph 4:1–6 or Col 3:9–17 or*
> *I Jn 4:9–15; Jn 11:45–52 or Jn 17:11b–19 (20–23)*

MOTHERING SUNDAY (LENT 4)

On 'Mothering' or 'Refreshment' Sunday, rose colour is sometimes used; together with the organ and flowers.

Mothering Sunday can be combined with Lent if its theme is **Our Lady of Sorrows**. For texts, see Missal September 15. CW *Readings: Exod 2:1–10; 2 Cor 1:3–7 or Col 3:12–17; Ps 34:11–20; 127:1–4; Jn 19:25–27 or Lk 2:33–35; Preface PHG p. 278 (second pref).*

HARVEST

CW offers

Year A	*Deuteronomy 8:7–18* or *Deuteronomy 28:1–14;*
	Psalm 65;
	2 Corinthians 9:6–15;
	Luke 12:16–30 or *Luke 17:11–19.*
Year B	*Joel 2:21–27;*
	Psalm 126;
	1 Timothy 2:1–7 or *1 Timothy 6:6–10;*
	Matthew 6:25–33.
Year C	*Deuteronomy 26:1–11;*
	Psalm 100;
	Philippians 4:4–9 or *Revelation 14:14–18;*
	John 6:25–35.

REMEMBRANCE SUNDAY

PHG recommended the original R: Sunday lections (inappropriately 'improved' by CW) as suitable themes for Remembrance. CW also provides a votive for Peace. In many places the traditional practice of a Solemn Requiem on this day is continued, with appropriate propers related to the Resurrection Hope and the duty of Prayer for the Dead. CW considers the Collects for the Third Sunday before Advent most suitable for Remembrance Sunday.

THE BISHOP

On the Anniversary of the Pope's Inauguration and the 'Episcopal Ordination' (Consecration) or Translation of the Diocesan or the Provincial Bishop, a class 2 Votive (p. xxi) may be said. Texts in the Missal, or CW p. 237. (In the Collect, change 'your servant now to be *enthroned*' to 'your chosen servant *N*'.)

THE MONARCH

Office and Mass: Josh 1:1–10; Prov 8:1–16; Rom 13:1–10; Rev 21:22–22:4; Ps 20; 101; 121; Mt 22:16–22; Lk 22:24–30.

Appendix 2: Local days

THE DEDICATION OF THE LOCAL CHURCH

is a Solemnity observed on the date of the church's Consecration; if this Solemnity falls on a Sunday in Advent, Lent or Easter the seasonal notes will indicate how to transfer it. (The Dedication of the Cathedral is a Festum.)

When the Day of Consecration is unknown, CW allows the first Sunday in October. R: and CW suggest the Sunday before All Saints, in order to focus on the unity between the Church on Earth and the Church in Heaven. See Introduction paragraph 5 (External Solemnities, etc.). Clergy who serve several (country) churches may observe their Dedications as they get around them Sunday by Sunday 'on suitable dates chosen locally' (CW).

Hymns: 1 & 2 EP: 169 (NEH 204); MP 170 (NEH 205)
Mass: Gl; Cr; R: Pref of Dedication (ASB 26)

R:		Mass	*II Chron 5:6–11 & 13–6:2 (in Eastertide, Acts 7:44–50) I Cor 3:9–13 & 16–17; Jn 4:19–24*		
CW	W	1st EP of foll;		II Chron 7:11–16	Gen 28:10–end
		Ps: 24		Jn 4:19–29	Rev 21:9–16
	W	MP		Hag 2:6–9	I Chron 29:6–11
		Ps: 48		Heb 10:19–25	Eph 2:8–end
		Mass	*Year A: I Kings 8:22–30 or Rev 21:9–14; Ps 122; Heb 12:18–24; Mt 21:12–16.*		
			Year B: Gen 28:11–18 or Rev 21:9–14; Ps 122; 2 Pet 2:1–10; Jn 10:22–29.		
			Year C: I Chron 29:6–19; Ps 122; Eph 2:19–22; Jn 2:13–22.		
		2 EP	Year A	Jer 7:1–11	I Kgs 8:22–30
			Ps: 132	I Cor 3:9–17	Heb 10:19–25
			Years B & C	Jer 7:1–11	
			Ps: 132	Lk 19:1–10	

THE DEDICATION OF THE CATHEDRAL

is a Festum throughout the Diocese: no 1 EP or Creed at mass, but otherwise as above.

THE PATRON OF A CHURCH, CITY OR TOWN
is a Solemnity; Gloria and Creed are said at Mass, a first EP is said. The readings used in the Office should be the CW Proper Readings given by the middle column of the ORDO, supplemented by readings for the first EP from the list below, or else readings from the Commons. Or the generous provision in the Weekday Missal may be found helpful.

Appropriate readings should be selected if neither the ORDO nor this Appendix nor the Weekday Missal make adequate provision. August 6 is traditionally the Title of Churches dedicated to Christ; August 15 of those dedicated to S Mary.

If this Solemnity falls on a Sunday in Advent, Lent or Easter, the seasonal notes will indicate how to transfer it. See Introduction, paragraph 5, External Solemnity.

THE PRINCIPAL PATRON OF A DIOCESE is a Solemnity *or* Festum. Anglican Diocesan Calendars tend not to use this term, but it is often clear that particular Saints are so regarded (e.g. Chichester: Ss Richard and Wilfrid; Truro: Ss Piran and Petroc). When more than one Saint is clearly regarded as of more than 'Memorial' status, they should all probably be regarded as Co-Principal Patrons. When such Calendars tend to assume that these Saints can displace a 'Green' Sunday, they may be regarded as Solemnities (1 EP; Gl and Cr at Mass). Rome and EAD prefer such Patrons only to be Festa; no 1 EP; Gl only.

THE TITLE OF THE LOCAL CHURCH is a Solemnity.

THE TITLE OF THE CATHEDRAL is not observed outside the Cathedral unless (which tends particularly to be true in 'Celtic' areas) he/she – may be regarded as also the Diocesan Patron.

WHEN A SOLEMNITY REQUIRES A FIRST EVENING PRAYER (CW):

HYMNS are the same as for the Second EP.

	Psalm	OT Reading	NT Reading
S Paul	149	Isa 49:1–13	Acts 22:3–16
Presentation	118	I Sam 1:19b–28	Heb 4:11–16
S Mark	19	Isa 52:7–10	Mk 1:1–15
Ss P and James	25	Isa 40:27–31	Jn 12:20–26
S Matthias	147	Isa 22:15–22	Phil 3:13b–4:1
Visitation	45	Songs 2:8–14	Lk 1:26–38
S Barnabas	1 & 15	Isa 42:5–12	Acts 14:8–28
S Thomas	27	Isa 35	Heb 10:35–11:1
S Mary Magdalen	139	Isa 25:1–9	II Cor 1:3–7
S James	144	Deut 30:11–20	Mk 5:21–43
Transfiguration	99 & 110	Exodus 24:12–18	Jn 12:27–36a
S Bartholomew	97	Isa 61:1–9	II Cor 6:1–10
Holy Cross Day	66	Isa 52:13–53:12	Eph 2:11–22
S Matthew	34	Isa 33:13–17	Mt 6:19–34
S Michael etc	91	II Kgs 6:8–17	Mt 18:1–6 & 10
S Luke	33	Hos 6:1–3	II Tim 3:10–17
Ss S and Jude	124, 125, & 126	Deut 32:1–4	Jn 14:15–26
S Andrew	48	Isa 49:1–9a	I Cor 4:9–16

Appendix 3

CW COMMONS

Arranged for use at mass; but available to be used at the Office when, for example, a Patron is to be celebrated.

*coincides with or overlaps Roman reading. †Reading supplied from R:

	1st READING		PSALMS	2nd READING	GOSPEL
	OT: Outside Eastertide	NT: Within Eastertide			
MARTYRS	II Chron 24:17–21*	Rev 12:10–12a*	31:1–5*	Rom 8:35–39*	Mt 10:16–22*
	Wisd 4:10–15		126*	II Cor 4:7–15*	Mt 10:28–39*
	Isa 43:1–7		3; 11	II Tim 2:3–7(8–13)*	Jn 12:24–26*
	Jer 11:18–20		44:19–24	I Pet 4:12–19*	Jn 15:18–21*
				Heb 11:32–40	Mt 16:24–26
BISHOPS	I Sam 16:1 & 6–13*	Acts 20:28–35*	15*; 96*	I Cor 4:1–5*	Jn 10:11–16*
AND	Isa 6:1–8*		110*	II Cor 4:1–10*	Jn 21:15–17*
PASTORS	Jer 1:4–10*		1; 16:5–11	II Cor 5:14–20*	Mt 11:25–30
	Ezek 3:16–21*			I Pet 5:1–4*	Mt 24:42–46
	Mal 2:5–7				

	1st READING		PSALMS	2nd READING	GOSPEL
	OT: Outside Eastertide	NT: Within Eastertide			
DOCTORS	I Kgs 3:(6−10)11−14* Wisd 7:7−10 & 15−16* Ecclus 39:1−10* Prov 4:1−9	Acts 13:26−33†	19:7−10* 37:30−35* 119:89−96* 119:97−104 34:11−17	I Cor 1:18−25* I Cor 2:1−10* I Cor 2:9−16* Eph 3:8−12* II Tim 4:1−8* Titus 2:1−18	Mt 5:13−19* Mt 23:8−12* Mk 4:1−9* Mt 13:52−58 Jn 16:12−15
VIRGINS	Song S 8:6−7* Hos 2:14−15 & 19−20*	Rev 19:1 & 5−9*	45†; 149†	II Cor 10:17−11.2*	Mt 19:3−12*
HOLY MEN AND WOMEN	Gen 12:1−14* Mic 6:6−8* Ecclus 2:7−13(14−17)* Prov 8:1−11	Rev 21:(1−4)5−7*	33:1−5 32; 119:1−8; 139:1−4(5−12); 145:8−14	Eph 3:14−19* Eph 6:11−18* Jas 2:14−17* I Jn 4:7−16* Heb 13:7−8 & 15−16	Mt 25:1−13* Mt 25:14−30* Jn 15:1−8* Jn 17:20−26* Mt 19:16−21
RELIGIOUS As for Virgins; and—	I Kgs 19:9−18* Prov 10:27−32 Isa 61:10−62.5	Acts 4:32−35*	34:1−8* 112:1−9* 131* 119:57−64 123	Phil 3:7−14* I Jn 2:15−17	Mt 11:25−30* Mt 19:3−12 Lk 9:57−62* Lk 12:32−37* Mt 19:23−30
MISSIONARIES	Isa 52:7−10 Isa 61:1−3a Ezek 34:11−16 Jonah 3:1−5	Acts 2:14 & 22−36 Acts 13:46−49 Acts 16:6−10 Acts 26:19−23	67; 87; 97; 100; 117	Rom 15:17−21 II Cor 5:11−6:2	Mt 9:35−38 Mt 28:16−20 Mk 16:15−20 Lk 5:1−11 Lk 10:1−9
Those who worked for the UNDER- PRIVILEGED	Isa 58:6−11*	Acts 4:32−35†	82; 146: 5−10	I Jn 3:14−18* Heb 13:1−3	Mt 5:1−12* Mt 25:31−46*
MARRIED	Tobit 8:4−7* Prov 31:10−31*	Rev 19:1 & 5−9†	128* 127	I Pet 3:1−9*	Mk 3:31−35* Lk 10:38−42*
RULERS	I Sam 16:1−13a I Kgs 3:3−14	Rev 3:14 & 20−22†	72:1−7 99	I Tim 2:1−6	Lk 14:27−33* Mk 10:42−45
SCHOLARS	Prov 8:22−31 Ecclus 44:1−15	Rev 21:5−7†	36:5−10 49:1−4	Phil 4:7−8*	Mt 13:44−46 & 52* Jn 7:14−18

Office of the Dead (a selection)

MP	Ps: 40, 42	Isa 25:6−9	Isa 38:10−20
		Phil 3:10−21	I Cor 15:51−end
EP	H: 350 vv 1 & 4−7 (NEH 327)	Lam 3:22−26 & 31−33	Isa 43:1−7
	Ps: 121, 130	Jn 14:1−6	Rev 1:9−18

Appendix 4

'LESSER FESTIVALS' AND 'COMMEMORATIONS'

in The Christian Year: Calendar, Lectionary and Collects=Common Worship.

This list contains two distinct categories:

(a) the *Roman type* names, followed (mostly without description) by: are those (only) of the CW 'lesser festivals' for which CW provides optional proper readings. Some, but not all, of these suggested readings coincide with Roman optional suggestions for the same Saint; those which do are marked †.

(b) the *Italic* names, with brief descriptions, are those recommended, as 'commemorations': i.e. for naming in the prayers of intercession and thanksgiving. The Liturgical Commission admitted that it had not been 'scrupulous in reflecting on questions of orthodoxy or even baptismal status' with regard to some of these. Your compiler, see front of volume, may be able to provide information about some of them. 'RefM' means 'Reformation Martyr'.

(BRACKETS) distinguish those who have not been canonised or enjoyed a traditional cultus in the Latin or Byzantine rites. Your compiler accepts that different ecclesiological presuppositions will lead different users to regard some of these as having been definitively raised to the altars of the Church; or as suited to a real but restricted cultus ('Beati'); or as orthodox Christians judged to have had cardinal and theological virtues to a heroic degree and deserving therefore a private cultus ('Venerabiles'); or as still needing to have the Holy Sacrifice offered for them. (Those listed for 'commemoration' on the CW list who have been canonised, or enjoyed a long-standing traditional cultus, are mostly omitted from this list since they are incorporated into the main body of the ORDO as having (CW) 'an established celebration in the wider church'.)

JAN:
2 Basil and Gregory: II Tim 4:1–8; Mt 5:13–19
2 *Seraphim, Monk*
2 (*Vedanayagam Samuel Azariah, Bishop*)
10 (*William Laud, Bishop, Martyr*)
11 (*Mary Slessor, Missionary*)
12 Aelred: Ecclus 15:1–6
13 Hilary: I Jn 2:18–25†; Jn 8:25–32
13 (*George Fox*)
17 Antony: Phil 3:7–14; Mt 19:16–26†
17 (*Charles Gore, Bishop*)
19 Wulfstan: Mt 24:42–46
20 *Richard Rolle, Religious*
21 Agnes: Rev 7:13–17
24 Francis de Sales: Prov 3:13–18; Jn 3:17–21
28 Thomas Aquinas: Wisd 7:7–10 & 15–16; I Cor 2:9–16; Jn 16:12–15
30 Charles: Ecclus 2:12–17; I Tim 6:12–16

FEB:
3 Anskar: Isa 52:7–10; Rom 10:11–15
14 Cyril and Methodius: Isa 52:7–10; Rom 10:11–15
15 (*Thomas Bray, Priest*)
17 (*Janani Luwum, Bishop, Martyr*: Ecclus 4:20–28; Jn 12:24–32)
23 Polycarp: Rev 2:8–11†
27 (*George Herbert, Priest*: Mal 2:5–7; Mt 11:25–30; Rev 19:5–9

MAR:
1 David: II Sam 23:1–4; Ps 89:19–22 & 24
7 Perpetua, etc.: Rev 12:10–12a; Wisd 3:1–7
8 (*Geoffrey Studdert Kennedy, Priest*)
8 (*Edward King, Bishop*: Heb 13:1–8)
17 Patrick: Ps 19:1–4 & 13–16; Lk 10:1–12 & 17–20
21 (*Thomas Cranmer*, Bishop, RefM.)
24 (*Walter Hilton, Religious*)
24 (*Oscar Romero, Bishop, Martyr*)
26 (*Harriet Monsell, Religious*)
31 (*John Donne, Priest*)

OIL IN INITIATION

1. The main thrust of the ancient Western, and particularly Roman, tradition is to use two distinct sets of terms:
   (a) line[i]re or ung(u)ere (or simply tangere) – to *smear* oil on; and
   (b) (con)signare – to 'seal' with the *sign* of (usually) the Cross.

2. The use of oil may feature at three points:
   (i) Before the act of Baptism, when the Oil of the Catechumens, often nowadays called the Oil of Baptism, is used. Historically, 1(a) terms were used, and the candidates were smeared on their *chests* and *backs* (in the modern Roman Rite, only on their chests) *not* on (the one place required in *Common Worship*!) their heads.
   Concepts of exorcism or of the Christian Athlete can be associated with this.
   (ii) Immediately after the act of baptism. Historically, a presbyter smeared (1(a)) *the top of the head* (*not* the forehead) of the new Christian with Chrism. This is still Roman practice.
   (iii) In Confirmation, when the Bishop sealed (1(b)) the *forehead* of the candidates, usually (but see 3, below) having dipped his thumb in Chrism. This is still Roman practice.

3. One way of reading the evidence is to see 2(ii) as a preliminary to 2(iii); the presbyter (as S. Ambrose's description appears to suggest) poured generously and smeared oil from the top of the head downwards, and the Bishop then thumbed the sign of the Cross on the already oily forehead. When the current Western practice of splitting 'Baptism' and 'Confirmation' results in 2(ii) and 2(iii) having several years between them, one could, catechetically, explain 2(ii) in 'Baptism' as a 'pointer' to 2(iii) in 'Confirmation'.

4. SUMMARY. If it is desired to use CW texts as they stand:
   (i) CW Section "Signing with the Cross":
   – Make the sign of the Cross on the **chest**. If using oil, use the "Oil of Baptism".
   (ii) CW Section "Baptism," after the words ". . . inheritance of the Saints in glory. Amen.":
   – Do **not** make the sign of the Cross. If using oil, simply smear Chrism on the **top** of the head, **saying nothing**.
   (iii) The sign of the Cross on the forehead is proper to Confirmation alone.

ADVENT AND DECEMBER

UNTIL DECEMBER 16

1 Nothing may displace the Sunday Mass and Office. Any Solemnity (e.g. Dedication or Patron) is transferred to the Monday. Festa and Memorials are suppressed. (CW orders a Festum to be so transferred to Monday, and allows Dedication and Patronal festivals except on Advent 1.)

2 Altars are not decorated with *flowers* except on Solemnities, Festa, and Advent 3; and apart from these days the *organ* and other instruments are only played at liturgical services to sustain singing.

3 **Office Hymns. Until 16 December: EH: MP 2 EP 1. *NEH: MP 2 EP 1.***

4 On the Sundays of Advent, *Te Deum* is said at MP even though the *Gloria* is not used at Mass.

5 A seasonal form of the **Penitential Rite** (Introduction 12) is given in PHG p. 128, 2a (=R:).

6 Of the two prefaces provided in the Roman missal, Advent (I) is to be used from Advent Sunday to 16 December. This **preface** is the first of the 'extended' CW prefaces. On memorials, *either* the *seasonal* preface is used, *or* that of the Saint.

7 November 29 is, in Anglican Calendars, a Day of Intercession for the Missionary Work of the Church.

DECEMBER 17–24

8 On December 17 the Great Antiphons begin. They are found at EH 734 and NEH 503, and they are all now a day later than the medieval/BCP dates given in EH and NEH. They are said before and after the Magnificat at EP. (PHG suggests other uses for these Antiphons.)

9 In the Roman rite, the second Advent **preface** is now used. This preface is the second of the 'extended' CW prefaces.

10 **Office Hymns: EH: MP 14 EP 5. *NEH: MP 19 EP5.***

11 On the remaining weekdays of December, the propers in the Daily Eucharistic Lectionary are according to the *date in the month*.

12 On the remaining weekdays of December, Memorials are indicated [within square brackets] which means the following: Mass and Office of the Feria. The Memorial may be *either* totally ignored; *or* its Collect may be said *after* the Collect of the day at MP and EP, and *instead* of the Collect of the day at Mass.

13 Advent 4 is the Sunday of the Fathers of the Old Testament, and of Our Lady seen as the climax of God's ancient Covenant and Scriptures. The ancient Western celebration of January 1 as the Solemnity of Mary, Mother of God (Theotokos), is not a duplication of this, since it concentrates more on Our Lady as guarantee of the dogmatic truths of the Incarnation: Christ, Man and God; one Person, two Natures. (CW provides the R: mass readings of this Solemnity.) 'The . . . Council of Ephesus used *Theotokos* . . . to affirm the oneness of Christ's person by identifying Mary as the Mother of God the Word incarnate.' (ARCIC 2005)

IMMACULATE CONCEPTION OF THE BVM

1 'The Immaculate Conception was a feast (and a doctrine) first developed in the West in the Anglo-Saxon England of the early eleventh century on an older and rather different Byzantine basis.' (Gregory Dix). (It had to fend off assaults by Norman Romanizers who pointed out that it was not observed by the Papal Court.)

2 'As a result of our study, the Commission offers the following agreements, which we believe significantly advance our consensus regarding Mary. We affirm together . . . that in view of her vocation to be the Mother of the Holy One, Christ's redeeming work reached "back" in Mary to the depths of her being and to her earliest beginnings.' (ARCIC 2005)

3 While CW only offers the Commons, we follow PHG, which provides the (R:) mass readings and the full provision for MP and EP (Collect 89) as being 'appropriate to the season of Advent'. 'In the night of the Advent expectation, Mary began to shine like a true *Stella Matutina*. For just as the Morning Star, together with the Dawn, precedes the rising of the Sun, so Mary from the time of her Immaculate Conception preceded the coming of the Saviour, the rising of the Sun of Righteousness.' (JP2). PPL urges a Novena.

4 The *Office Hymns* now used are not in EH or NEH but may be obtained from the Compiler. The Common Hymns are 213, 214, 215 (NEH 180, 181, 183). EH 229 vv 1–3 & 7 is appropriate.

5 S John Diego Cuahtlatoatzin (Dec 9) was the visionary who saw our Lady of Guadalupe (Dec 12), Patron of the Americas. They have both been added optionally to the Universal Calendar as an expression of the Church's universality. For obtaining the Collects, see *PRAENOTANDA*.

S NICOLAS, BISHOP, PATRON: Mass: Isa 61:1–3; I Tim 6:6–11; Mk 10:13–16
1 EP: Ezek 34:11–16, Mt 25:14–30   MP: Isa 6:1–8, I Cor 4:1–6
2 EP: Isa 52:7–10; I Tim 4:1–5   Psalms, 1, 15, 23 (CW and PHG.)

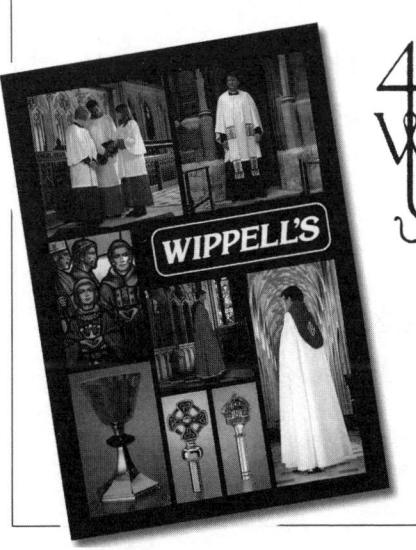

✠ *SUNDAY*   **ADVENT 1**

2	P	MP	Ps: 44	Mic 4:1–7	Isa 1:1–20
				I Thess 5:1–11	Rev 14:13 – 15:4
R: Ps I		Mass	*no Gl; Cr; Pref of Advent (1)*		
			CW: Isa 2:1–5; Ps 122; Rom 13:11–14; Mt 24:36–44		
			R: Isa 2:1–5; Ps 122; Rom 13:11–14; Mt 24:37–44 (The Day of the Lord)		
		EP		Isa 52:1–12	Isa 2:10–end
			Ps: 9	Mt 24:15–28	Jn 3:1–21

MONDAY   **S Francis Xavier, Pr**

3	W	MP	Ps: 1, 2, 3	Isa 25:1–9	Isa 3:1–15
				Mt 12:1–24	Mk 1:1–20
		Mass	*or of the Saint*		
			Isa 4:2–6; Ps 122; Mt 8:5–11		
		EP		Isa 42:18–end	Isa 4:2–end
			Ps: 4, 7	Rev 19	Rev 6

TUESDAY   **Feria (S John of Damascus, Pr, Dr)**

4	P	MP	Ps: 5, 6, 8	Isa 26:1–13	Isa 5:1–17
	(or W)			Mt 12:22–37	Mk 1:21–end
		Mass	*of Sunday or the day in Advent; no Gl or Cr; Pref of Advent (1) (or of the Saint)*		
			(*Nicolas Ferrar, Dcn, Rel*)		
			Isa 11:1–10; Ps 72:1–4 & 18–end; Lk 10:21–24		
		EP		Isa 43:1–13	Isa 5:18–end
			Ps: 9, 10	Rev 20	Rev 7

WEDNESDAY   **Feria**

5	P	MP	Ps: 119: 1–32	Isa 28:1–13	Isa 6
				Mt 12:38–end	Mk 2:1–22
		Mass	*as Tuesday*		
			Isa 25:6–10a; Ps 23; Mt 15:29–37		
		EP		Isa 43:14–end	Isa 8:16 – 9:7
			Ps: 11, 12, 13	Rev 21:1–8	Rev 8

THURSDAY   **Feria (S Nicolas, B: see p. xxxvi)**

6	G	MP	Ps: 14, 15, 16	Isa 28:14–end	Isa 9:8 – 10:4
	(or W)			Mt 13:1–23	Mk 2:23 – 3:12
		Mass	*as Tuesday (or of the Saint)*		
			Isa 26:1–6; Ps 118:18–27a; Mt 7:21 & 24–27		
		EP		Isa 44:1–8	Isa 10:5–23
			Ps: 18	Rev 21:9–21	Rev 9

FRIDAY   **S Ambrose, B, Dr**

7	W	MP	Ps: 17, 19	Isa 29:1–14	Isa 10:24 – 11:9
				Mt 13:24–43	Mk 3:13–end
		Mass	*of the Saint (First Friday: Sacred Heart, see p. 38)*		
			Isa 29:17–24; Ps 27:1–4 & 16–17; Mt 9:27–31		

              IMMACULATE CONCEPTION OF THE BVM (PHG) (see p. xxxvi)

	W	1 EP		Ecclus 24:17–22	◁
			Ps: 113, 147:12–20	Rom 8:28–30	◁

SATURDAY

8	W	MP	Ps: 46, 87	Isa 61:10 – 62:5	◁
				I Cor 1:26–30	◁
		Mass	*Gl; Cr; Proper Pref (or ASB 6 or CW Annunciation)*		
			Gen 3:9–15 & 20; Ps 98:1–5; Eph 1:3–6 & 11–12; Lk 1:26–38		
	P	1 EP of foll		Isa 44:24 – 45:13	Isa 14:3 — 27
			Ps: 24, 25	Rev 22:6–end	Rev 11

✠ *SUNDAY*   **ADVENT 2**

9   P   MP   Ps: 80   Amos 7   Isa 11:1–9
                                    Lk 1:5–20   Rev 20:11–21

R: Ps II   Mass   *no Gl; Cr; Pref of Advent (1)*
                  CW: Isa 11:1–10; Ps 72:1–7 & 18–19; Rom 15:4–13; Mt 3:1–12
                  R: Isa 11:1–10; Ps 72; Rom 15:4–9; Mt 3:1–12 (Our Baptism in the Spirit)

           2 EP   I Kgs 18:17–39   Isa 11:10 – 12 end
                  Ps: 11, 28   Jn 1:19–28   Lk 1:1–25

MONDAY   **Feria**

10   P   MP   Ps: 27, 30   Isa 30:1–18   Isa 17
                                    Mt 14:1–12   Mk 4:21–end

           Mass   *of Sunday or the day in Advent; no Gl or Cr; Pref of Advent (1) (**The Holy House**)*
                  Isa 35; Ps 85:7–end; Lk 5:17–26

           EP   Isa 45:14–end   Isa 18
                Ps: 26, 28, 29   I Thess 1   Rev 12

TUESDAY   **Feria (☐ S Damasus, Pp)**

11   P   MP   Ps: 32, 36   Isa 30:19–end   Isa 19:1–17
(or W)   Mt 14:13–end   Mk 5:1–20

           Mass   *as Monday (or of the Saint)*
                  Isa 40:1–11; Ps 96:1 & 10–end; Mt 18:12–14

           EP   Isa 46   Isa 19:18–end
                Ps: 33   I Thess 2:1–12   Rev 13

WEDNESDAY   **Feria (☐ Our Lady of Guadalupe: see p. xxxvi, note 5)**

12   P   MP   Ps: 34   Isa 31   Isa 21:1–12
(or W)   Mt 15:1–20   Mk 5:21–end

           Mass   *of Monday (or of Our Lady)*
                  Isa 40:25–end; Ps 103:8–13; Mt 11:28–end

           EP   Isa 47   Isa 22:1–14
                Ps: 119:33–56   I Thess 2:13–end   Rev 14

THURSDAY   **S Lucy, V, M**

13   R   MP   Ps: 37   Isa 32   Isa 24
                                    Mt 15:21–28   Mk 6:1–13

           Mass   *of the Saint (**Samuel Johnson**)*
                  Isa 41:13–20; Ps 145:1 & 8–13; Mt 11:11–15

           EP   Isa 48:1–11   Isa 28:1–13
                Ps: 39, 40   I Thess 3   Rev 15

FRIDAY   **S John of the Cross, Pr, Dr**

14   W   MP   Ps: 31   Isa 33:1–22   Isa 28:14–end
                                    Mt 15:29–end   Mk 6:14–29

           Mass   *of the Saint*
                  Isa 48:17–19; Ps 1; Mt 11:16–19

           EP   Isa 48:12–end   Isa 29:1–14
                Ps: 35   I Thess 4:1–12   Rev 16

SATURDAY   **Feria**

15   P   MP   Ps: 41, 42, 43   Isa 35   Isa 29:15–end
                                    Mt 16:1–12   Mk 6:30–end

           Mass   *as Monday*
                  Ecclus 48:1–4 & 9–11; Ps 80:1–4 & 18–end; Mt 17:10–13

P (or   1 EP of Advent 3   Isa 49:1–13   Isa 30:1–18
Rose)   Ps: 45, 46   I Thess 4:13–end   Rev 17

✠ *SUNDAY*
16 P (or Rose)

R: Ps III

ADVENT 3

	MP	Ps: 68:1–19	Zeph 3:14–20	Isa 25:1–9
			Phil 4:4–7	Rev 21:9 – 22:5
	Mass	no Gl; Cr; Pref of Advent (1) or (2)		
		CW: Isa 35:1–10; Ps 146:4–10; Jas 5:7–10; Mt 11:2–11		
		R: Isa 35:1–6a & 10; Ps 146; Jas 5:7–10; Mt 11:2–11 (S John Baptist)		
	2 EP		Isa 5:8–30	Isa 26
		Ps: 12, 14	Acts 13:13–41	I Tim 1:12 – 2:7

MONDAY
17 P

Feria (O Sapientia: see pp. xxxv–xxxvi, notes 8–13)

	MP	Ps: 44	Isa 38:1–8, 21–22	Isa 30:19–end
			Mt 16:13–end	Mk 7:1–23
	Mass	see p. xxxv, note 11.		
		no Gl or Cr; Pref of Advent (2) (***Eglantine Jebb***)		
		Gen 49:2 & 8–10; Ps 72:1–5 & 18–end; Mt 1:1–17		
	EP		Isa 49:14–25	Isa 31
		Ps: 47, 49	I Thess 5:1–11	Rev 18

TUESDAY
18 P

Feria (O Adonal)

	MP	Ps: 48, 52	Isa 38:9–20	Isa 38:1–20
			Mt 17:1–13	Mk 7:24 – 8:10
	Mass	as Monday (Obit of Michael, second Bishop of Ebbsfleet, in 1999)		
		Jer 23:5–8; Ps 72:1–2 & 12–13 & 18–end; Mt 1:18–24		
	EP		Isa 50	Isa 40:1–11
		Ps: 50	I Thess 5:12–end	Rev 19

WEDNESDAY
19 P

Feria (O Radix)*

	MP	Ps: 144, 146	Isa 39	Isa 40:12–end
			Mt 17:14–21	Mk 8:11 – 9:1
	Mass	as Monday		
		Judg 13:2–7 & 24–25; Ps 71:3–8; Lk 1:5–25		
	EP		Isa 51:1–8	Isa 41
		Ps: 10, 57	II Thess 1	Rev 20

THURSDAY
20 P

Feria (O Clavis)

	MP	Ps: 46, 95	Zeph 1:1 – 2:3	Isa 42:1–17
			Mt 17:22–end	Mk 9:2–32
	Mass	as Monday (***Our Lady of the Annunciation: 2***)		
		Isa 7:10–14; Ps 24:1–6; Lk 1:26–38		
	EP		Isa 51:9–16	Isa 42:18 – 43:13
		Ps: 4, 9	II Thess 2	Rev 21:1–14

FRIDAY
21 P

Feria (O Oriens) [□ S Peter Canisius, Pr, Dr]*

	MP	Ps: 121, 122, 123	Zeph 3:1–13	Isa 43:14 – 44:5
			Mt 18:1–20	Mk 9:33–end
	Mass	as Monday (Anniversary of the Episcopal Ordination in 1996 of David, Bishop in Wales.		
		Appendix I) (***Our Lady of the Visitation: 3***)		
		Zeph 3:14–18; Ps 33:1–4 & 11–12 & 19–end; Lk 1:39–45		
	EP		Isa 51:17–end	Isa 44:6–23
		Ps: 80, 84	II Thess 3	Rev 21:15 – 22:5

SATURDAY
22 P

Feria (O Rex)*

	MP	Ps: 124, 125, 126, 127	Zeph 3:14–end	Isa 44:24 – 45:13
			Mt 18:21–end	Mk 10:1–31
	Mass	as Monday		
		I Sam 1:24–28; Ps 113 ; Lk 1:46–56		
	1 EP of Advent 4		Isa 52:1–12	Isa 45:14–end
		Ps: 89:1–37	Jude	Rev 22:6–end

---

* Ember Days. See Introduction, paragraph 25.

✠ *SUNDAY* **ADVENT 4**

23 P MP Ps: 144 Mic 5:2–5a Isa 32:1–8
                     Lk 1:26–38 Rev 22:6–end

R: Ps IV Mass *no Gl; Cr; Pref of Advent (2)*
                CW: Isa 7:10–16; Ps 80:1–8 & 18–20; Rom 1:1–7; Mt 1:18–25
                R: Isa 7:10–14; Ps 24; Rom 1:1–7; Mt 1:18–24 (our Lady)

          2 EP I Sam 1:1–20 Isa 40:1–11
                Ps: 113, 126 Rev 22:6–21 Lk 1:26–45

MONDAY **(Morning)**

24 P MP Ps: 45, 113 Mal 1:1 & 6–end Isa 46
                              Mt 19:1–12 Mk 10:32–end

          Mass *as last Monday*
                II Sam 7:1–5 & 8–11 & 16; Ps 89:2 & 19–27; Lk 1:67–79

CHRISTMAS EVE, CHRISTMAS DAY
Notes for Christmastide See page 5

WEDNESDAY **S Stephen, First Martyr**

26 R MP H: 31 (NEH 218) Jer 26:12–15 ◁
              Ps: 13, 31:1–8, 150 Acts 6 (=R:) ◁

          Mass *Gl; Pref of Christmas*
                CW: from: II Chron 24:20–22; Acts 7:51–60; Ps 119:161–168; Gal 2:16b–20;
                Mt 10:17–22
                R: Acts 6:8–10 & 7:54–9; Ps 31; Mt 10:17–22

                                                        [EP of the Saint
        W EP of Christmas H: 17 (NEH 19) Isa 41:1–5 Ps 57, 86; Gen 4:1–10
                    Ps: 19 Jn 12:20–26 Mt 23:34–end]

THURSDAY **S John, Apostle and Evangelist**

27 W MP Hymn from Common Exod 33:12–end ◁
              Ps: 21, 147:13–21 I Jn 2:1–11 (=R:) ◁

          Mass *Gl; Pref of Christmas*
                CW: Exod 33:7–11a; Ps 117; I Jn 1; Jn 21:19b–25
                R: I Jn 1:1–4; Ps 97; Jn 20:2–8

                                                        [EP of the Saint:
        W EP of Christmas H: 17 (NEH 19) Isa 41:8–16 Ps 97: Isa 6:1–8
                    Ps: 45 Jn 12:27–33 1 Jn 5:1–12]

FRIDAY **Holy Innocents**

28 R MP H: 34 (NEH 218) Baruch 4:21–27 ◁
              Ps: 36, 146 Mt 18:1–10 ◁

          Mass *Gl; Pref of Christmas*
                CW: Jer 31:15–17; Ps 124; I Cor 1:26–29; Mt 2:13–18
                R: I Jn 1:5 – 2:2; Mt 2:13–18

                                                        [EP of the Saints:
        W EP of Christmas H: 17 (NEH 19) Isa 41:17–20 Ps 123, 128: Isa 49:14–25
                    Ps: 132 Jn 12:34–37 Mk 10:13–16]

SATURDAY **In the Octave of Christmas**

29 *[S Thomas a Becket, B, M (see p. xxxv, note 12)]*
        W MP H: 18 (NEH 20) Jonah 1 Isa 55
                Ps: 19, 20 Col 1:1–14 Jn 1:14–18

          Mass *Gl; Pref of Christmas*
                I Jn 2:3–11; Ps 96:1–4; Lk 2:22–35

        W 1 EP of Christmas I:
                H: 17 (NEH 19) Isa 57:15–end Isa 60:1–12
                Ps: 132 Jn 1:1–18 Mt 11:2–6

           1 EP of Holy Family:
                H: 46 (NEH 45) Prov 4:1–6 ◁
                Ps: 122 Lk 2:40–end ◁

✠
24-25
NATIVITY OF THE LORD
CHRISTMAS EVE and CHRISTMAS DAY   *GOLD OR WHITE*

All the masses of Christmas—*including* the Vigil Mass (see note 1 below) — are celebrated in white vestments, with Gloria, Creed (Kneel for the *Incarnatus*), and Preface of the Incarnation (see note 4 below).

EVE   Evening ('Vigil') Mass: *Isa 62:1–5; Ps 89:3–4 & 15–16 & 26 & 28; Acts 13:16–17 & 22–25*
                Mt (1–17) 18–end

	1 EP	Zech 2 (R: Isa 11:1–10)	Zech 2:10–end
	Ps: 85	Rev 1:1–8	Titus 2:11 – 3:7

NIGHT   Midnight Mass:
                CW = R: Isa 9:2–7; Ps 96; Titus 2:11–14; Lk 2:1–14

DAY   MP   Ps: 110, 117   Isa 62:1–5   Isa 9:2–7
                                        Mt 1:18–25   Lk 2:1–20

          Mass at Dawn:
                CW: Isa 62:6–12; Ps 97; Titus 3:4–7; Lk 2 (1–7) 8–20
                R: Isa 62:11–12; Ps 97; Titus 3:4–7; Lk 2:15–20

          Mass of the Day:
                CW: Isa 52:7–10; Ps 98; Heb 1:1–4 (5–12); Jn 1:1–14
                R: Isa 52:7–10; Ps 98; Heb 1:1–6; Jn 1:1–18 or 1–5 & 9–14

	2 EP	Isa 65:17–25	Isa 35
	Ps: 8	Phil 2:5–11	I Jn 4:7–end

NOTES FOR CHRISTMASTIDE AND EPIPHANY

1 **The Eve.** The Vigil mass of Christmas is the first of the four masses of Christmas, and is celebrated festally as such. Its Collect in the Roman Rite is the ancient one which CW mistakenly assigns to the Advent mass in *purple* vestments said in the *earlier* part of the 24th. This Collect is also used at 1 EP.

2 **Penitential Rite.** Seasonal forms (Introduction, Paragraph 12) are given in PHG: *Christmas* p. 196, 1; *Epiphany* p. 233, a and b (all=R:).

3 **Collects.** *Eve*: see Note 1. *Midnight*: CW gives the Roman Collect in a better translation than R:. *Dawn*: the R: Collect, which is not in CW, is also used at MP. *Day*: CW continues to offer Cranmer's elegant composition.

The ancient Christmas Collect *Almighty God who wonderfully created . . .* was introduced by 1928 for Christmas II, transferred by ASB and CW to Christmas I, (where it will unfortunately be in competition with the Holy Family) and is now the Roman Collect for Christmas Day itself.

On *ferial days* from Christmas until the Sunday after Ephiphany, R: has a different Collect for each day. Anglican custom expects the Christmas Day and Epiphany Collects to be used until the following Sundays, and otherwise the Collect of the previous Sunday to be used. Your compiler recommends that it is best *either* to use the daily Roman Collects: *or* to stay with *Almighty God who wonderfully created . . .* until Epiphany, and thereafter to use the Epiphany Collect. **Memorials:** see page xxxv note 12.

4 **Prefaces.** The CW 'extended' Preface is a lengthened version of the Roman Preface. R: offers two more Christmas Prefaces. PHG gives us a version of the Roman Epiphany Preface on p. 238 (b); and the Roman Preface for the Baptism on p. 231. On the Feasts of Christmas Week, the Christmas Prefaces are used. On memorials after January 1, the Preface of the Season or of the Saint is used.

5 **Evening Prayer.** The great festival of the Incarnation should dominate its octave. Accordingly, from S Stephen to the Holy Innocents, Rome, endorsed by PHG but not CW, has *MP only* of the Festum; EP of Christmastide (H:17 NEH 19). *Your Order follows this usage,* while giving readings for the Saints *in the right-hand column* for those who follow the other practice, or who need to treat these Saints as Patronal Solemnities. (The readings in both columns are CW.)

6 **Office hymns until Epiphany: EH: MP 18 EP 17 *NEH: MP 20 EP 19*.**

DECEMBER 2007 *R: CW Year A. Weekday Lectionaries Year 2*

✠ *SUNDAY*			**CHRISTMAS 1 (CW)**		
30	W	MP	Ps: 105:1–11	Isa 35:1–6	Isa 40:1–11
				Gal 3:23–29	Col 1:1–20
R: Ps I		Mass	*Gl; Cr; Pref of Christmas*		
			CW: Isa 63:7–9; Ps 148; Heb 2:10–18; Mt 2:13–23		
		2 EP	H: 17	Isa 49:7–13	Isa 40:12–end
			Ps: 132	Phil 2:1–11	Phil 2:1–11
OR			**HOLY FAMILY (ROMAN & PHG)**		
	W	MP	Ps: 132	Isa 35	◁
				Col 1:1–20	◁
		Mass	*Gl; Cr; Pref of Christmas*		
			Ecclus 3:2–6 & 12–14; Ps 128; Col 3:12–21; Mt 2:13–15 & 19–end		
		2 EP	H: 46 (NEH 45)	Isa 41:21–end	◁
			Ps: 84, 122	Phil 2:1–11	◁
MONDAY			**In the Octave of Christmas** [*S Silvester, Pp (see p. xxx, note 12)*]		
31	W	MP	Ps: 102	Jonah 3–4	Isa 62
				Col 1:24 – 2:7	Jn 6:41–58
		Mass	*Gl; Pref of Christmas (**John Wycliff**)*		
			I Jn 2:18–21; Ps 96:1 & 11–end; Jn 1:1–18		
EITHER		1 EP of The Holy Name of Jesus*		Jer 23:1–6	Numbers 6:22–26
			Ps: 148	Col 2:8–15	Lk 21:25–36
OR		1 EP of Mary Mother of God (R:)*		Gen 17:1–12a & 15–16	◁
			Ps: 90, 148	Col 2:8–15	◁

* Hymn from tomorrow's EP.

JANUARY 2008

TUESDAY			**THE HOLY NAME OF JESUS (CW)**		
1	W	MP	H: 238 (NEH 291)	Gen 17:1–13	Deut 10:12 – 11:1
			Ps: 103, 150	Rom 2:17–29	Rom 2:17–end
		Mass	*Gl; Cr; Pref of Christmas*		
			Num 6:22–27; Ps 8; Gal 4:4–7; Lk 2:15–21		
		2 EP	H: 237 (NEH 153)	Deut 30: (1–10) 11-20	Deut 30
			Ps: 115	Acts 3:1–16	Col 2:8–15
OR			**MARY MOTHER OF GOD (ROMAN)**		
	W	MP	H: 214 (NEH 181)	Mic 5:2–5a	◁
			Ps: 103, 150	Heb 2:9–17 (=R:)	◁
		Mass	*Gl; Cr; Pref I of BVM*		
			Num 6:22–27; Ps 67; Gal 4:4–7; Lk 2:16–21 (given by PHG & CW)		
		2 EP	H: 613:1 & 3–6		
			(NEH 33)	Baruch 4:36 – 5:4	◁
			Ps: 115	Eph 2:11–22	◁
WEDNESDAY			*Ss Basil the Great and Gregory Nazianzen, Bs and Drs*		
2	W	MP	Ps: 18:1–30	Ruth 1	Isa 63:1–6
				Col 2:8–end	Mt 1:18–end
		Mass	*of the Saints; no Gl; Pref of Christmas (**S Seraphim of Sarov, Rel**)*		
			*(**Vedanayagam Samuel Azariah, B**)*		
			1 Jn 2:22–28; Ps 98:1–4; Jn 1:19–28		
			(Printed in Weekday Missal as 'Readings for 2–12 January: 2 January')		
		EP		Isa 60:1–12	Isa 63:7–end
			Ps: 45, 46	Jn 1:35–42	I Thess 1
THURSDAY			*Feria (The Most Holy Name of Jesus)*		
3	W	MP	Ps: 127, 128, 131	Ruth 2	Isa 64
				Col 3:1–11	Mt 2
		Mass	*CW: of Sunday. Weekday Missal: 'Masses for Weekdays of the Christmas Season'*		
			no Gl or Cr; Pref of Christmas		
			I Jn 2:29 – 3:6; Ps 98:2–7; Jn 1:29–34		
			Holy Name: Phil 2:1–11; Ps 8; Lk 2:21–24		
		EP		Isa 60:13–end	Isa 65:1–16
			Ps: 2, 110	Jn 1:43–end	I Thess 2:1–16

FRIDAY
4   W   MP   Ps: 89:1–37   Ruth 3   Isa 65:17–end
                                  Col 3:12 – 4:1   Mt 3:1 – 4:11
         Mass   *as Thursday (First Friday: Sacred Heart, see p. 38)*
                 I Jn 3:7–10; Ps 98:1 & 8–end; Jn 1:35–42
         EP   Isa 61   Isa 66:1–9
                 Ps: 85, 87   Jn 2:1–12   I Thess 2:17 – 3:end

SATURDAY
5   W   MP   Ps: 8, 48   Ruth 4:1–17   Isa 66:10–end
                                 Col 4:2–end   Mt 4:12 – 5:16
         Mass   *as Thursday (First Saturday: Immaculate Heart, see p. 38)*
                 I Jn 3:11–21; Ps 100; Jn 1:43–end

✠   **EPIPHANY OF THE LORD**
         1 EP   H: 38 (NEH 46)   Isa 49:1–13   Isa 42:1–9
                 Ps: 96, 97   Jn 4:7–26   Rom 15:8–21

SUNDAY
6   W   MP   H: 40 (NEH 48)   Jer 31:7–14   Isa 49:1–13
                    Ps: 113, 132   Jn 1:29–34   Lk 3:15–22
         Mass   *Gl; Cr; Pref of Epiphany (p. 5, note 4)*
                 CW: Isa 60:1–6; Ps 72: (1–9) 10–15; Eph 3:1–12; Mt 2:1–12
                 R: Isa 60:1–6; Ps 72; Eph 3:2–3a & 5–6; Mt 2:1–12
         2 EP   H: 38 (NEH 46)   Isa 60:1–9 (10–22) (= R:)   Isa 60:9–end
                 Ps: 98, 100   Jn 2:1–11   Jn 2:1–11

Because of a laudable desire to be very subtle, the CW revisers impose a diverting complexity upon the period after Epiphany this year. (See *PRAENOTANDA*)

CW title and **Collect**	CW **readings**	Roman title	BCP title
January 6 Epiphany and also numbered as "The 1st Sunday of Epiphany"	Epiphany	Epiphany	Epiphany
January 13 Baptism of the Lord and also called "The 2nd Sunday of Epiphany"	Baptism	Baptism	1st Sunday after Epiphany
January 20 "The 3rd Sunday of Epiphany"	**As for the 2nd Sunday of Epiphany**	2nd of the Year	Septuagesima
January 27 "The 4th Sunday of Epiphany"	**As for the 3rd Sunday of Epiphany**	3rd of the Year	Sexagesima
February 3 "Next before Lent" OR The Presentation	Next before Lent	4th of the Year	Quinquagesima

MONDAY | | | *Feria (☐ S Raymund of Penyafort, Pr)* | | |

7	W	MP	H: 40 (NEH 48)	Baruch 1:15 – 2:10	Hos 2:14–3 end
			Ps: 71	Mt 20:1–16	Mt 5:17–end
R: Ps II		Mass	*CW: of Epiphany; R: from 'Masses for weekdays of the Christmas season'.*		
			no Gl or Cr; Pref of Christmas or Epiphany (or of the Saint).		
			I Jn 3:22 – 4:6; Ps 2:7–end; Mk 4:12–17 & 23–end (Printed in Weekday Missal as 'Readings		
			for 2–12 January: 7 January or Monday after Epiphany'.)		
		EP	H: 38 (NEH 46)	Isa 63:7–end	Hos 4:1–11
			Ps: 72, 75	I Jn 3	I Thess 4:1–12

TUESDAY | | | *Feria* | | |

8	W	MP	H: 40 (NEH 48)	Baruch 2:11–end	Hos 5:8 – 6:6
			Ps: 73	Mt 20:17–28	Mt 6:1–18
		Mass	*as Monday*		
			I Jn 4:7–10; Ps 72:1–8; Mk 6:34–44		
		EP	H: 38 (NEH 46)	Isa 64	Hos 8
			Ps: 74	I Jn 4:7–end	I Thess 4:13 – 5:11

WEDNESDAY | | | *Feria* | | |

9	W	MP	H: 40 (NEH 48)	Baruch 3:1–8	Hos 9
			Ps: 77	Mt 20:29–end	Mt 6:19–end
		Mass	*as Monday*		
			I Jn 4:11–18; Ps 72:1 & 10–13; Mk 6:45–52		
		EP	H: 38 (NEH 46)	Isa 65:1–16	Hos 10
			Ps: 119:81–104	I Jn 5:1–12	I Thess 5:12–end

THURSDAY | | | *Feria* | | |

10	W	MP	H: 40 (NEH 48)	Baruch 3:9 – 4:4	Hos 11
			Ps: 78:1–39	Mt 23:1–12	Mt 7
		Mass	*as Monday (**William Laud, B, M**)*		
			I Jn 4:19 – 5:4; Ps 72:1 & 18–end; Lk 4:14–22		
		EP	H: 38 (NEH 46)	Isa 65:17–end	Hos 12
			Ps: 78:40–end	I Jn 5:13–end	II Thess 1

FRIDAY | | | *Feria* | | |

11	W	MP	H: 40 (NEH 48)	Baruch 4:21–30	Hos 13:1–14
			Ps: 55	Mt 23:13–28	Mt 8:1–17
		Mass	*as Monday (**Mary Slessor**)*		
			I Jn 5:5–13; Ps 147:12–end; Lk 5:12–16		
		EP	H: 38 (NEH 46)	Isa 66:1–11	Hos 14
			Ps: 69	II Jn	II Thess 2

SATURDAY | | | *Feria (S Aelred of Rievaulx, Abbot; Benedict Biscop, Ab)* | | |

12	W	MP	H: 40 (NEH 48)	Baruch 4:36 – 5–end	Joel 1
			Ps: 76, 79	Mt 23:29–end	Mt 8:18–end
		Mass	*as Monday (or of the Saint)*		
			I Jn 5:14–end; Ps 149:1–5; Jn 3:22–30		
			BAPTISM OF THE LORD		
	W	1 EP of foll	Isa 61	◁ [Joel 2:1–14]	
			Ps: 36	Titus 2:11–14 & 3:4–7	◁ [II Thess 3]

✠ SUNDAY
13   W   MP   **THE BAPTISM OF THE LORD**

	MP	Ps: 89:19–29	Exod 14:15–22	◁ [Isa 42:1–12]
			I Jn 5:6–9	◁ [Jn 4:1–26 (27–42)]
	Mass	*Gl; Cr on Sunday; R: Proper Pref; CW, of Epiphany (p. 5 note 4)*		
		CW: Isa 42:1–9; Ps 29; Acts 10:34–43; Mt 3:13–17		
		R: Isa 42:1–4 & 6–7; Ps 29; Acts 10:34–38; Mt 3:13–17		
	2 EP	H: NEH 58 (EH 38)	Josh 3:1–8 & 14–17	◁ [Isa 43:1–13]
		Ps: 46, 47	Heb 1:1–12	◁ [Jn 2:20–36a]

'ORDINARY TIME' – 'PER ANNUM' – 'THE GREEN SEASON' – BEGINS
1st WEEK of YEAR

MONDAY
14   G   *Feria*

R: Ps I

MP	Ps: 80, 82	Gen 1:1–19	Joel 2:15–end
		Mt 21:1–17	Mt 9:1–17
Mass	*CW: Collect of Epiphany 2; R: of the first week of the year; no Gl or Cr; Common Pref*		
	I Sam 1:1–8; Ps 116:10–15; Mk 1:14–20		
EP		Amos 1	Joel 3
	Ps: 85, 86	I Cor 1:1–17	Gal 1

TUESDAY
15   G   *Feria*

MP	Ps: 87, 89:1–18	Gen 1:20 – 2:3	Amos 1
		Mt 21:18–32	Mt 9:18–34
Mass	*as Monday*		
	I Sam 1:9–20; Ps I Sam 2:1 & 4–8; Mk 1:21–28		
EP		Amos 2	Amos 2
	Ps: 89:19–end	I Cor 1:18–end	Gal 2

WEDNESDAY
16   G   *Feria*

MP	Ps: 119:105–128	Gen 2:4–end	Amos 3
		Mt 21:33–end	Mt 9:35 – 10:23
Mass	*as Monday*		
	I Sam 3:1–10 & 19–20; Ps 40:1–4 & 7–10; Mk 1:29–39		
EP		Amos 3	Amos 4
	Ps: 91, 93	I Cor 2	Gal 3

THURSDAY
17   W   *S Antony, Abbot*

MP	Ps: 90, 92	Gen 3	Amos 5
		Mt 22:1–14	Mt 10:24–end
Mass	*of the Saint (**Charles Gore, B**)*		
	I Sam 4:1–11; Ps 44:10–15 & 24, 25; Mk 1:40–end		
EP		Amos 4	Amos 6
	Ps: 94	I Cor 3	Gal 4:1 – 5:1

FRIDAY
18   G (or W)   *Feria (Confession of S Peter; Unity Week; see p. xxvii)*

MP	Ps: 88, 95	Gen 4:1–16, 25–26	Amos 7
		Mt 22:15–33	Mt 11
Mass	*as Monday (or of the Apostle)*		
	I Sam 8:4–7 & 10–end; Ps 89:15–18; Mk 2:1–12		
EP		Amos 5:1–17	Amos 8
	Ps: 102	I Cor 4	Gal 5:2–end

SATURDAY
19   G (or W)   *Our Lady on Saturday* or the Feria*
(S Wulfstan, B, Rel; EAD Solemnity in Worcester)

MP	Ps: 96, 97, 100	Gen 6:1–10	Amos 9
		Mt 22:34–end	Mt 12:1–21
Mass	*Introduction Paragraph 26(b) (or of the Saint)*		
	I Sam 9:1–4 & 17–19 & 10:1; Ps 21:1–6; Mk 2:13–17		
G 1 EP of foll*		Amos 5:18–end	Obadiah
	Ps: 104	I Cor 5	Gal 6

---

* For 'Our Lady on Saturday' see Introduction Paragraph 26(b), and Hymns page xxiii.

✠ SUNDAY | | | **2nd SUNDAY and WEEK of YEAR; CW see page 7; BCP SEPTUAGESIMA**

20	G	MP	Ps: 113	Amos 3:1–8	Gen 1:1 – 2:3
				I Jn 1:1–4	Rev 21:1–7
R: Ps II		Mass	*Gl; Cr; Sunday Pref. (UNITY: see Introduction Appendix 1)*		
			CW: Isa 49:1–7; Ps 40:1–12; I Cor 1:1–9; Jn 1:29–42		
			R: Isa 49:3 & 5–6; Ps 40; I Cor 1:1–3; Jn 1:29–34 (The Lamb of God)		
		2 EP		Eccles 3:1–11	Gen 2:4–end
			Ps: 33	I Pet 1:3–12	Mk 10:1–16

MONDAY | | | **S Agnes, V, M**

21	R	MP	Ps: 98, 99, 101	Gen 6:11 – 7:10	Gen 3
				Mt 24:1–14	Mt 15:29 – 16:12
		Mass	*of the Saint*		
			I Sam 15:16–23; Ps 50:8–10 & 16–17 & 24; Mk 2:18–22		
		EP		Amos 6	Gen 4:1–16
			Ps: 103, 105	I Cor 6:1–11	Rom 1

TUESDAY | | | **Feria (S Vincent, Dcn, M)**

22	W (or R)	MP	Ps: 103, 106	Gen 7:11–end	Gen 6:5–end
				Mt 24:15–28	Mt 16:13–end
		Mass	*of Sunday (CW: Collect of Epiphany 3); no Gl or Cr; Common Pref (or of the Saint)*		
			I Sam 16:1–13; Ps 89:19–27; Mk 2:23–end		
		EP		Amos 7	Gen 7
			Ps: 107	I Cor 6:12–end	Rom 2

WEDNESDAY | | | **Feria**

23	G	MP	Ps: 110, 111, 112	Gen 8:1–14	Gen 8:1–14
				Mt 24:29–end	Mt 17:1–23
		Mass	*as Tuesday (**Espousals of our Lady**)*		
			I Sam 17:32–33 & 37 & 40–51; Ps 144:1–2 & 9–10; Mk 3:1–6		
		EP		Amos 8	Gen 8:15 – 9:17
			Ps: 119:129–152	I Cor 7:1–24	Rom 3

THURSDAY | | | **S Francis de Sales, B, Dr**

24	W	MP	Ps: 113, 115	Gen 8:15 – 9:7	Gen 11:1–9
				Mt 25:1–13	Mt 17:24 – 18:14
		Mass	*of the Saint*		
			I Sam 18:6–9 & 19:1–7; Ps 56:1–2 & 8–end; Mk 3:7–12		
		EP		Amos 9	Gen 11:27 – 12:10
			Ps: 114, 116, 117	I Cor 7:25–end	Rom 4

FRIDAY | | | **Conversion of S Paul, Apostle**

25	W	MP	H: 226 vv4 & 6	Ezek 3:22–27	Isa 56:1–8
			Ps: 66, 147:13–21	Phil 3:1–14	Gal 1:11–end (=R:)
		Mass	*of the Saint; Gl; R; Pref of Apostles; CW, of Saints*		
			CW: Acts 9:1–22; Ps 67; (Gal 1:11–16a); Mt 19:27–30		
			R: Acts 22:3–16 or 9:1–22; Ps 117; Mk 16:15–18		
		EP	H: NEH 154	Ecclus 39:1–10	Jer 1: 4–10
			Ps: 119:41–56	Col 1:24 – 2:7	Phil 3:1–14

SATURDAY | | | **Ss Timothy and Titus, Bs**

26	W	MP	Ps: 120, 121, 122	Gen 11:1–9	Gen 15
				Mt 25:31–end	Mt 19:1–15
		Mass	*of the Saints*		
			CW: Isa 61:1–3a; Ps 100; II Tim 2:1–8 or Titus 1:1–5; Lk 10:1–9		
			(R: II Tim 1:1–8 or Titus 1:1–5; Lk 10:1–9)		
	G	1 EP of foll		Hos 2:2–17	Gen 16
			Ps: 118	I Cor 9:1–14	Rom 6

JANUARY – FEBRUARY

The *Presentation*, according to CW, may be celebrated *either* on Sunday February 3 *or* on Saturday February 2. In either case it is, for CW, a Solemnity with a 1 EP and the Creed at Mass. (According to R: it is observed on Friday, with *no* 1 EP: and, additionally, an 'External Solemnity' – all Masses and Offices including a 1 EP – may be observed on Sunday.) We print the entire provision separately for insertion according to local decision.

Presentation of the Lord

[IEP	Ps: 118	I Sam 1:19b–28		Exod 13:1–16
		Heb 4:11–16		Gal 4:1–7]
W	MP	Ps: 48; 146	Exod 13:1–16 (=R:)	I Sam 1:21–end
			Rom 12:1–5	Heb 10:1–10
	Mass	*Ceremonies*; Gl; Pref of Presentation (Missal or CW)*		
		CW: Mal 3:1–5; Ps 24:(1–6) 7–10; Heb 2:14–18; Lk 2: 22–40		
		R: Mal 3:1–4; Ps 24; Heb 2:14–18; Lk 2:22–32 (33–40)		
	(2)EP	HL 208 (NEH 156*)	Hag 2:1–9	Hag 2:1–9
		Ps: 122, 132	Jn 2:18–22	Rom 12:1–5

* In H: NEH 156, NEH seems curiously intent on eliminating *Theotokos*. The Presentation ceremonies traditionally take place before the main mass (R: & PHG pp. 283 ff); PHG envisages they might follow it (pp. 280ff). R: and PHG both envisage the omission of the Penitential Rite.

HOLY OILS

We talk about 'the holy oils'. The oil of the sick, and the oil of baptism with which we touch the candidate for baptism before he is baptized – traditionally, upon the chest – are sacramentals demanding our respect, but it is the Chrism which goes back to within a stone's throw of the New Testament; is full of significance; and calls for greater reverence. It is also a potential source of catechesis as we draw our people into a deeper understanding of the Paschal Mystery.

'We are called Christians because we are anointed with the oil of God'*; 'by it Christians are made and priests and kings and prophets'†, a phrase associated with the oil of chrism in the ancient and modern liturgies of East and West. Since the second century it has been called the oil of eucharist because it is consecrated by a prayer of thanksgiving, just as the eucharistic elements are. As the Lord breathed the Holy Spirit upon his disciples‡, your bishop breathes the Spirit upon the Chrism which you will take back to your people. S Cyril of Jerusalem informed his neophytes that they should 'not mistake the Chrism for ordinary ointment. Just as the bread of the Eucharist after the invocation of the Holy Spirit is not ordinary bread but the Body of Christ, so also the holy Chrism after the invocation is no more merely ointment, but the gracious endowment of Christ and the Holy Spirit, being made operative by the presence of his Divinity'§.

The current liturgical books encourage you to teach the faithful about the oils as you (or lay members of your congregation) bring them into your church, either before the Maundy Thursday Mass of the Last Supper, or at some other suitable time. When you baptize, by ancient custom, immediately after the act of water-baptism, you daub the top of the head of the new christian with Chrism: an action which can be seen as a pointer and preliminary to Confirmation. Your people will be interested to know that this is also the oil used in the ordination of priests and bishops, in the consecration of altars and churches, and in the coronation of christian monarchs.

The oils are kept reverently in an aumbry, but not in an aumbry or tabernacle in which the Blessed Sacrament is reserved. Nor should they be kept in a tabernacle which has the appearance of being used for the reservation of the Blessed Sacrament. Where the font is still used for baptisms, it may be appropriate to reserve the oils nearby. If no suitable aumbry is available, perhaps the church safe or a decent place in the priest's house will have to serve. The aumbry for the oils sometimes has *OLEA SANCTA – THE HOLY OILS* – on the door, or a purple veil hanging in front of it. A recent idea is to have an aumbry with a glass door and an internal light, so that the people, being able to see the oils, may easily be instructed. At the end of the year, what remains of the three oils is decently burnt, preferably in the oil lamp which burns before the Blessed Sacrament.

* Theophilus of Antioch (*c*. 180).   † Aphraates *Dem*.23.3 (*c*. 340).   ‡ John 20:22.   § *Cat*. xxi.3 (348).

✠ *SUNDAY*   **3rd SUNDAY and WEEK of YEAR; CW see page 7; BCP SEXAGESIMA**

27 G	MP	Ps: 71:1–6 & 15–17	Hag 2:1–9	Gen 3
			I Cor 3:10–17	I Cor 6:12–end
R: Ps III	Mass	*Gl; Cr; Sunday Pref*		
		CW: Isa 9:1–4; Ps 27:1 & 4–12; I Cor 1:10–18; Mt 4:12–23		
		R: Isa 8:23 – 9:3; Ps 27; I Cor 1:10–13 & 17; Mt 4:12–17 (18–23) (The Light of the World)		
	2 EP		Gen 28:10–22	Gen 37
		Ps: 34	Phil 1–16	Lk 10:25–37

MONDAY   **S Thomas Aquinas, Pr, Dr**

28 W	MP	Ps: 123, 124, 125, 126	Gen 11:27 – 12:9	Gen 17:1–22
			Mt 26:1–16	Mt 19:16 – 20:16
	Mass	*of the Saint*		
		II Sam 5:1–7 & 10; Ps 89:19–27; Mk 3:22–30		
	EP		Hos 2:18 – 3: end	Gen 18
		Ps: 127, 128, 129	I Cor 9:15–end	Rom 7

TUESDAY   **Feria**

29 G	MP	Ps: 132, 133	Gen 13:2–end	Gen 19:1–3 & 12–29
			Mt 26:17–35	Mt 20:17–end
	Mass	*of Sunday (CW: Collect of Epiphany 4); no Gl or Cr; Common Pref*		
		II Sam 6:12–15 & 17–19; Ps 24:7–end; Mk 3:31–end		
	EP		Hos 4:1–16	Gen 21
		Ps: 134, 135	I Cor 10:1–13	Rom 8:1–17

WEDNESDAY   **Bl Charles Stuart, M or the Feria ('Red Letter' in 1662)**

30 R or G	MP	Ps: 119:153–end	Gen 14	Gen 22:1–19
			Mt 26:36–46	Mt 21:1–22
	Mass	*of the Blessed or as Tuesday or, following 1662, Festum with Gloria*		
		II Sam 7:4–17; Ps 89:19–27; Mk 4:1–20		
	EP		Hos 5:1–7	Gen 23
		Ps: 136	I Cor 10:14 – 11:1	Rom 8:18–end

THURSDAY   **S John Bosco, Pr**

31 W	MP	Ps: 143, 146	Gen 15	Gen 24:1–28
			Mt 26:47–56	Mt 21:23–end
	Mass	*of the Saint*		
		II Sam 7:18–19 & 24–29; Ps 132:1–5 & 11–15; Mk 4:21–25		
	EP		Hos 5:8 – 6:6	Gen 24:29–end
		Ps: 138, 140, 141	I Cor 11:2–16	Rom 9

F E B R U A R Y

FRIDAY   *Feria (S Brigid, V; IRELAND Festum)*

1 G (or W)	MP	Ps: 142, 144	Gen 16	Gen 25:7–11 & 19–end
			Mt 26:57–end	Mt 22:1–33
	Mass	*as Tuesday (or of the Saint) (First Friday: Sacred Heart, see p. 38)*		
		II Sam 11:1–10 & 13–17; Ps 51:1–5 & 9; Mk 4:26–34		
	EP		Hos 6:7 – 7:2	Gen 27:1–40
		Ps: 145	I Cor 11:17–end	Rom 10

SATURDAY   **Our Lady on Saturday (or the Feria) (Presentation see p. 11)**

2 W (or G)	MP	Ps: 147	Gen 17:1–22	Gen 27:41–28 end
			Mt 27:1–10	Mt 22:34 – 23:12
	Mass	*Introduction Paragraph 26(b)*		
		(First Saturday: Immaculate Heart, see p. 38)		
		(Anniversary of the Episcopal Ordination in 1994 of Martyn, third Bishop of Beverley.)		
		II Sam 12:1–7 & 10–17; Ps 51:11–16; Mk 4:35–end		
G	1 EP of foll		Hos 8	Gen 29:1–20
		Ps: 148, 149, 150	I Cor 12:1–11	Rom 11

NOTES FOR LENT

1 The faithful are encouraged to see Lent as their preparation for the *Paschal* Mystery of the Death and Resurrection of the Lord, the Easter Triduum, rather than as a mere imitation of the Forty Days in the Wilderness. Preachers might notice that CW texts now follow Rome in expecting congregations to understand the word 'Paschal'. Those who are to be baptized and/or confirmed at Easter are prepared for the Sacraments, and the rest of the faithful express their penitence sacramentally and in communal Services of Penitence (LHWE pp. 38 ff). Ash Wednesday is a day of fasting and abstinence (p. xiv).

2 *On Sundays in Lent*, any Solemnity (e.g. Dedication or Patron) is transferred to the Monday; Festa and Memorials are suppressed. (CW also allows a Festum to be transferred to Monday, and permits a Dedication or Patronal Festival on Sundays 2, 3, and 4).

3 *On Weekdays in Lent*, Solemnities and Festa are observed; Memorials are indicated [within square brackets] which means the following: Mass and Office are of the Feria. The memorial may be *either* totally ignored *or* its collect may be said *after* the Collect of the day at MP and EP, and *instead* of the Collect of the day at Mass. (The new R: Calendar for England has moved S Chad from 2 March to 26 October; and S Cuthbert from 20 March to 4 September: to get them out of Lent. CW permits this optionally. Local Saints will prefer to have a non-Lenten date found for them: e.g. as of a Translation.)

4 **Office Hymns: EH: Sundays: MP 65 EP 66; Ferias: MP 67 or 68 EP 69. *NEH: MP 59 EP 60.***

5 Altars are not decorated with *flowers* except on Solemnities, Festa, and Lent 4, Refreshment Sunday; and apart from these days the organ and other instruments are only played at liturgical services to sustain poor singing. All use of *Alleluia* is avoided.

6 *Prefaces:* R: provides, in the Weekday Missal, four Lenten Prefaces, the first of which beautifully brings out the character of Lent as preparation for the *Pascha*, followed now in this by the (less generously provided) CW prefaces. R: also encourages marking Lent 1 with the Litany at the Entrance of the Mass.

7 **Sunday Themes and Readings**

   (a) On *Lent 1*, CW and Rome remember the Temptation in the Wilderness.

   (b) On *Lent 2*, Rome recalls the Transfiguration (Lent calls us to a participation in the Lord's own Paschal Transfiguration). CW transferred this perception to the Sunday *before* Lent.

   (c) On *Lent 3, 4, and 5* CW and Rome reflect an ancient Christian association of Lent with Eschatological, Paschal, and Redemptive themes. Rome (see also CW) allows (even in Years B and C) the Year A Gospels (together with their associated readings and proper prefaces) which are given below. These are the readings anciently used in the preparation of candidates for Baptism and Confirmation. They may also be used on weekdays. (Compare also the Byzantine rite.)

   ### Roman Sundays in Year A

   3 Living Water [The Samaritan Woman]
   Exod 17:3–7; Rom 5:1–2 & 5–8; Jn 4:5–42 (or 5–15 & 19–26 & 39–42)

   4 Enlightenment [the Man Blind from Birth]
   1 Sam 6:1 & 6–7 & 10–13; Eph 5:8–14; Jn 9:1–41 (or 1 & 6–9 & 13–17 & 34–38)

   5 New Life [Lazarus]
   Ezek 37:12–14; Rom 8:8–11; Jn 11:1–45 (or 3–7 & 17–27 & 33b–45)

8 Customary ways of observing Lent include: *Thursdays* Eucharistic Adoration *Fridays* Way of the Cross and penitential celebrations *Saturdays* Rosary. PPL urges also: venerating relics of the Cross; reading the Passion; the *Via Matris*.

✠ *SUNDAY*   **4th SUNDAY and WEEK of YEAR; CW NEXT BEFORE LENT *OR***
                        PRESENTATION; BCP QUINQUAGESIMA

3   G   MP   Ps: 72   Exod 34:29–35   Gen 12:1–9
                                                  II Cor 4:3–6   I Cor 12:4–end
R: Ps IV   Mass   *Gl; Cr; Sunday Pref*
                        CW: Exod 24:12–18; Ps 2; II Pet 1:16–21; Mt 17:1–9
                        R: Zeph 2:3 & 3:12–13; Ps 146; I Cor 1:26–31; Mt 5:1–12 (Our Nothingness)
                 2 EP   Ecclus 48:1–10   Gen 41:1–40
                        Ps: 84   Mt 17: (1–8) 9–23   I Jn 4:7–end

MONDAY   **Feria (Ss Gilbert of Sempringham, Comp, Rel)**
4   G   MP   Ps: 1, 2, 3   Gen 37:1–11   Gen 31:1–9 & 14–21
         (or W)   Gal 1   Mt 23:13–end
                 Mass   *of Sunday; no Gloria or Creed; Common Pref (or of the Saints)*
                        II Sam 15:13–14 & 30 & 16:5–13; Ps 3; Mk 5:1–20
                 EP   Jer 1   Gen 31:22 – 32:2
                        Ps: 4, 7   Jn 3:1–21   Rom 12

TUESDAY   **S Agatha, V, M**
5   R   MP   Ps: 5, 6, 8   Gen 37:12–end   Gen 32:3–30
                                                  Gal 2:1–10   Mt 24:1–28
                 Mass   *of the Saint*
                        II Sam 18:9–10 & 14 & 24–25 & 30–19:3; Ps 86:1–6; Mk 5:21–end
                 EP   Jer 2:1–13   Gen 33
                        Ps: 9, 10   Jn 3:22–end   Rom 13

(✠) *WEDNESDAY*   **ASH WEDNESDAY**
6   P   MP   Ps: 38   Dan 9:3–6 & 17–19   Isa 58
                                                  I Tim 6:6–19   Mk 2:13–22
R: Ps IV   Mass   *of the day; the penitential rite is omitted; Blessing & imposition of Ashes takes place after the Homily;*
                        R: Pref 4 of Lent; CW, Pref 1 of Lent
                        CW: Joel 2:1–2 & 12–17; Ps 51:1–18; II Cor 5:20b – 6:10; Mt 6:1–6 & 16–21
                        R: Joel 2:12–18; Ps 51; II Cor 5:20 – 6:2; Mt 6:1–6 & 16–18
                 EP   Isa 1:10–18 [R: Isa 58:1–12]   Dan 9:3–19
                        Ps: 102 or 102:1–17   Lk 15:11–32   Heb 3:12 – 4:13

THURSDAY   **Feria**
7   P   MP   Ps: 14, 15, 16   Gen 39   Gen 35:1–20
                                                  Gal 2:11–end   Mt 24:29–end
                 Mass   *of the day; Pref of Lent*
                        Deut 30:15–end; Ps 1; Lk 9:22–25
                 EP   Jer 2:14–32   Gen 37
                        Ps: 18   Jm 4:1–26   Rom 14

FRIDAY   **Feria [□ S Jerome Emiliani; □ S Josephine Bakhita, V;**
                        Bl Pius IX, Pp]
8   P   MP   Ps: 17, 19   Gen 40   Gen 39
                                                  Gal 3:1–14   Mt 25:1–30
                 Mass   *of the day; Pref of Lent*
                        Isa 58:1–9a; Ps 51:1–5 & 17–18; Mt 9:14–15
                 EP   Jer 3:6–22   Gen 40
                        Ps: 22   Jn 4:27–42   Rom 15

SATURDAY   **Feria**
9   P   MP   Ps: 20, 21, 23   Gen 41:1–24   Gen 41:1–40
                                                  Gal 3:15–22   Mt 25:31–end
                 Mass   *of the day; Pref of Lent*
                        Isa 58:9b–end; Ps 86:1–7; Lk 5:27–32
            P   1 EP of foll   Jer 4:1–18   Gen 41:41–end
                        Ps: 24, 25   Jn 4:43–end   Rom 16

✠ SUNDAY
10   P

R: Ps I

LENT 1 see Notes for Lent

P	MP	Ps: 119:1–16	Jer 18:1–11	Gen 27:1–40
			Lk 18:9–14	Heb 4:14 – 5:10

Mass   *Cr; R: Proper Pref; CW, of Lent*
CW: Gen 2:15–17 & 3:1–7; Ps 32; Rom 5:12–19; Mt 4:1–11
R: Gen 2:7–9 & 3:1–7; Ps 51; Rom 5:12 (13–16) 17–19;
Mt 4:1–11 (Christ The Second Adam)

2 EP		Deut 6:4–9 and 16–25	Gen 42
	Ps: 50:1–15	Lk 15:1–10	Lk 22:1–23

MONDAY
11   P

Feria [□ Our Lady of Lourdes]

P	MP	Ps: 27, 30	Gen 41:25–45	Gen 43:1–14
			Gal 3:23 – 4:7	Mt 26:1–30

Mass   *of the day; Pref of Lent*
Lev 19:1–2 & 11–18; Ps 19:7–end; Mt 25:31–end

EP		Jer 4:19–end	Gen 43:15–end
	Ps: 26, 28, 29	Jn 5:1–18	Phil 1

TUESDAY
12   P

Feria

P	MP	Ps: 32, 36	Gen 41:46 – 42:5	Gen 44
			Gal 4:8–20	Mt 26:31–56

Mass   *as Monday*
Isa 55:10–11; Ps 34:4–6 & 21–22; Mk 6:7–15

EP		Jer 5:1–19	Gen 45:1–15
	Ps: 33	Jn 5:19–29	Phil 2

WEDNESDAY
13   P

Feria*

P	MP	Ps: 34	Gen 42:6–17	Gen 45:16 – 46:7
			Gal 4:21 – 5:1	Mk 26:57–end

Mass   *as Monday*
Jonah 3; Ps 51:1–4 & 16–17; Lk 11:29–32

EP		Jer 5:20–end	Gen 46:26 – 47:12
	Ps: 119:33–56	Jn 5:30–end	Phil 3

THURSDAY
14   W

Ss Cyril, Monk, and Methodius, B, Patrons of Europe

W	MP	[Ps: 37]	[Gen 42:18–28]	[Gen 47:13–end]
			[Gal 5:2–15]	[Mt 27:1–26]

Mass   *of the Saints; Gl, no Cr; R: Pref of Patrons, CW of Saints (**S Valentine, B & M**)*
Office Readings from Appendix 3, 'Missionaries'
CW = R: Acts 13:46–49; Ps 117; Lk 10:1–9

EP		[Jer 6:9–21]	[Gen 48]
	[Ps: 39, 40]	[Jn 6:1–15]	[Phil 4]

FRIDAY
15   P

Feria [S Sigfrid, B]*

P	MP	Ps: 31	Gen 42:29–end	Gen 49:1–32
			Gal 5:16–end	Mt 27:27–56

Mass   *as Monday (**Thomas Bray, Pr**)*
Ezek 18:21–28; Ps 130; Mt 5:20–26

EP		Jer 6:22–end	Gen 49:33–50 end
	Ps: 35	Jn 6:16–27	Col 1:1–20

SATURDAY
16   P

Feria*

P	MP	Ps: 41, 42, 43	Gen 43:1–15	Exod 1:1–14 & 22 – 2:10
			Gal 6	Mt 27:57–28 end

Mass   *as Monday*
Deut 26:16–end; Ps 119:1–8; Mt 5:43–end

P	1 EP of foll		Jer 7:1–20	Exod 2:11–22
		Ps: 45, 46	Jn 6:27–40	Col 1:21 – 2:7

---

* Ember Masses Introduction paragraph 25.

✠ *SUNDAY*   **LENT 2**

17 P   MP   Ps: 74   Jer 22:1–9   Gen 28:10–end
                                              Mt 8:1–13   Heb 10:19–end

R: Ps II   Mass   *Cr; Pref of Lent. R: Proper Preface*
                      Gen 12:1–4a; Ps 121; Rom 4:1–5 & 13–17; Jn 3:1–17
                      R: Gen 12:1–4a; Ps 33; II Tim 1:8b–10; Mt 17:1–9 (The Transfiguration)

               2 EP   Num 21:4–9   Gen 43:1–15 (16–26) 27–end
                      Ps: 135   Lk 14:27–33   Lk 22:24–53

MONDAY   *Feria*

18 P   MP   Ps: 44   Gen 43:16–end   Exod 2:23 – 3 end
                                              Heb 1   Jn 1:1–28

               Mass   *of the day; Pref of Lent*
                      Dan 9:4–10; Ps 79:8–9 & 12 & 14; Lk 6:36–38

               EP   Jer 7:21–end   Exod 4:1–23
                      Ps: 47, 49   Jn 6:41–51   Col 2:8 – 3:11

TUESDAY   *Feria*

19 P   MP   Ps: 48, 52   Gen 44:1–17   Exod 4:27 – 6:1
                                              Heb 2:1–9   Jn 1:29–end

               Mass   *as Monday*
                      Isa 1:10 & 16–20; Ps 50:8 & 16–end; Mt 23:1–12

               EP   Jer 8:1–15   Exod 6:2–13 & 7:1–7
                      Ps: 50   Jn 6:52–59   Col 3:12 – 4:1

WEDNESDAY   *Feria*

20 P   MP   Ps: 119:57–80   Gen 44:18–end   Exod 7:8–end
                                              Heb 2:10–end   Jn 2

               Mass   *as Monday*
                      Jer 18:18–20; Ps 31:4–5 & 14–18; Mt 20:17–28

               EP   Jer 8:18 – 9:11   Exod 8:1–19
                      Ps: 59, 60, 67   Jn 6:60–end   Col 4:2–end

THURSDAY   *Feria* [□ *S Peter Damian, B, Dr*]

21 P   MP   Ps: 56, 57, 63   Gen 45:1–15   Exod 8:20 – 9:12
                                              Heb 3:1–6   Jn 3:1–21

               Mass   *as Monday*
                      Jer 17:5–10; Ps 1; Lk 16:19–end

               EP   Jer 9:12–24   Exod 9:13–end
                      Ps: 61, 62, 64   Jn 7:1–13   Phil

FRIDAY   □ **The Chair of S Peter, Ap**

22 W   MP   [Ps: 51, 54]   [Gen 45:16–end]   [Exod 10:1–20]
                                              [Heb 3:7–end]   [Jn 3:22–end]

               Mass   *of the Festum. See Intro Appendix 1, p. xxvii*
                      [Gen 37:3–4 & 12–13 & 17–28; Ps 105:16–22; Mt 21:33–43 & 45–46]

               EP   [Jer 10:1–16]   [Exod 10:21 – 11–end]
                      [Ps: 38]   [Jn 7:14–24]   [Eph 1]

SATURDAY   *Feria* [*S Polycarp, B, M*]

23 P   MP   Ps: 68   Gen 46:1–7, 28–end   Exod 12:1–20
                                              Heb 4:1–13   Jn 4:1–26

               Mass   *as Monday*
                      Micah 7:4–15 & 18–20; Ps 103:1–4 & 9–12; Lk 15:1–3 & 11–end

        P   1 EP of foll   Jer 10:17–24   Exod 12:21–36
                      Ps: 65, 66   Jn 7:25–36   Eph 2

✠ **SUNDAY**
24 P MP — **LENT 3**

✠ SUNDAY **24**	P	MP	Ps: 46	Amos 7:10–17 — Gen 29:1–20
				II Cor 1:1–11 — Heb 12:14–end
R: Ps III		Mass	Cr; Pref of Lent	
			CW: Exod 17:1–7; Ps 95; Rom 5:1–11; Jn 4:5–42	
			R: Exod 17:3–7; Ps 95; Rom 5:1–2 & 5–8;	
			Jn 4:5–42 (see p. 13) (The Samaritan Woman: Living Water)	
		2 EP		Josh 1:1–9 — Gen 44:1 – 45:8
			Ps: 40	Eph 6:10–20 — Lk 22:54–end

MONDAY **25**	P	MP	Ps: 71	Gen 47:1–27 — Exod 12:37–end
				Heb 4:14 – 5:10 — Jn 4:27–end
		Mass	of the day; Pref of Lent	
			II Kgs 5:1–15; Ps 42:1–2 & 43:1–4; Lk 4:24–30	
		EP		Jer 11:1–17 — Exod 13:1–16
			Ps: 72, 75	Jn 7:37–52 — Eph 3

Feria

TUESDAY **26**	P	MP	Ps: 73	Gen 47:28 – 48–end — Exod 13:17 – 14:14
				Heb 5:11 – 6:12 — Jn 5:1–23
		Mass	as Monday	
			Song of the Three 2 & 11–20a*: Ps 25:3–10; Mt 18:21–end	
		EP		Jer 11:18 – 12:6 — Exod 14:15–end
			Ps: 74	Jn 7:53 – 8:11 — Eph 4:1–16

Feria

WEDNESDAY **27**	P	MP	Ps: 77	Gen 49:1–32 — Exod 15:1–26
				Heb 6:13–end — Jn 5:24–end
		Mass	as Monday (**George Herbert, Pr**)	
			Deut 4:1 & 5–9; Ps 147:13–end; Mt 5:17–19	
		EP		Jer 13:1–11 — Exod 15:27 – 16:35
			Ps: 119:81–104	Jn 8:12–30 — Eph 4:17–30

Feria

THURSDAY **28**	P	MP	Ps: 78:1–39	Gen 49:33– 50–end — Exod 17
				Heb 7:1–10 — Jn 6:1–21
		Mass	as Monday (**Foundation of SSC: Votive of the Holy Cross?**)	
			Jer 7:23–28; Ps 95:1–2 & 6–end; Lk 11:14–23	
		EP		Jer 14 — Exod 18
			Ps: 78:40–end	Jn 8:31–47 — Eph 4:31 – 5:21

Feria

FRIDAY **29**	P	MP	Ps: 55	Exod 1:1–14 — Exod 19
				Heb 7:11–end — Jn 6:22–40
		Mass	as Monday	
			Hos 14:2–10; Ps 81:6–10 & 13 & 16; Mt 12:28–34	
		EP		Jer 15:10–end — Exod 20:1–21
			Ps: 69	Jn 8:48–end — Eph 5:22 – 6:9

MARCH

SATURDAY
1 W

S David, B (WALES Solemnity; elsewhere Festum)

SATURDAY **1**	W	MP	[Ps: 76, 79]	[Exod 1:22 – 2:10] — [Exod 22:20 – 23:17]
				[Heb 8] — [Jn 6:41–end]
		Mass	Office: Appendix 3.	
			of the Saint; Gl; Cr in Wales, Pref of Saints (Missal, National Appendix)	
			[Hos 5:15 – 6:6; Ps 51:1–2 & 17–end; Lk 18:9–14]	
	P (or	1 EP of foll		Jer 16:10 – 17:4 — Exod 23:20–end
	Rose)		Ps: 81, 84	Jn 9:1–17 — Eph 6:10–end

* Apocryphal/Deuterocanonical Books, 'Prayer of Azariah and Song of the three young men/Jews/Children'. King James-based and Vulgate-based Bibles have different verse systems; we follow the former.

✠ SUNDAY **LENT 4**

2   P (or Rose)   MP   Ps: 19   Isa 43:1–7   Gen 32:3–30

R: Ps IV   Eph 2:8–14   Heb 13:1–21

    Mass   *Cr; Pref of Lent; MOTHERING SUNDAY, p. xxvii*
       CW: I Sam 16:1–13; Ps 23; Eph 5:8–14; Jn 9:1–41
       R: I Sam 16:1 & 6–7 & 10–13; Ps 23; Eph 5:8–14; Jn 9:1–41 (see page 13)
       (The Man Blind from Birth: Enlightenment)

    2 EP   Mic 7   Gen 45:16 – 46:7
       Ps: 31:1–8 (9–16)   James 5   Lk 23:1–25

MONDAY   *Feria*

3   P   MP   Ps: 80, 82   Exod 2:11–22   Exod 24
       Heb 9:1–14   Jn 7:1–24

    Mass   *of the day; Pref of Lent*
       Isa 65:17–21; Ps 30:1–5 & 8 & 11–12; Jn 4:43–end

    EP   Jer 17:5–18   Exod 25:1–22
       Ps: 85, 86   Jn 9:18–end   I Tim 1:1–17

TUESDAY   *Feria* [□ *S Casimir*]

4   P   MP   Ps: 87, 89:1–18   Exod 2:23 – 3:20   Exod 28:1–4 & 29:1–9
       Heb 9:15–end   Jn 7:25–end

    Mass   *as Monday*
       Ezek 47:1–9 & 12; Ps 46:1–8; Jn 5:1–3 & 5–16

    EP   Jer 18:1–12   Exod 29:38 – 30:16
       Ps: 89:19–end   Jn 10:1–10   I Tim 1:18 – 2 end

WEDNESDAY   *Feria* [*S Piran; Solemnity of the Patron in CORNWALL*]

5   P   MP   Ps: 119:105–128   Exod 4:1–23   Exod 32
       Heb 10:1–18   Jn 8:1–30

    Mass   *as Monday*
       Isa 49:8–15; Ps 145:8–17; Jn 5:17–30

    EP   Jer 18:13–end   Exod 33
       Ps: 91, 93   Jn 10:11–21   I Tim 3

THURSDAY   *Feria*

6   P   MP   Ps: 90, 92   Exod 4:27 – 6:1   Exod 34
       Heb 10:19–25   Jn 8:31–end

    Mass   *as Monday*
       Exod 32:7–14; Ps 106:19–23; Jn 5:31–47

    EP   Jer 19:1–13   Exod 35:20 – 36:7
       Ps: 94   Jn 10:22–end   I Tim 4

FRIDAY   *Feria** [*Ss Perpetua and Felicity, Ms*]

7   P   MP   Ps: 88, 95   Exod 6:2–13   Exod 40:17–end
       Heb 10:26–end   Jn 9

    Mass   *as Monday*
       Wisd 2:1 & 12–22; Ps 34:15–end; Jn 7:1–2 & 10 & 25–30

    EP   Jer 19:14 – 20:6   Lev 6:8–end
       Ps: 102   Jn 11:1–16   I Tim 5

SATURDAY   *Feria* [□ *S John of God, Rel; S Felix, B*]

8   P   MP   Ps: 96, 97, 100   Exod 7:8–end   Lev 19:1–18 & 30–end
       Heb 11:1–16   Jn 10:1–21

    Mass   *as Monday* (**Edward King, B; Geoffrey Studdert Kennedy, Pr**)
       Jer 11:18–20; Ps 7:1–2 & 8–10; Jn 7:40–52

    P†   1 EP of foll   Jer 20:7–end   Lev 25:1–24
       Ps: 104   Jn 11:17–27   I Tim 6

---

* Episcopal Ordination in 2002 of Keith, second Bishop of Richborough.
† Before this EP, cross, statues, and pictures may be veiled in purple.

✠ *SUNDAY*
9 P MP **LENT 5***

| | | | Ps: 86 | Jer 31:27–37 | Exod 2:23 – 3:20 |
| | | | | Jn 12:20–33 | Mt 20:17–28 |

R: Ps I Mass *Cr; Pref of Lent (CW: Pref of Fifth Sunday onwards)*
CW: Ezek 37:1–14; Ps 130; Rom 8:6–11; Jn 11:1–45
R: Ezek 37:12–14; Ps 130; Rom 8:8–11; Jn 11:1–45
(see p. 13) (Lazarus: New Life)

| | | 2 EP | | Lam 3:19–33 | Exod 6:2–13 |
| | | | Ps: 30 | Mt 20:17–34 | Lk 23:26–49 |

MONDAY
10 P MP **Feria [SCOTLAND: S John Ogilvie, Pr; Festum]**

| | | | Ps: 98, 99, 101 | Exod 8:1–19 | Num 6 |
| | | | | Heb 11:17–31 | Jn 10:22–end |

Mass *of the day; Pref I of Passion (CW: Pref of Fifth Sunday onwards)*
Susanna 1–9 & 15–17 & 19–30 & 33–62; Ps 23; Jn 8:1–11

| | | EP | | Jer 21:1–10 | Num 9:15–end & 10:29–end |
| | | | Ps: 103, 105 | Jn 11:28–44 | Titus 1:1 – 2:8 |

TUESDAY
11 P MP **Feria**

| | | | Ps: 106 | Exod 8:20–end | Num 11:10–23 |
| | | | | Heb 11:32 – 12:2 | Jn 11:1–44 |

Mass *as Monday*
Num 21:4–9; Ps 102:1–3 & 16–23; Jn 8:21–30

| | | EP | | Jer 22:1–5, 13–19 | Num 12 |
| | | | Ps: 107 | Jn 11:45–end | Titus 2:9–3 end |

WEDNESDAY
12 P MP **Feria**

| | | | Ps: 110, 111, 112 | Exod 9:1–12 | Num 13:1–3 and 17–end |
| | | | | Heb 12:3–13 | Jn 11:45–end |

Mass *as Monday*
Dan 3:14–20 & 24–25 & 28; Song of the Three 29–34; Jn 8:31–42

| | | EP | | Jer 22:20 – 23:8 | Num 14:1–25 |
| | | | Ps: 119:129–152 | Jn 12:1–11 | II Tim 1 |

THURSDAY
13 P MP **Feria**

| | | | Ps: 113, 115 | Exod 9:13–end | Num 16:1–35 |
| | | | | Heb 12:14–end | Jn 12:1–19 |

Mass *as Monday*
Gen 17:3–9; Ps 105:4–9; Jn 8:51–59

| | | EP | | Jer 23:9–32 | Num 16:36–17 end |
| | | | Ps: 114, 116, 117 | Jn 12:12–19 | II Tim 2 |

FRIDAY
14 P MP **Feria**

| | | | Ps: 139 | Exod 10 | Num 20 |
| | | | | Heb 13:1–16 | Jn 12:20–end |

Mass *as Monday (**There is a new Roman Collect today for Our Lady of Sorrows**)*
Jer 20:10–13; Ps 18:1–6; Jn 10:31–end

| | | EP | | Jer 24 | Num 22:1–35 |
| | | | Ps: 130, 131, 137 | Jn 12:20–36a | II Tlm 3 |

SATURDAY
15 P MP **Feria (S JOSEPH? See PRAENOTANDA)**

| | | | Ps: 120, 121, 122 | Exod 11 | Num 22:36 – 23:26 |
| | | | | Heb 13:17–end | Jn 13 |

Mass *as Monday*
Ezek 37:21–end; Jer 31:10–13 or Ps 121; Jn 11:45–end

| | R | 1 EP of foll | | Jer 25:1–4 | Num 23:27 – 24 end |
| | | | Ps: 118 | Jn 12:36b–end | II Tim 4 |

---

* Confusion may arise from the fact that this Sunday is no longer called 'Passion Sunday' in the Roman Rite, which has transferred this title to next Sunday (Palm Sunday). But the Roman Office allows the use of the 'Passion' Hymns on the Weekdays of this Week: MP 95 or 96 (NEH 78 or 517); EP 94 (NEH 79). CW continues talk of 'Passiontide'.

HOLY WEEK AND THE END OF LENT

Lent lasts until the Evening of Maundy Thursday. The Mass of the Last Supper until the EP of Easter Sunday inclusively constitutes the Easter Triduum, which is of even greater antiquity than the Season of Lent.

1   From Palm Sunday onwards, Solemnities are transferred to after Low Sunday; Festivals and Memorials are suppressed.

2   **The Chrism Mass** provides the Oils for use at Baptism and Confirmation at Easter and thereafter. It should take place towards the end of Lent at a time when priests and peoples can easily gather. (Oils in Initiation: see p. xxxiv and 12.)

In some places, the Oils are subsequently 'received' into Parish Churches, and their purpose explained. Before the Mass of the Lord's Supper is a popular time for this, but undeniably complicates the occasion. Earlier in Holy Week, or at MP on Good Friday or Holy Saturday, may be convenient occasions.

3   **Confessions and Penitential Celebrations** for the whole Christian community (LHWE pp. 38 ff) should take place at the end of Lent, *before* the Easter Triduum, but not immediately before the Mass of the Lord's Supper.

4   **PALM SUNDAY** The colour of the day is red. Palms are held during the Palm gospel and procession, but not during the Passion gospel. The processional cross is carried unveiled. After the procession, when the celebrant arrives at the altar, he reverences (and censes) it. Then he goes to his chair and Mass begins with the collect of the day. Rome allows, for pastoral reasons, one or both of the readings before the Passion to be omitted.

The Passion gospel may be read by three deacons or by laymen. If possible, the priest should read the part of Christ. The Passion may be read by the deacon of the Mass, or if necessary by the celebrant. Neither lights nor incense are used. At the beginning the greeting and signing of the book are omitted. At the end the book is not kissed. LHWE permits the omission of the Creed.

5   **MAUNDY THURSDAY** Before the Evening, holy water stoups are emptied, the Blessed Sacrament taken to a private place of reservation, and lamps extinguished. Those who have concelebrated or communicated with the Bishop in the morning may celebrate concelebrate or communicate again in the evening.

6   The practice of attenuating the Office during the Triduum, mentioned by LHWE (p. 90), was discontinued by Rome in 1971.

✠ SUNDAY			**PALM SUNDAY OF THE LORD'S PASSION**		
16	R	MP	H: 95 or 96 (NEH 78)	Zech 9:9–12	Exod 10:21–11 end
			Ps: 61, 62	Lk 16:19–31	Mt 26
R: Ps II		Mass	*Cr; Pref Proper (CW: 'from the Fifth Sunday of Lent')*		
			Gospel for Palms Ceremony: Mt 21:1–11		
			CW: Isa 50:4–9a; Ps 31:9–16; Phil 2:5–11; Mt 26:14 – 27:66 or 27:11–54		
			R: Isa 50:4–7; Ps: 22; Phil 2:6–11; Mt 26:14 – 27:66 or 27:11–54		
		EP	H: 94 (NEH 79)	Isa 5:1–7	Isa 52:13–53 end
			Ps: 80	Mt 21:33–46	Lk 19:29–end

MONDAY			**MONDAY IN HOLY WEEK**		
17	P	MP	H: 95 or 96 (NEH 78)	Lam 1:1–12a	◁
			Ps: 41	Lk 22:1–23	Jn 14:1–14
		Mass	*of the day; R: Pref of Passion II; CW, Pref of Fifth Sunday onwards*		
			CW: Isa 42:1–9; Ps 36:5–11; Heb 9:11–15; Jn 12:1–11		
			*ASB = R: = LHWE: Isa 42:1–7; Ps 27:1–3 & 16–17; Jn 12:1–11		
		EP	H: 94 (NEH 79)	Lam 2:8–19	Lam 2:18–19
			Ps: 25	Col 1:18–23	Jn 14:15–end

TUESDAY			**TUESDAY IN HOLY WEEK**		
18	P	MP	H: 95 or 96 (NEH 78)	Lam 3:1–18	Lam 3:1–30
			Ps: 27	Lk 22:24–53 (or 39–53)	Jn 15:1–16
		Mass	*as Monday*		
			CW: Isa 49:1–7; Ps 71:1–14; I Cor 1:18–31; Jn 12:30–36		
			*ASB = R: = LHWE: Isa 49:1–6; Ps 71:1–6 & 15–16; Jn 13:21–33 & 36–38		
		EP	H: 94 (NEH 79)	Lam 3:40–51	Lam 3:40–51
			Ps: 55:13–22	Gal 6:11–18	Jn 15:17–end

WEDNESDAY			**WEDNESDAY IN HOLY WEEK**		
19	P	MP	H: 95 or 96 (NEH 78)	Jer 11:18–20 or Wisd 1:16 – 2:1 & 2:12–22	Isa 42:1–9
			Ps: 102	Lk 22:54–71	Jn 16:1–15
		Mass	*as Monday*		
			CW: Isa 50:4–9a; Ps 70: Heb 12:1–3; Jn 13:21–32		
			*ASB = R: = LHWE: Isa 50:4–9a; Ps 69:7–9 & 32–35; Mt 26:14–25		
		EP	H: 94 (NEH 79)	Isa 63:1–9	Num 21:4–9
			Ps: 88	Rev 14:18 – 15:4	Jn 16:16–end

THURSDAY			**THURSDAY IN HOLY WEEK (Morning)**		
20	P	MP	H: 95 or 96 (NEH 78)	Lev 16:2–24	Exod 24:1–11
			Ps: 42, 43	Lk 23:1–25	Jn 17
	P	EP	H: 331 (NEH 308)	Exod 11	Lev 16:2–24
			vv 2–4		
			Ps: 39	Eph 2:11–18	◁ or Jn 13:1–35

* Readings at Mass: ASB = R: = LHWE: are the originally Roman propers authorised by ASB p. 1074 and repeated in LHWE, printed in the Weekday Missal. Psalms are adjusted to the CW verse numbers.

THE EASTER TRIDUUM

1   **THE EASTER FAST**, more ancient than Lent, should be observed both on Friday and Saturday, until the Vigil.

2   **R:** the following anthem is said before Benedictus and Magnificat from EP on Maundy Thursday to Holy Saturday: **Christ humbled himself for us, and, in obedience, accepted death**. Good Friday add **even death on a cross.**
Holy Saturday add **Therefore God raised him to the heights and gave him the name which is above all other names**.

3   **MAUNDY THURSDAY** For the evening Mass of the Lord's Supper, white vestments are worn, the altar is decorated as on feasts, and the cross is veiled in white. Bells may

be rung at *Gloria in excelsis* and then are silent until the Easter Vigil. The Washing of Feet may follow the Sermon. The Creed is omitted. The Institution Narrative begins *Who in this night when* . . . It is appropriate that authorised lay people take Communion to the sick or elderly at Communion time. Immediately after the post-communion prayer the procession to the altar of repose follows, where the watch takes place. John 13–17 may be read. After midnight, flowers and candles are removed; one lamp or two candles are to be left burning. After the procession altars are privately stripped and crosses removed (or covered with a purple veil).

If there will be no Good Friday Liturgy in the same church, the Blessed Sacrament is replaced in the Tabernacle and Mass ends in the ordinary way.

4   **GOOD FRIDAY** The colour for the day is red. Public MP is encouraged. For the Solemn Liturgy, which should begin about 3 pm but may for pastoral reasons take place between noon and 9 pm, the sacred ministers wear Mass vestments throughout. The altar should be completely bare at the start of the service. Afterwards, it is stripped again, the Cross and four candles being left upon it.

The Passion According To John, Chapters 18 & 19, is, according to ancient tradition (preserved in CW and the Roman Rite) read in its entirety at the Solemn Liturgy. CW, and BCP allow it to be divided: MP Jn 18; Liturgy Jn 19:1–37; EP Jn 19:38–end.

The priest may remove his chasuble and shoes to venerate the Cross; and *Stabat Mater* (EH 115, NEH 97) or another piece about our compassionate Mother is added to the texts which may accompany the Veneration.

5   **HOLY SATURDAY BEFORE THE VIGIL** The *Anglican* tradition has been for a Liturgy of the Word – 'Antecommunion' or 'Altar Prayers' – in purple stole (and cope); MP; and EP; the 'Principal Service' readings should be used at the main Office attended by the faithful. *Rome* recommends the Office of Readings, and Morning Prayer, with the participation of the people – or at least 'some celebration of the Word of God, or some suitable act of devotion'. Representations of Christ crucified or entombed or visiting Hell, or of our Lady of Sorrows, may be placed in Church for the veneration of the faithful.

EP must be said, and veiled statues and pictures unveiled, before the Vigil.

6   **THE EASTER VIGIL** is the 'Solemnity of Solemnities', and the people (even those who will be away from their home parishes on holiday) are urged to see it as the greatest observance of the Christian Year and the foretaste of the Everlasting Easter; and as the Celebration of the Resurrection Night rather than as a service that happens at the end of Holy Saturday. The dignity and festive character of the Vigil may be enhanced if smaller groups and parishes celebrate it together. Both Rome and LHWE are adamant that there *must still only be one Paschal Candle*; LHWE adds that 'if it is desired to take Easter Candles back to other churches, they may be lit from the first candle at the end of the service and carried in procession out of the building'.

The Vigil should begin after nightfall and end before daybreak; the bonfire should, if possible, be big enough for its flames truly to scatter the darkness of this Night; and the Paschal Candle should be large. The marking of the Candle is compulsory.

The service of Light and Fire should precede the Vigil readings from the OT: for the Christian tradition, the OT is not a period of darkness but a divine dispensation illuminated and elucidated by Christ our Light: 'only in the light of Resurrection can we comprehend the unfolding revelation of the prophecies that point to the Paschal Mystery'. The 'Light of Christ' is proclaimed at: church door; mid-church; sanctuary.

The sacred ministers wear white Mass vestments throughout. At *Gloria in excelsis* bells are rung (and statues and pictures unveiled). At the Gospel incense is carried, but not candles. Before he shows the *Lamb of God* the priest may briefly address any new communicants. After the Mass, the Blessed Sacrament is replaced in the aumbry or tabernacle. Priests who celebrate or concelebrate the Vigil Mass may celebrate or concelebrate the Mass of Easter Day. Those who receive Holy Communion at the Vigil Mass may communicate again at Mass on Easter Day. But they *have* already fulfiled their Easter duty.

THE EASTER TRIDUUM

THURSDAY
20 W   Mass   **MAUNDY THURSDAY EVENING**

Gl; R: Pref of Eucharist; CW, Proper Pref
CW: Exod 12:1–4 (5–10) 11–14; Ps 116:1 & 10–17;
I Cor 11:23–26; Jn 13:1–17 & 31b–35
R: Exod 12:1–8 & 11–14; Ps 116:12–13 & 15–16bc & 17–18; I Cor 11:23–26;
Jn 13:1–15

(✠) *FRIDAY*
21 R   MP   **GOOD FRIDAY, IN THE LORD'S PASSION**

The Solemn Liturgy

H: 95 or 96 (NEH 78)	Gen 22:1–18	Gen 22:1–18
Ps: 69	Heb 10:1–10	see note, or ◁

Readings (CW = R:): Isa 52:13 – 53:12; Ps 22 (R: 31:2 & 6 & 12–13 & 15–17 & 25);
Heb 4:14–16 & 5:7–9; Jn 18 & 19 (see note)

EP

H: 94 (NEW 79)	Lam 5:15–22	Isa 50:4–10
Ps: 130, 143	Col 1:18–23	see note; or I Pet 2:11–end

SATURDAY
22 P   **HOLY SATURDAY**

CW 'Principal Service': Job 14:1–14 or Lam 3:1–9 & 19–24; Ps 31:1–4 & 15–16;
I Pet 4:1–8; Mt 27:57–66 or Jn 19:38–42
CW: MP: Ps 142; Hos 6:1–6; Jn 2:18–22
CW: EP: Ps 116; Job 19:21–27; I Jn 5:5–12
1961: MP: Zech 9:9–12 & I Pet 2:19–end; EP: Job 19:21–27 & Jn 2:13–22
R: MP: Hos 5:15d – 6:2; Office of Readings Heb 4:1–13; EP I Pet 1:18–21
Byzantium: Liturgy: I Cor 5:6–9 & Gal 3:13–14; Mt 27:62–66

22–23 W   ### EASTER TIME
EASTER NIGHT: THE EASTER VIGIL

There should be at least three readings before the Epistle and Gospel. The account of the Crossing of the Red Sea (Exodus) must always be read. (CW and LHWE make suggestions additional to those listed).

Roman Rite	**CW (or LHWE)**
1. *Gen 1:1–2:2	*Gen 1:1–2:4a
(or 1:1 & 26–31a)	(or 1:1–5 & 26–end: LHWE)
	*Gen 7:1–5 & 11–18 & 8:6–18 & 9:8–13
2. *Gen 22:1–18	*Gen 22:1–18
(or 22:1–2 & 9a & 10–13 & 15–18)	(or 22:1–2 & 9–13 & 15–18: LHWE)
3. *Exod 14:15–15:1	*Exod 14:10–31 & 15:20–21
	(or Exod 14:15 – 15:1a: LHWE)
4. Isa 54:5–14	(Isa 54:5–14: LHWE)
5. *Isa 55:1–11	*Isa 55:1–11
6. *Baruch 3:9–15 & 32 – 4:4	*Baruch 3:9–15 & 32 – 4:4
7. Ezek 36:16–17a & 18–28	Ezek 36:24–28
	*Ezek 37:1–14
Rom 6:3–11	Rom 6:3–11
Mt 28:1–10	Mt 28:1–10

For Reading 7, R: allows, where baptisms are happening, Isa 12:2–6.
[In Churches where the Vigil is not observed, the Principal Eucharist on Easter Sunday morning is the Great Easter Liturgy; it may start with the blessing of the Paschal Candle (LHWE).
It fittingly includes Baptisms and Confirmations or else the Renewal of Baptismal Vows (e.g., CW 'Initiation' pp. 127–8) after the Gospel; if so, the Creed is omitted.]

* Readings from the ancient Roman Vigil.

✠ *SUNDAY*   **EASTER DAY IN THE LORD'S RESURRECTION**
23   W   MP   Ps: 114; 117   Exod 14:10–18 & 26 – 15:2   Exod 12:1–14
                                                     Rev 15:2–4   Rev 1:4–18
R: Ps I   Mass   *Gl; (R: Seq compulsory: EH 130 NEH 519) Cr; R: Pref I of Easter; CW, Pref of Easter.*

                          CW: Acts 10:34–43; Ps 118*:1–2 & 14–24; Col 3:1–4; Jn 20:1–18 (or Mt 28:1–10)
                          R: Acts 10:34a & 37–43; Ps 118*:1–2 & 16ab–17 & 22–23; Col 3:1–4 (or I Cor 5:6b–8);
                          Jn 20:1–9 (or Mt 28:1–10 or, at an Evening Mass, Lk 24:13–35)
                          *[OT readings: see Note 7 below. For those who particularly desire an OT reading, CW provides
                          Isa 65:17–25]*

               EP   Song of Sol 3:2–5 & 8:6–7   Exod 14:5–end
                          Ps: 105 or 66:1–11   Rev 1:12–18   Jn 20: (1–10) 11–23

* Ps 118, last of the Passover Hallel psalms, quoted by the Lord and in the Easter Kerygma. Verses 24 & 1 are anciently associated
with the readings at Rome and Byzantium.

NOTES FOR EASTER WEEK ONLY

1 During the octave of Easter, that is, from Easter Day *until the evening of Low Sunday*, two alleluias are
added to the dismissals at the end of Mass, and at the end of Morning and Evening Prayer, and to
the response. Throughout Eastertide, Alleluia is added to all Antiphons or 'Sentences' which do not
already have it.

2 In R: from Easter Sunday MP to the EP of Low Sunday, before Benedictus and Magnificat, this
antiphon is used: **This is the day which was made by the Lord: let us rejoice and be glad.
Alleluia.**

3 Preface: In CW, the *'short* preface' is the ancient Western Easter preface, which comes down to us
via BCP. According to ancient custom, R: orders this preface, *and no other*, to be used until Low Sunday
inclusive. Your Compiler urges its exclusive use during the Octave instead of the CW 'extended
Preface'.

NOTES FOR ALL EASTERTIDE

4 A **SOLEMNITY** falling on a Sunday in Eastertide is transferred to the Monday. (CW allows
Dedications and Patronal Festivals.) A **Festum** falling on a Sunday in Eastertide is omitted (Roman
rules) or *may* be transferred to the first available weekday (CW).

5 **According to the provisions of *The Liturgy of the Hours*, the Office Hymns for
Eastertide begin on Easter Day. EH: MP 123 EP 125 (122 may be used optionally at
MP on Ferias after Easter Week).**
NEH: Sundays: MP 100 EP 101; Ferias: MP 124 EP 101.

6 Prefaces: the CW provision is very austere. After Low Sunday (see note 3 above) your Compiler
urges the use also of ASB 14 = R:4, and of ASB 15 and/or R: prefaces 2, 3, and 5. (Unlike CW, R:
draws upon Prefaces in the ancient Western Sacramentaries.)

7 The Paschal Candle is lit at Mass and Evening Prayer on Easter Day and daily during the octave;
and thereafter on Sundays and greater feasts until the evening of Pentecost. It may be lit at other
liturgical services according to custom.

8 *Regina Coeli* is recited instead of *Angelus* until the evening of Pentecost.

9 R: and CW provide *all three* Sunday Eucharistic readings from the New Testament throughout
Eastertide.

10 On weekdays from Low Sunday until Pentecost, propers at mass are taken *either* from the Daily
Eucharistic Lectionary (Weekday Missal) which is R: = CW, *or* from the previous Sunday (Friday and
Saturday after Ascension, from the Ascension).

11 During the Easter Season it is particularly suitable to use the Asperges (Sprinkling) for the
Penitential Rite, to remind us of our Baptism (Introduction Paragraph 12). See Introduction
Paragraph 17 for the Creed.

12 The 'Julian' (Eastern) Easter this year is April 27.

MONDAY
24 W MP
MONDAY IN EASTER WEEK

	Ps: 111, 117, 146	Exod 12:1–14	Exod 15:1–18
		I Cor 15:1–11	Lk 24:1–12
Mass	*of the day; Gl; (Seq ad lib) Pref (I) of Easter (****Our Lady of the Way****)*		
	Acts 2:14 & 22–32; Ps: 16:1–2 & 6–end; Mt 28:8–15		
EP		Song of Sol 1:9 – 2:7	Isa 12
	Ps: 135	Mk 16:1–8	Rev 7:9–end

TUESDAY
25 W MP
TUESDAY IN EASTER WEEK

	Ps: 112, 147:1–12	Exod 12:14–36	Isa 25:1–9
		I Cor 15:12–19	I Pet 1:1–12
Mass	*as Monday*		
	Acts 2:36–41; Ps: 33:4–5 & 18–end; Jn 20:11–18		
EP		Song of Sol 2:8–end	Isa 26:1–19
	Ps: 136	Lk 24:1–12	Mt 28:1–15

WEDNESDAY
26 W MP
WEDNESDAY IN EASTER WEEK

	Ps: 113, 147:13–end	Exod 12:37–end	Isa 61
		I Cor 15:20–28	I Pet 1:13–end
Mass	*as Monday*		
	Acts 3:1–10; Ps: 105:1–9; Lk 24:13–35		
EP		Song of Sol 3	Song of Sol 2:8–end
	Ps: 105	Mt 28:16–end	Mt 28:16–end

THURSDAY
27 W MP
THURSDAY IN EASTER WEEK

	Ps: 114, 148	Exod 13:1–16	Job 14:1–15
		I Cor 15:29–34	I Thess 4:13–end
Mass	*as Monday (see p. 32)*		
	Acts 3:11–end; Ps: 8; Lk 24:35–48		
EP		Song of Sol 5:2 – 6:3	Dan 12
	Ps: 106	Lk 7:11–17	Mk 16

FRIDAY
28 W MP
FRIDAY IN EASTER WEEK

	Ps: 115, 149	Exod 13:17 – 14:14	Zeph 3:14–end
		I Cor 15:35–50	Acts 17:16–31
Mass	*as Monday*		
	Acts 4:1–12; Ps: 118:1–4 & 22–26; Jn 21:1–14		
EP		Song of Sol 7:10 – 8:4	II Kgs 4:8–37
	Ps: 107	Lk 8:41–end	Jn 21:1–14

SATURDAY
29 W MP
SATURDAY IN EASTER WEEK

	Ps: 116, 150	Exod 14:15–end	Jer 31:1–14
		I Cor 15:51–end	Acts 26:1–23
Mass	*as Monday*		
	Acts 4:13–21; Ps: 118:1–4 & 14–21; Mk 16:9–15		
W 1 EP of foll		Song of Sol 8:5–7	Mic 7:7–end
	Ps: 145	Jn 11:17–44	Jn 21:15–end

Low Sunday, in Western Christendom, is 'Divine Mercy Sunday'. In an Hour of Mercy before the End Time, the believer, even if perplexed by doubt, is drawn by the Risen Lord to reach out with trusting Faith to His Sacred Heart, pierced source (for all Christians as well as for the Paschal neophytes) of the Waters of Regeneration and the Blood of Redemption. (Acts 17:30–31; Mt 28:17; Jn 20:27–8 & 19:34; cf the Gallican collect now used in R: for this Sunday, and the Byzantine Festival, around this time of *Zoodochos Pege*, which also visits themes of Healing Streams but has a greater Marian bias). The old English title 'Mother of Mercy,' beloved of S Richard of Chichester, Bishop Grandisson of Exeter, and so many other saintly Anglicans, seems particularly suitable.

✠ *SUNDAY*

DIVINE MERCY SUNDAY

2nd SUNDAY and WEEK within EASTERTIDE (BCP EASTER 1)

30	W	MP	Ps: 81:1–10	Exod 12:1–17	Isa 52:1–12
				I Cor 5:6b–8	Lk 24:13–35
		Mass	*Gl; Cr; Pref of Easter*		
			CW: Acts 2:14a & 22–32; Ps 16; I Pet 1:3–9; Jn 20:19–31		
			R: Acts 2:42–47; Ps 118:2–4 & 13–15 & 22–24; I Pet 1:3–9;		
			Jn 20:19–31 (Our Easter Joy)		
		2 EP		Dan 6: (1–5) 6–23	Isa 54
			Ps: 30:1–5	Mk 15:46 – 16:8	Jn 20:24–end

MONDAY

ANNUNCIATION OF THE LORD (Transferred)

31	W	MP	H: 214 (NEH 181)	I Sam 2:1–10 (R: I Chron 17:1–15)	Isa 52:7–12
R: Ps II			Ps: 111 & 113	Rom 5:12–21	Heb 2:5–end
		Mass	*Gl; Cr; (Kneel for Incarnatus); R and CW Proper Prefaces*		
			CW: Isa 7:10–14; Ps 40:5–11; Heb 10:4–10; Lk 1:26–38		
			R: Isa 7:10–14; Ps 40; Heb 10:4–10; Lk 1:26–38		
		EP		Isa 52:1–12	I Sam 2:1–10
			Ps: 131, 146	Heb 2:5–18	Mt 1:18–23

A P R I L

TUESDAY

Feria (S JOSEPH? See PRAENOTANDA)

1	W	MP	Ps: 5, 6, 8	Exod 15:22 – 16:10	Deut 2:1–25
				Col 1:15–end	Acts 2:1–21
		Mass	*no Gl or Cr; Pref of Easter*		
			Acts 4:32–end; Ps 93; Jn 3:7–15		
		EP		Deut 1:19–40	Deut 2:26 – 3:5
			Ps: 9, 10	Jn 20:11–18	Acts 2:22–end

WEDNESDAY

Feria (☐ S Francis de Paola, hermit)

OBIT OF JOHN PAUL THE GREAT, 2005

2	W	MP	Ps: 119:1–32	Exod 16:11–36	Deut 3:18–end
				Col 2:1–15	Acts 3:1 – 4:4
		Mass	*as Tuesday (or of the Saint)*		
			Acts 5:17–26; Ps 34:1–8; Jn 3:16–21		
		EP		Deut 3:18–end	Deut 4:1–24
			Ps: 11, 12, 13	Jn 20:19–end	Acts 4:5–31

THURSDAY

Feria

3	W	MP	Ps: 14, 15, 16	Exod 17	Deut 4:25–40
				Col 2:16 – 3:11	Acts 4:32 – 5:11
		Mass	*as Tuesday*		
			Acts 5:27–33; Ps 34:1 & 15–end; Jn 3:31–end		
		EP		Deut 4:1–14	Deut 5:1–21
			Ps: 18	Jn 21:1–14	Acts 5:12–end

FRIDAY

Feria (☐ S Isidore, B, Dr)

4	W	MP	Ps: 17, 19	Exod 18:1–12	Deut 5:22–end
				Col 3:12 – 4:1	Acts 6:1 – 7:16
		Mass	*as Tuesday (or of the Saint) (First Friday: Sacred Heart, see p. 38)*		
			Acts 5:34–end; Ps 27:1–5 & 16–17; Jn 6:1–15		
		EP		Deut 4:15–31	Deut 6
			Ps: 22	Jn 21:15–19	Acts 7:17–34

SATURDAY

Feria (☐ S Vincent Ferrer, Pr)

5	W	MP	Ps: 20, 21, 23	Exod 18:13–end	Deut 7:1–11
				Col 4:2–end	Acts 7:35 – 8:4
		Mass	*as Tuesday (or of the Saint) (First Saturday: Immaculate Heart, see p. 38)*		
			Acts 6:1–7; Ps 33:1–5 & 18–19; Jn 6:16–21		
	W	1 EP of foll		Deut 4:32–40	Deut 7:12–end
			Ps: 24, 25	Jn 21:20–end	Acts 8:4–25

✠ SUNDAY			**3rd SUNDAY and WEEK within EASTERTIDE (BCP EASTER 2)**	
6	W	MP	Ps: 23	Isa 40:1–11	Isa 55
				I Pet 5:1–11	Mk 5:21–end
R: Ps III		Mass	*Gl; Cr; Pref of Easter*		
			CW: Acts 2:14a & 36–41; Ps 116:1–3 & 10–17; I Pet 1:17–23; Lk 24:13–35		
			R: Acts 2:14 & 22–33; Ps 16:1–2a & 5 & 7–11; I Pet 1:17–21;		
			Lk 24:13–35 (Christ With Us On the Road)		
		2 EP	Hag 1:13 – 2:9	Deut 4:25–40
			Ps: 48	I Cor 3:10–17	Rev 2:1–17

MONDAY			**☐ S John Baptist de la Salle, Pr**	
7	W	MP	Ps: 27, 30	Exod 19	Deut 8
				Lk 1:1–25	Acts 8:26–end
		Mass	*of the Saint*		
			Acts 6:8–end; Ps 119:17–24; Jn 6:22–29		
		EP	Deut 5:1–22	Deut 9:1–10
			Ps: 26, 28, 29	Eph 1:1–14	Acts 9:1–31

TUESDAY			**Feria (The Annotine Easter)**	
8	W	MP	Ps: 32, 36	Exod 20:1–21	Deut 9:11–end
				Lk 1:26–38	Acts 9:32–end
		Mass	*no Gl or Cr; Pref of Easter*		
			Acts 7:51 – 8:1; Ps 31:1–5 & 16; Jn 6:30–35		
		EP	Deut 5:22–end	Deut 10
			Ps: 33	Eph 1:15–end	Acts 10:1–23

WEDNESDAY			**Feria**	
9	W	MP	Ps: 34	Exod 24	Deut 11:1–12
				Lk 1:39–56	Acts 10:24–end
		Mass	*as Tuesday (or of the Saint) (**Dietrich Bonhoeffer, M**)*		
			Acts 8:1–8; Ps 66:1–6; Jn 6:35–40		
		EP	Deut 6	Deut 11:13–end
			Ps: 119:33–36	Eph 2:1–10	Acts 11:1–18

THURSDAY			**Feria**	
10	W	MP	Ps: 37	Exod 25:1–22	Deut 12:1–14
				Lk 1:57–end	Acts 11:19–end
		Mass	*as Tuesday (**William Law, Pr; William of Ockham**)*		
			Acts 8:26–end; Ps 66:7–8 & 14–end; Jn 6:44–51		
		EP	Deut 7:1–11	Deut 15:1–18
			Ps: 39, 40	Eph 2:11–end	Acts 12:1–24

FRIDAY			**Feria (☐ S Stanislas, B, M)**	
11	W (or R)	MP	Ps: 31	Exod 28:1–4a, 29–38	Deut 16:1–20
				Lk 2:1–20	Acts 12:25 – 13:12
		Mass	*as Tuesday (or of the Saint) (**George Selwyn, B**)*		
			Acts 9:1–20; Ps 117; Jn 6:52–9		
		EP	Deut 7:12–end	Deut 17:8–end
			Ps: 35	Eph 3:1–13	Acts 13:13–43

SATURDAY			**Feria**	
12	W	MP	Ps: 41, 42, 43	Exod 29:1–9	Deut 18:9–end
				Lk 2:21–40	Acts 13:44 – 14:7
		Mass	*as Tuesday*		
			Acts 9:31–42; Ps 116:10–15; Jn 6:60–69		
	W	1 EP of foll	Deut 8	Deut 19
			Ps: 45, 46	Eph 3:14–end	Acts 14:8–end

✠ *SUNDAY*
13 W
R: Ps IV

		4th SUNDAY and WEEK within EASTERTIDE (BCP EASTER 3)	
MP	Ps: 106:6–24	Neh 9:6–15	Num 13:1–2 & 17–end
		I Cor 10:1–13	Lk 7:11–17

Mass *Gl; Cr; Pref of Easter*
  CW: Acts 2:42–47; Ps 23; I Pet 2:19–25; Jn 10:1–10
  R: Acts 2:14a & 36–41; Ps 23; I Pet 2:20–25; Jn 10:1–10 (The Good Shepherd)

2 EP		Ezra 3:1–13	Deut 5:1–21
	Ps: 29:1–10	Eph 2:11–22	Rev 2:18 – 3:6

MONDAY
14 W

		Feria	
MP	Ps: 44	Exod 32:1–14	Deut 21:22 – 22:8
		Lk 2:41–end	Acts 15:1–21

Mass *no Gl or Cr; Pref of Easter*
  Acts 11:1–18; Ps 42:1–2, 43:1–4; Jn 10:11–18

EP		Deut 9:1–21	Deut 24:5–end
	Ps: 47, 49	Eph 4:1–16	Acts 15:22–35

TUESDAY
15 W

		Feria	
MP	Ps: 48, 52	Exod 32:15–34	Deut 26
		Lk 3:1–14	Acts 15:36 – 16:5

Mass *as Monday*
  Acts 11:19–26; Ps 87; Jn 10:22–30

EP		Deut 9:23 – 10:5	Deut 28:58–end
	Ps: 50	Eph 4:17–end	Acts 16:6–end

WEDNESDAY
16 W

		Feria	
MP	Ps: 119:57–80	Exod 33	Deut 29:10–end
		Lk 3:15–22	Acts 17:1–15

Mass *as Monday (**Isabella Gilmore**)*
  Acts 12:24 – 13:5; Ps 67; Jn 12:44–end

EP		Deut 10:12–end	Deut 30
	Ps: 59, 60, 67	Eph 5:1–14	Acts 17:16–end

THURSDAY
17 W

		Feria	
MP	Ps: 56, 57, 63	Exod 34:1–10, 27–end	Deut 31:1–13
		Lk 4:1–13	Acts 18:1–23

Mass *as Monday*
  Acts 13:13–25; Ps 89:1–2 & 20–26; Jn 13:16–20

EP		Deut 11:8–end	Deut 31:14–29
	Ps: 61, 62, 64	Eph 5:15–end	Acts 18:24 – 19:7

FRIDAY
18 W

		Feria	
MP	Ps: 51, 54	Exod 35:20 – 36:7	Deut 31:30 – 32:14
		Lk 4:14–30	Acts 19:8–20

Mass *as Monday*
  Acts 13:26–33; Ps 2; Jn 14:1–6

EP		Deut 12:1–14	Deut 32:15–47
	Ps: 38	Eph 6:1–9	Acts 19:21–end

SATURDAY
19 W
(or R)

		Feria (S Alphege, B, M) ELECTION OF BENEDICT XVI, 2005	
MP	Ps: 68	Exod 40:17–end	Deut 33
		Lk 4:31–37	Acts 20:1–16

Mass *as Monday (or of the Saint)*
  Acts 13:44–52; Ps 98:1–5; Jn 14:7–14

W	1 EP of foll	Deut 15:1–18	Deut 32:48–end & 34
	Ps: 65, 66	Eph 6:10–end	Acts 20:17–end

✠ SUNDAY
20
W   MP

R: Ps I   Mass

           2 EP

5th SUNDAY and WEEK within EASTERTIDE (BCP EASTER 4)

Ps: 30	Ezek 37:1–12	Num 22:1–35
	Jn 5:19–29	Jn 11:1–44

Gl; Cr; Pref of Easter
CW: Acts 7:55–60; Ps 31:1–5 & 15–16; I Pet 2:2–10; Jn 14:1–14
R: Acts 6:1–7; Ps 33; I Pet 2:4–9; Jn 14:1–12 (Our Royal Priesthood)

	Zech 4:1–10	Deut 10:12 – 11:1
Ps: 147:1–12	Rev 21:1–14	Rev 3:7–end

MONDAY
21
W   MP

           Mass

           EP

Feria (S Anselm B, Dr)

Ps: 71	Num 9:15–end; 10:33–end	Josh 1
	Lk 4:38–end	Acts 21:1–16

as Tuesday (or of the Saint)
Acts 14:5–18; Ps 118:1–3 & 14–15; Jn 14:21–26

	Deut 16:1–20	Josh 2
Ps: 72, 75	I Pet 1:1–12	Acts 21:17–36

TUESDAY
22
W   MP

           Mass

Feria

Ps: 73	Num 11:1–33	Josh 3
	Lk 5:1–11	Acts 21:37 – 22:22

no Gl or Cr; Pref of Easter
Acts 14:19–end; Ps 145:10–end; Jn 14:27–end

S GEORGE, M, PATRON OF ENGLAND

R   1 EP

H: 185	Jer 15:15–21	◁
Ps: 111, 116	Heb 11:32 – 12:2	◁

WEDNESDAY
23
R   MP

           Mass

           2 EP

H: 180	Josh 1:1–9	◁
Ps: 5, 146	Eph 6:10–20	◁

Gl; Cr; Pref of Martyrs (or Patrons) (CW of Saints)
CW: Rev 12:7–12; Ps: 126; II Tim 2:3–13; Jn 15:18–21

H: 181	Isa 43:1–7	◁
Ps: 3, 11	Jn 15:1–8	◁

THURSDAY
24
W   MP
(or R)

           Mass

           EP

Feria (□ S Adalbert, B, M; □ S Fidelis de Sigmaringen, Pr, M;
S Mellitus, B) INAUGURATION OF BENEDICT XVI, 2005

Ps: 78:1–39	Num 13:1–3, 17–end	Josh 9:3–end
	Lk 5:27–end	Acts 24:24 – 25:12

as Tuesday (or of the Saint)
Acts 15:17– 21; Ps 96:1–3 & 7–10; Jn 15:9–11

	Deut 19	Josh 4:1 – 5:1
Ps: 78:40–end	I Pet 2:11–end	Acts 22:23 – 23:11

FRIDAY
25
R   MP

           Mass

           EP

S Mark Ev

Ps: 37:23–41, 148	Isa 62:6–10 or Ecclus 51:13–30	Ezek 1:1–14
	Acts 12:25 – 13:13 (R: Eph 4:1–16)	Acts 15:35–end

Gl; R: Pref of Apostles (II); CW, Pref of Saints
CW: Acts 15:35–41; Ps 119:9–16; Eph 4:7–16; Mk 13:5–13
R: I Pet 5:5–14; Ps 89; Mk 16:15–20

	Ezek 1:4–14	Isa 62:6–10
Ps: 45	II Tim 4:1–11	II Tim 4:1–11

SATURDAY
26
W   MP

           Mass

W   1 EP of foll

Feria

Ps: 76, 79	Num 14:26–end	Josh 23
	Lk 6:12–26	Acts 28:1–15

*as Tuesday (**Our Lady of Good Counsel**)*
Acts 16:1–10; Ps 100; Jn 15:18–21

	Deut 24:5–end	Josh 24:1–28
Ps: 81, 84	I Pet 3:13–end	Acts 28:16–end

ASCENSION AND PENTECOST

1. Modern liturgical reforms emphasise a primitive concept of the fifty days of Eastertide as a unitary festival, a Week of Weeks, 'the One Day', 'the Great Sunday'. That is why the Paschal candle burns from Easter Night until Pentecost Evening, when it is removed (and placed near the font). **However**, recent Roman directions allow the BCP-style Whitmonday: Mass and Office 'as yesterday'.

2. ***Rogations***, instituted in Gaul around 475 'to repel calamities', became spring processions to ask that God 'give and preserve to our use the kindly fruits of the earth.' They are Class 2 votives (page xxi); CLC pp 231 and 115. We have Synodical encouragement for processing the relics of Saints on these days; and Monday has been episcopally designated (EXETER) Feast of the Translation of the Relics. The R: = CW masses for Monday, Tuesday, and Wednesday do NOT have Rogation themes.

3. Rome now provides a ***Vigil*** mass for Ascension (as well as Pentecost), the Collect of which is used at 1 EP (God, whose Son this day ascended into the heavens as his Apostles stood by; grant us we beseech/beg thee/you, that, according to his promise, he may ever be with us upon earth and that we may be worthy to live with him in heaven.) The Tridentine = BCP = CW collect for Ascension *day* is now restored by R: as an option!

4. ***Prefaces from Ascension to Pentecost (exclusively) (including Sunday)***
   CW: 'From the day after Ascension Day until the Day of Pentecost'. R: Either of the Ascension or of Easter [even on Memorials]. CW *Short* Preface *for Ascension* is traditional.

5. ***Weekday Masses after Pentecost Sunday***
   According to R:, any 'green' Sunday Collect may be used, and CW (p. 406) offers Roman Sunday Collect 10 (= BCP Easter 5) in its Cranmerian translation. Mass readings come from the Week of the Year.

6. ***Weekday Masses after Trinity Sunday***
   CW expects the Trinity collect to be used; Rome both provides a collect and allows optionally any Sunday collect to be used. Mass readings come from the Week of the Year.

7. ***Hymns from Ascension to Pentecost (exclusively) (including Sunday)***
   MP 141 (NEH 128) EP 154 (NEH 138) [or, optionally, on Memorials, of the Saint].

8. Between Ascension and Pentecost, Evening Prayer has the Holy Spirit as its theme in both the Office Hymn and the Readings.

9. ***Ascension on Sunday***
   For those observing the Ascension, with the English Roman Catholic Church, on the Sunday following, the CW office readings can be:

   Wednesday EP: Deut 28:58–end; I Pet 5 (Pss 91, 93)

   Thursday MP: Num 20:1–13; Lk 7:11–17 (Pss 90, 92)
   EP: Exod 35:30 – 36:1; Gal 5:13–26 (Ps 94)

   Friday MP: Num 21:4–9; Lk 7:18–35
   EP: Num 11:16–17 & 24–29; I Cor 2 } (unless SS P & J, as CW orders, are kept today.)

   Saturday MP: Num 21:4–9; Lk 7:18–35 (unless SS P & J, as R: orders, are kept today.)
   EP: of the Ascension, tomorrow.

(Tridentinists and Prayer Book enthusiasts will presumably not wish to make this transference.)

Mass in the Roman Rite provides *Acts 18:1–8; Ps 98; Jn 16:16–20* as the readings for Thursday if the Ascension is transferred to Sunday.

THE MAY DEVOTION TO OUR LADY,

so long traditional, suits well the Paschal celebration of Humanity, restored and deified. In the words of the great Russian Orthodox lay theologian Vladimir Lossky, 'freed from the limitations of time, Mary can be the cause of that which is before her; can preside over that which comes after her. She obtains eternal benefits. It is through her that men and angels receive grace. No gift is received in the Church without the assistance of the Mother of God, who is herself the first-fruits of the glorified Church. Thus, having attained to the limits of becoming, she necessarily watches over the destinies of the Church and of the Universe.' One of the greatest of the Greek fathers, S. Gregory Palamas, wrote that the All-Holy Mother of God 'is herself alone the boundary of created and uncreated nature, and nobody could come to God except through her . . . she is the Treasury and President of the Wealth of the Godhead . . . she stewards and encompasses God's graces . . .'. PPL comments that the May Devotion 'highlights the earthly role played by the glorified Queen of Heaven, here and now, in the celebration of Baptism, Confirmation, and Eucharist.' As well as the Rosary (especially on Saturdays), the Akathist hymn to Our Lady of Victories seems appropriate (see p. xxvi).

1. Many priests begin the May Devotion with a (Class 2 – see p. xxi) votive of Our Lady on the first free day. **May 3**, in ancient 'Celtic' Calendars, was her Conception (in Poland, Solemnity of our Lady Queen of Poland, and in Russia the Feast of her Icon in the great Pechersk Monastery, fountainhead of the cenobitic monastic life in that country): which may suggest texts from December 8 appropriately adapted with Paschal Alleluias.

2. On the **Friday in Easter Week*** Byzantium emphasises the role of the Mother of God in pouring Christ's healing streams upon us (Zoodochos Pege: originally the Dedication of the ancient Sanctuary of the Mother of God of the Living Fountain beside its miraculous stream at Constantinople; the panorthodox chapel in the shrine church at Walsingham has this dedication). Collection of Masses (Int P 26b ii) mass 31 visits this theme.

3. The **Visitation of Our Lady** was deliberately moved in 1969 to associate it with May 31, the day long connected with the celebration of Our Lady as Mediatrix of All Graces, as an appropriate conclusion to the May devotion. This year it 'absorbs' the Immaculate Heart.

4. Rome moved **Ss Philip and James** from May 1 to May 3 to accommodate S Joseph the Craftsmen on the Workers' festival. (EAD allows either date.) But he never caught on, least of all in England, and after Vatican II was reduced from a Solemnity to an Optional Memorial.

* May 2 in this year's Julian Calendar.

May 1 **S Joseph the Workman** (Optional Memorial) MP and EP as on March 19
Mass: Gen 1:26 – 2:3; or Col 3:14–15 & 17 & 23–24; Ps 90; Mt 13: 54–58

Ss Philip and James Aps MAY 2 (CW) OR MAY 3 (R:)?

R	MP	Ps: 139, 146	Prov 4:10–18	Isa 30:15–21
			James 1:1–12	Jn 6:1–14
	Mass	*Gl; R: Pref of Apostles (II); CW, Pref of Saints*		
		CW: Isa 30:15–21; Ps 119:1–8; Eph 1:3–10; Jn 14:1–14		
		R: I Cor 15:1–8; Ps 19; Jn 14:6–14		
	EP		Job 23:1–12	Job 23:1–12
		Ps: 149	Jn 1:43–51	Jn 1:43–end

COLLISIONS IN LATE MAY

MAY	R: Calendar for England	Common Worship
24 Sat	Aldhelm†	(The Wesleys†)
25 Sun	SUNDAY* (of CORPUS CHRISTI)	SUNDAY*
26 Mon	Philip Neri*	Augustine† Philip† (Calvin†)
27 Tues	Augustine*	Feria

* Compulsory.　† Optional.

✠ SUNDAY   **6th SUNDAY and WEEK within EASTERTIDE (BCP EASTER 5)**

27 W MP   Ps: 73:21–28   Job 14:1–2 & 7–15 & 19:23–27a   Num 22:36 – 23:12
                                      I Thess 4:13–18   Rom 6:1–14

R: Ps II Mass *Gl; Cr; Pref of Easter*
                CW: Acts 17:22–31; Ps 66:7–18; I Pet 3:13–22; Jn 14:15–21
                R: Acts 8:5–8 & 14–17; Ps 66; I Pet 3:15–18; Jn 14:15–21 (The Spirit of Truth)

          2 EP   Zech 8:1–13   Deut 28:1–14
                Ps: 87, 36:5–10   Rev 21:22 – 22:5   Mk 4:1–20

MONDAY   *Feria (Rogation Day) (S Peter Chanel, Pr, M;*
                                ☐ S Louis Marie Grignion de Montfort, Pr)

28 W MP   Ps: 80, 82   Num 16:1–35   Deut 7:6–13
     (or R)   Lk 6:27–38   Mt 6:5–18

          Mass *of Sunday; no Gl or Cr; Pref of Easter: Rogations: see p. 30*
                Acts 16:11–15; Ps 149:1–5; Jn 15:26 – 16:4

          EP   Deut 26   Deut 8
                Ps: 85, 86   I Pet 4:1–11   Mt 6:19–end

TUESDAY   **S Catharine of Siena V & Dr Patron of Europe***

29 W MP   [Ps: 87, 89:1–18]   [Num 16:36–end]   [Deut 11:8–21]
                                      [Lk 6:39–end]   [Lk 5:1–11]

          Mass *Office Readings from Appendix 3: Doctors*
                Gl; no Cr; Pref of Patrons or (CW) Saints
                R: I Jn 1:5 – 2:2; Ps 45:10–11 & 13b–16; Mt 25:1–13
                CW: Prov 8:1 & 6–11; Ps 34:11–17; Mt 25:1–13 or Jn 17:12–26
                [Acts 16:22–34; Ps 138; Jn 16:5–11]

          EP   [Deut 26]   [I Kgs 8:22–43]
                [Ps: 89:19–end]   [I Pet 4:12–end]   [Jas 5:1–18]

WEDNESDAY   *Feria (Rogation Day) (☐ S Pius, V, Pp)*

30 W MP   Ps: 119:105–128   Num 17:1–11   Joel 2:21–27
                                      Lk 7:1–10   Jn 6:22–40

          Mass *as Monday (or of the Saint) (**Pandita Mary Ramabai**)*
                Acts 17:15 & 22 – 18:1c; Ps 148:1–2 & 11–end; Jn 16:12–15

✠   **ASCENSION OF THE LORD** *(SEE P. 30 FOR TRANSFERENCE)*

          1 EP of foll   II Sam 23:1–5   Song of the Three 29–37
                Ps: 15, 24   Col 2:20–3:4   Mt 28:16–end

M A Y
THURSDAY

1   W MP   H: 141 (NEH 128)   Isa 52:7–15   II Kgs 2:1–15
                Ps: 110   Heb 7:(11–25) 26–28 (R: Eph 4:1–24) Jn 17

          Mass *Gl; Cr; Pref of the Ascension*
                CW: Acts 1:1–11; Ps 47; Eph 1:15–23; Lk 24:44–53
                R: Acts 1:1–11; Ps 47:2–3 & 6–9; Eph 1:17–23; Mt 28:16–20

          2 EP H: 144 (NEH 129)   Song of the Three 29–37   II Sam 23:1–5
                                      or II Kgs 2:1–15
                Ps: 8   Rev 5   Heb 1

FRIDAY   *S Athanasius, B, Dr (SS P & J? see p. 31)*

2   W MP   Ps: 88, 95   Num 20:1–13   Judg 2:6–end
                                      Lk 7:11–17   Heb 2

          Mass *of the Saint (First Friday: Sacred Heart, see p. 38)*
                Acts 18:9–18; Ps 47:1–6; Jn 16:20–23

          EP   Exod 35:30 – 36:1   Judg 4
                Ps: 102   Gal 5:13–26   Heb 3

SATURDAY   *Feria (SS P & J? see p. 31)*

3   W MP   Ps: 96, 97, 100   Num 21:4–9   Judg 5
                                      Lk 7:18–35   Heb 4:1–13

          Mass *no Gl or Cr; Pref see p. 30 (First Saturday: Immaculate Heart, see p. 38)*
                Acts 18:23–end; Ps 47:1–2 & 7–end; Jn 16:23–28

        W 1 EP of foll   Num 11:16–17, 24–29   Judg 6:1–24
                Ps: 104   I Cor 2   Heb 4:14 – 5:10

* Episcopal Ordination of John Richards, first Bishop of Ebbsfleet, 1994.

✠ SUNDAY   7th SUNDAY and WEEK within EASTERTIDE

4 W	MP	H: see p. 31	Isa 65:17–25	Isa 52:1–12
		Ps: 104:26–35	Rev 21:1–8	Eph 4:1–16
R: Ps III	Mass	*Gl; Cr; Pref see p. 30*		
		CW: *Acts 1:6–14; Ps 68:1–10 & 32–35; I Pet 4:12–14 & 5:6–11; Jn 17:1–11*		
		R: *Acts 1:12–14; Ps 27:1 & 4 & 7–8a; I Pet 4:13–14 & 16; Jn 17:1–11 (The Spirit of Prayer)*		
	2 EP	II Sam 23:1–5		Isa 62
		Ps: 47	Eph 1:15–23	Rev 5

MONDAY   Feria [Hymns, Prefaces, see p. 30]

5 W	MP	Ps: 98, 99, 101	Num 22:1–35	Ezek 11:14–20
			Lk 7:36–end	Acts 2:12–36
	Mass	*no Gl or Cr*		
		Acts 19:1–8; Ps 68:1–6; Jn 16:29–end		
	EP		Num 27:15–23	Wisd 1:1–7
		Ps: 103, 105	I Cor 3	Acts 2:37–end

TUESDAY   Feria

6 W	MP	Ps: 106	Num 22:36 – 23:12	Ezek 37:1–14
			Lk 8:1–15	I Cor 12:1–13
	Mass	*as Monday*		
		Acts 20:17–27; Ps 68:9–10 & 18–19; Jn 17:1–11		
	EP		I Sam 10:1–10	Wisd 7:15 – 8:21
		Ps: 107	I Cor 12:1–13	I Cor 12:27–13 end

WEDNESDAY   Feria

7 W	MP	Ps: 110, 111, 112	Num 23:13–end	I Kgs 19:1–18
			Lk 8:16–25	I Cor 2
	Mass	*as Monday*		
		Acts 20:28–end; Ps 68:27–28 & 32–end; Jn 17:11–19		
	EP		I Kgs 19:1–18	Wisd 9
		Ps: 119:129–152	Mt 3:13–end	I Cor 3

THURSDAY   Feria

8 W	MP	Ps: 113, 115	Num 24	II Sam 23:1–5
			Lk 8:26–39	Eph 6:10–20
	Mass	*as Monday (**Julian of Norwich**) (**Our Lady, Mediatrix of Grace;** **Mother of Fairest Love**)*		
		Acts 22:30 & 23:6–11; Ps 16:1 & 5–end; Jn 17:20–end		
	EP		Ezek 11:14–20	Exod 35:30 – 36:1
		Ps: 114, 116, 117	Mt 9:35 – 10:20	Gal 5:13–end

FRIDAY   Feria

9 W	MP	Ps: 139	Num 27:12–end	Num 11:16–17 & 24–29
			Lk 8:40–end	II Cor 5:14 – 6:10
	Mass	*as Monday*		
		Acts 25:13–21; Ps 103:1–2 & 11–12 & 19–20; Jn 21:15–19		
	EP		Ezek 36:22–28	Jer 31:31–34
		Ps: 130, 131, 137	Mt 12:22–32	II Cor 3

SATURDAY   Feria

10 W	MP	Ps: 120, 121, 122	Num 32:1–27	Num 27:15–end
			Lk 9:1–17	Mt 9:35 – 10:20
	Mass	*as Monday (**Our Lady Queen of Apostles**)*		
		Acts 28:16–20 & 30–31; Ps: 11:4–end; Jn 21:20–25		
	R	1 EP of Pentecost H: 154 (NEH 138) Deut 16:9–15		Gen 11:1–9
		Ps: 48	Jn 15:26 – 16:15	Acts 18:24 – 19:7
		R: *Vigil Mass: Gen 11:1–9 (or Exod 19:3–8a & 16–20b; or Ezek 37:1–14; or Joel 3:1–5);*		
		Ps: 104; Rom 8:22–27; Jn 7:37–39). The Vigil Collect is used at 1 EP.		

✠ SUNDAY			**PENTECOST**		**(Whitsunday)**
11	R	MP	H: 151 (NEH 136)	Gen 11:1–9	Joel 2:28–end
			Ps: 87	Acts 10:34–48	Rom 8:1–17
		Mass	*Gl; (R: Seq ad lib: EH 155 NEH 520) Cr; Pref (18)*		
			CW: Acts 2:1–21; Ps 104:26–36 & 37b; I Cor 12:3b–13; Jn 20:19–23		
			R: Acts 2:1–11; Ps 104:1 & 24 & 29–31 & 34; I Cor 12:3b–7 & 12–13; Jn 20:19–23		
		2 EP	H: 154 (NEH 138)	Joel 2:21–32	Isa 11:1–9
			Ps: 67, 133	Acts 2:14–21 (22–38)	Rom 8:18–end

'ORDINARY TIME' – 'PER ANNUM' – 'THE GREEN SEASON' – RESUMES   **6th WEEK OF YEAR**

MONDAY			*Feria (☐ Ss Nereus and Achilleus, Ms; ☐ S Pancras, M)*		
12	G (or R)	MP	Ps: 123, 124, 125, 126	Josh 1	Judg 6:25–end
				Lk 9:18–27	Heb 5:11–6 end
R: Ps II		Mass	*of Sunday; no Gl or Cr; Common Pref*		
			Jas 1:1–11; Ps 119:65–72; Mk 8:11–13		
		EP		Job 1	Judg 7
			127, 128, 129	Rom 1:1–17	Heb 7

TUESDAY			*Feria (☐ Our Lady of Fatima)**		
13	G (or W)	MP	Ps: 132, 133	Josh 2	Judg 10:17 – 11:8
				Lk 9:28–36	Heb 8
		Mass	*as Monday (or of our Lady)*		
			Jas 1:12–18; Ps 94:12–18; Mk 8:14–21		
		EP		Job 2	Judg 11:29 – 12:7
			134, 135	Rom 1:18–end	Heb 9:1–14

WEDNESDAY			**S Matthias, Apostle***		
14	W	MP	Ps: 16, 147:1–12	I Sam 2:27–35	Isa 22:15–22
				Acts 2:37–47	Mt 7:15–27
		Mass	*Gl; R: Pref of Apostles (II); CW, Pref of Saints*		
			CW: Acts 1:15–26; Ps 15; I Cor 4:1–7; Jn 15:9–17		
			R: Acts 1:15–17 & 20–26; Ps 113; Jn 15:9–17		
		EP		I Sam 16:1–13a	I Sam 16:1–13
			Ps: 80	Mt 7:15–27	I Cor 4:1–8

THURSDAY			*Feria*		
15	G	MP	Ps: 143, 146	Josh 4:1 – 5:1	Judg 16:4–end
				Lk 9:51–end	Heb 10:19–end
		Mass	*as Monday*		
			Jas 2:1–9; Ps 34:1–7; Mk 8:27–33		
		EP		Job 4	Ruth 1
			Ps: 138, 140, 141	Rom 2:17–end	Heb 11

FRIDAY			*Feria**		
16	G	MP	Ps: 142, 144	Josh 5:2–end	Ruth 2
				Lk 10:1–16	Heb 12:1–13
		Mass	*as Monday (**Caroline Chisholm**)*		
			Jas 2:14–24 & 26; Ps 112; Mk 8:34 – 9:1		
		EP		Job 5	Ruth 3
			Ps: 145	Rom 3:1–20	Heb 12:14–end

SATURDAY			*Our Lady on Saturday or the Feria**		
17	W (or G)	MP	Ps: 147	Josh 6:1–20	Ruth 4:1–17
				Lk 10:17–24	Heb 13
		Mass	*Introduction Paragraph 26(b)*		
			Jas 3:1–10; Ps 12:1–7; Mk 9:2–13		
	W	1 EP of foll		Exod 34:1–10	Isa 61
			Ps: 97, 98	Mk 1:1–13	II Tim 1:3–14

* Ember Days, see Introduction paragraph 25. Our Lady of Fatima: see p. 38.

CORPUS CHRISTI is now officially known in the Roman Church as The Body and Blood of Christ, and, where, as now in the English Roman Catholic Church, it is not regarded as a Day of Obligation, is to be observed on the following Sunday. (See Introduction Para 5C4.) CW says that 'the Thursday after Trinity Sunday may be observed as a day of Thanksgiving for the Holy Communion (sometimes known as Corpus Christi), and may be kept as a festival'; readings were authorised by CW. The CW **short** preface for Maundy Thursday is suitable. R: Preface of the Eucharist.

Since there will be clergy who will wish to follow the English RC transference of this Solemnity to the following Sunday, we give here the propers for insertion according to local decision.

THE BODY AND BLOOD OF CHRIST, CORPUS CHRISTI
Mass: Gl; Cr; Proper Pref; WHITE. The Sequence (EH 317; NEH 521) is traditionally sung before the Gospel.

CW		R: YEAR A (2008)	R: YEAR B (2009)	R: YEAR C (2010)
1 EP	H: 326 (NEH 268) Ps: 110, 111	◁	◁	◁
	Exod 16:2–15	◁	◁	◁
	Jn 6:22–35	◁	◁	◁
MP	H: 330 (NEH 269) Ps: 147	◁	◁	◁
	Deut 8:2–16	Exod 24:1–11*	Deut 8:2–16*	◁
	I Cor 10:1–17	Heb 9:11–15*	I Cor 10:1–17*	◁
Mass	Gen 14:18–20	Deut 8:2–3 & 14–16	Exod 24:3–8	Gen 14:18–20
	Ps 116:10–17	Ps 147:12–end	Ps 116:12–end	Ps 110
	I Cor 11:23–26	I Cor 10:16–17	Heb 9:11–15	I Cor 11:23–26
	Jn 6:51–58	Jn 6:51–58	Mk 14:12–16 & 22–26	Lk 9:11–17
2 EP	H: 326 (NEH 268) Ps: 23, 42, 43	◁	◁	◁
	Prov 9:1–5	◁	◁	◁
	Lk 9:11–17	◁	◁	Mk 14:12–25*

*Those who use the R: 3 year cycle and use an Anglican Office can avoid duplicating the mass reading by using these alternatives, mostly from the 1961 Lectionary.

BENEDICTION, PROCESSIONS, AND EXPOSITION OF THE BLESSED SACRAMENT are services clearly lawful under Canon B.5.2 if 'the minister having the cure of souls' considers them 'suitable' and uses, or 'permits another minister, to use' them. (The requirement of Canon B.5.3 that such services shall be 'neither contrary to, nor indicative of any departure from, the doctrine of the Church of England in any *essential* matter' need create no anxiety since ARCIC 1979 endorsed by Lambeth 1988 held that 'differences of practice' in this area can 'coexist with real consensus on the *essentials*'. A form was offered in Celebrating Common Prayer as commended by the then Archbishop of Canterbury.) If a reading and the Our Father are incorporated, Benediction etc come within the umbrella of CW pp 21–24 A Service Of The Word.

The *Assistant Curates Society* publishes a small, cheap *Rite of Eucharistic Exposition and Benediction* giving many alternatives for these most flexible of services. The traditional '**V** Thou gavest/You gave them Bread from Heaven **R** Containing in itself all sweetness' no longer appears in Roman texts but (Elliot) 'is still widely used.'

An Anglican variant called 'Devotions' (Exposition and prayers, but no physical act of Blessing) is now authorised by Rome for *laypeople* to perform; but is unsuitable if a priest is available. 'In the full rite of Benediction the blessing of the people with the Sacred Host as the climax of the service reminds them inescapably of the fact that, in our relation with God, it is He, and not we, who is the primary agent and who takes the initiative' (Eric Mascall).

✠ SUNDAY   **TRINITY SUNDAY**
18   W   MP   Ps: 86:8–13   Exod 3:1–6 & 13–15   Isa 6:1–8
                                              Jn 17:1–11   Mk 1:1–13
          Mass   *Gl; Cr; Pref of the Trinity*
                  CW: Isa 40:12–17 & 27–31; Ps 8; II Cor 13:11–13; Mt 28:16–20
                  R: Exod 34:4–6 & 8–9; Song of Three 29–34; II Cor 13:11–13; Jn 3:16–18
          2 EP   H: 159   Isa 6:1–8   Isa 40:12–end
                  Ps: 93, 150   Jn 16:5–15   I Pet 1:3–12

                                                              7th WEEK of YEAR

MONDAY   **Feria (S Dunstan, B)**
19   G   MP   Ps: 1, 2, 3   Josh 7:1–15   I Sam 1
        (or W)   Lk 10:25–37   Jas 1
R: Ps III   Mass   *see p. 30, note 6; no Gl or Cr; Common Pref (or of the Saint)*
                     Jas 3:13–end; Ps 19:7–end; Mk 9:14–29
          EP   Job 7   I Sam 2:1–21
                  Ps: 4, 7   Rom 4:1–12   Mk 1:14–31

TUESDAY   **Feria (□ S Bernardine of Sienna, Pr)**
20   G   MP   Ps: 5, 6, 8   Josh 7:16–end   I Sam 2:22–end
        (or W)   Lk 10:38–end   Jas 2:1–13
          Mass   *as Monday (or of the Saint)* (**Alcuin, Dcn**)
                  Jas 4:1–10; Ps 55:7–9 & 24; Mk 9:30–37
          EP   Job 8   I Sam 3
                  Ps: 9, 10   Rom 4:13–end   Mk 1:32–end

WEDNESDAY   **Feria (□ Ss Christopher Magallanes, Pr, Ms, Comp, Ms; S Helen)**
21 G (or   MP   Ps: 119:1–32   Josh 8:1–29   I Sam 4
       W or R)   Lk 11:1–13   Jas 2:14–end
          Mass   *as Monday (or of the Saints)* (**Our Lady of Vladimir**)
                  Jas 4:13–end; Ps 49:1–2 & 5–10; Mk 9:38–40
                  CORPUS CHRISTI? see p. 35. OTHERWISE:–
          EP   Job 9   I Sam 7
                  Ps: 11, 12, 13   Rom 5:1–11   Mk 2:1–22

THURSDAY   **Feria (□ S Rita of Cascia, Rel)**
22   G   MP   Ps: 14, 15, 16   Josh 8:30–end   I Sam 8
        (or W)   Lk 11:14–28   Jas 3
          Mass   *as Monday (or of the Saint)*
                  Jas 5:1–6; Ps 49:13–20; Mk 9:41–end
          EP   Job 10   I Sam 9:1–25
                  Ps: 18   Rom 5:12–end   Mk 2:23 – 3:12

FRIDAY   **Feria**
23   G   MP   Ps: 17, 19   Josh 9:3–26   I Sam 9:26 – 10:16
                                             Lk 11:29–36   Jas 4
          Mass   *as Monday*
                  Jas 5:9–12; Ps 103:1–4 & 8–13; Mk 10:1–12
          EP   Job 11   I Sam 10:17–end
                  Ps: 22   Rom 6:1–14   Mk 3:13–end

SATURDAY   **Our Lady on Saturday or the Feria (see p. 31)**
24   W   MP   Ps: 20, 21, 23   Josh 10:1–15   I Sam 11
        (or G)   Lk 11:37–end   Jas 5
          Mass   *Introduction Paragraph 26(b)* (**Our Lady Help of Christians**)
                  Jas 5:13–end; Ps 141:1–4; Mk 10:13–16
          G   1 EP of foll (**CORPUS CHRISTI? see p. 35**) Job 12   I Sam 12
        (or W)   Ps: 24, 25   Rom 6:15–end   Mk 4:1–34

✠ *SUNDAY*

25

R: Ps IV

8th SUNDAY and WEEK of YEAR; TRINITY 1
(CORPUS CHRISTI? see p. 35)

MP	Ps: 21, 23	Jer 33:1–11	Jer 5:1–19
		Acts 8:4–25	Acts 9:1–22 (23–31)
Mass	*Gl; Cr; Sunday Pref [PROPER 3]*		
	CW: Lev 19:1–2 & 9–18; Ps 119:33–40; I Cor 3:10–11 & 16–23; Mt 5:38–48		
	R: Isa 49:14–15; Ps 62; I Cor 4:1–5; Mt 6:24–34 (God's unfailing love)		
2 EP		Amos 9:5–15	I Kgs 3:5–14
	Ps: 18:1–20 or 21–30	Eph 6:1–20	Jn 13:1–20

MONDAY

26 W

See p. 31

MP	Ps: 27, 30	Josh 14	I Sam 13
		Lk 12:1–12	I Pet 1:1–21
Mass	*of the Saint*		
	I Pet 1:3–9; Ps 111; Mk 10:17–27		
EP		Job 13	I Sam 14:1–23
	Ps: 26, 28, 29	Rom 7:1–6	Mk 4:35 – 5:20

TUESDAY

27 W
(or G)

See p. 31

MP	Ps: 32, 36	Josh 21:43 – 22:8	I Sam 14:24–48
		Lk 12:13–21	I Pet 1:22 – 2:10
Mass			
	I Pet 1:10–16; Ps 98:1–5; Mk 10:28–31		
EP		Job 14	I Sam 15
	Ps: 33	Rom 7:7–end	Mk 5:21–end

WEDNESDAY

28 G

Feria

MP	Ps: 34	Josh 22:9–end	I Sam 16
		Lk 12:22–31	I Pet 2:11 – 3:7
Mass	*no Gl or Cr; Common Pref (**Lanfranc, B**)*		
	I Pet 1:18–end; Ps 147:13–end; Mk 10:32–45		
EP		Job 15	I Sam 17:1–30
	Ps: 119:33–56	Rom 8:1–11	Mk 6:1–29

THURSDAY

29 G

Feria

MP	Ps: 37	Josh 23	I Sam 17:31–54
		Lk 12:32–40	I Pet 3:8 – 4:6
Mass	*as Wednesday*		
	I Pet 2:2–5 & 9–12; Ps 100; Mk 10:46;–end		

SACRED HEART? see p. 38. OTHERWISE:–

EP		Job 16:1 – 17:2	I Sam 17:55 – 18:16
	Ps: 39; 40	Rom 8:12–17	Mk 6:30–end

FRIDAY

30 G
(or W)

Feria (S Joan of Arc)

MP	Ps: 31	Josh 24:1–28	I Sam 19
		Lk 12:41–48	I Pet 4:7–end
Mass	*as Wednesday (or of the Saint) (**Josephine Butler; Apolo Kivebulaya, Pr**)*		
	I Pet 4:7–13; Ps 96:10–end; Mk 11:11–26		
EP		Job 17:3–end	I Sam 20:1–17
	Ps: 35	Rom 8:18–30	Mk 7:1–23

SATURDAY

31 W

Visitation of the BVM (see p. 31, note 3)

MP	H: 229	I Sam 2:1–10 [R: Song of S 2:8–14 & 8:6–7]	◁
	Ps: 85, 150	Mk 3:31–35	◁
Mass	*of the Festival; Gl; R: Pref of the BVM; CW, of the Annunciation; or ASB 6*		
	CW: Zeph 3:14–18; Ps 113; Rom 12:9–16; Lk 1:39–49 (50–56)		
	R: Zeph 3:14–18 or Rom 12:9–16; Ps = Isa 12:2–6; Lk 1:39–56		
G	1 EP of foll	Job 18	I Sam 21:1 – 22:5
	Ps: 45, 46	Rom 8:31–end	Mk 7:24 – 8:10

SACRED HEART. One of the most popular English devotions before 1559 and one of the most commonly used votive masses was the Five Wounds. This devotion to the Suffering Humanity of our loving Saviour received a broader Biblical and doctrinal form in the Western Church as the Sacred Heart of Jesus came to be celebrated on the second Friday after Trinity Sunday. (It is also common to say a public Class 2 votive of the Sacred Heart [as long as there is no solemnity or festum] on the first Friday of each month, except during Lent. White vestments.)

'In Biblical language, the Heart (Leb) indicates the centre of human life, the point where reason, will, temperament and sensitivity converge, where the person finds his unity and his interior orientation.'* It is because the loving Heart of Jesus the consubstantial Word is intimately at one with His Father that He feels our transgressions as a wound.

The following lectionary provision, to supplement CW, draws upon Roman materials. Other hymns: see especially NEH 89; EH 71 & 413 (=NEH 63 & 382); AMR 211.

THE SACRED HEART of JESUS *Mass: Gl; Cr; Proper Pref. WHITE.*			
	YEAR A (2008)	YEAR B (2009)	YEAR C (2010)
1 EP (Thursday)	H: 419 pt 1 (NEH 385) Ps: 113; 146	◁	◁
	Hos 11:1–9	Ezek 34:11–16	Deut 7:6–11
	Lk 15:3–7	Jn 7:37–39	Mt 11:25–30
MP (Friday)	H: 419 pt 2 (NEH 386) Ps: 36; 61	◁	◁
	Jer 31:1–11 & 31–4	◁	◁
	Rom 8:28–end (=R:)	◁	◁
Mass	Deut 7:6–11	Hos 11:1 & 3–4 & 8c–9	Ezek 34:11–16
	Ps 103:1–2 & 3–4 & 6–7 & 8 & 10	Ps Isa 12:2–3 & 4bcd & 5–6	Ps 23:1–3a & 3b–4 & 5–6
	I Jn 4:7–16	Eph 3:8–12 & 14–19	Rom 5:5b–11
	Mt 11:25–30	Jn 19:31–37	Lk 15:3–7
2 EP (Friday)	H: 419 pt 3 (NEH 385) Ps: 110; 111	◁	◁
	Ezek 34:11–16	Deut 7:6–11	Hos 11:1–9
	Rom 5:5b–11	Jn 20:26–29	Eph 3:8–19

The Immaculate Heart of Mary is kept on the Saturday after the Sacred Heart except when, as this year, it is displaced by a superior celebration. Mary kept and pondered in her heart all the great deeds of God. 'According to Mt 5:8, the Immaculate Heart is a heart which, with God's grace, has come to a perfect interior unity and therefore "sees God".'* Because her Immaculate (Ps 119: 80: *Tamin, amomos*: perfectly fitted to be a sacrifice to the Lord) Heart is attuned to Him (Luke 1:49, 2:19, 2:51) and to the needs of others (John 2:3), even before the Hour of the Lord's Glory (John 2:4) the intercession of her heart mediates through shared obedience (John 2:5) the first Sign of the fullness of His Kingdom (John 2:11). 'To be "devoted" to the Immaculate Heart of Mary means therefore to embrace this attitude of heart, which makes the *fiat* – "your will be done" – the defining centre of one's whole life,'* that the Kingdom may come.

There is a custom of saying a public Class 2 votive of the Immaculate Heart of Mary [as long as there is no solemnity or festum] on the first Saturday of each month, except during Lent (and MP may be a votive of the observance). The **Fatima** visionaries believed that our Lady called for communions of reparation on first Saturdays.

CW (p. 307), Presentation, Extended Preface, lines 1–3 and 11–end, is suitable.

The Roman Collection of Masses (Int Para 26b ii) gives variety for the celebration (Mass 26).

* Pope Benedict XVI.

THE IMMACULATE HEART OF MARY *Mass: no Gl or Cr; Pref of our Lady*
Mass readings: Isa 61:9–11; Ps I Sam 2:1 & 4–8; Lk 2:41–51

✠ SUNDAY 1

		9th SUNDAY and WEEK of YEAR	TRINITY 2
G	MP	Ps: 37:1–18	Deut 5:1–21	Jer 7:1–16
			Acts 21:17–39a	Acts 13:1–13 (14–26)

R: Ps I   Mass   *Gl; Cr; Sunday Pref [PROPER 4]*
CW: Deut 11:18–21 & 26–28; Ps 31:1–5 & 19–24; Rom 1:16–17 & 3:22b–28;
Mt 7:21–29
R: Deut 11:18 & 26–28; Ps 31; Rom 3:21–25 & 28; Mt 7:21–27 (Keep My Words)

	2 EP		Ruth 2:1–20a	I Kgs 8:22–30 (9:1–3)
		Ps: 33	Lk 8:4–15	Jn 13:21–end

MONDAY 2   *Feria (☐ Ss Marcellinus & Peter, Ms)*

G	MP	Ps: 44	Judg 2	I Sam 22:6–end
(or R)			Lk 13:1–9	II Pet 1
	Mass	*of Sunday; no Gl or Cr; Common Pref (or of the Saints)*		
		II Pet 1:2–7; Ps 91:1–2 & 14–end; Mk 12:1–12		
	EP		Job 19	I Sam 23
		Ps: 47, 49	Rom 9:1–18	Mk 8:11 – 9:1

TUESDAY 3   *Ss Charles Lwanga, Comp, Ms*

R	MP	Ps: 48, 52	Judg 4:1–23	I Sam 24
			Lk 13:10–21	II Pet 2
	Mass	*of the Saints*		
		II Pet 3:11–15 & 17–18; Ps 90:1–4 & 10 & 14 & 16; Mk 12:13–17		
	EP		Job 21	I Sam 25:2–42
		Ps: 50	Rom 9:19–end	Mk 9:2–29

WEDNESDAY 4   *Feria (TRURO: Solemnity of S Petroc, Ab, Co Principal, Patron: see p. xxix)*

G	MP	Ps: 119:57–80	Judg 5	I Sam 26
(or W)			Lk 13:22–end	II Pet 3
	Mass	*as Monday (or of the Saint)*		
		II Tim 1:1–3 & 6–12; Ps 123; Mk 12:18–27		
	EP		Job 22	I Sam 28:3–end
		Ps: 59, 60, 67	Rom 10:1–10	Mk 9:30–end

THURSDAY 5   *S Boniface (EXETER: Solemnity of the Patron)*

W	MP	Ps: 56, 57, 63	Judg 6:1–24	I Sam 31
			Lk 14:1–11	Jude
	Mass	*of the Saint*		
		II Tim 2:8–15; Ps 25:4–12; Mk 12:28–34		
	EP		Job 23	II Sam 1
		Ps: 61, 62, 64	Rom 10:11–end	Mk 10:1–31

FRIDAY 6   *Feria (☐ S Norbert, B)*

G	MP	Ps: 51, 54	Judg 6:25–end	II Sam 2:1 – 3:1
(or W)			Lk 14:12–24	I Jn 1:1 – 2:6
	Mass	*as Tuesday (First Friday: Sacred Heart: see p. 38) (or of the Saint)* (**Ini Kopuria**)		
		II Tim 3:10–end; Ps 119:161–168; Mk 12:35–37		
	EP		Job 24	II Sam 3:17–end
		Ps: 38	Rom 11:1–12	Mk 10:32–end

SATURDAY 7   *Our Lady on Saturday or the Feria*

W	MP	Ps: 68	Judg 7	II Sam 5:1–12
(or G)			Lk 14:25–end	I Jn 2:7–end
	Mass	*Introduction Paragraph 26(b) (First Saturday: Immaculate Heart, see p. 38)*		
		II Tim 4:1–8; Ps 71:7–16; Mk 12:38–44		
G	1 EP of foll		Job 25–26	II Sam 6
		Ps: 65, 66	Rom 11:13–24	Mk 11:1–26

✠ SUNDAY			**10th SUNDAY and WEEK of YEAR**		**TRINITY 3**
8	G	MP	Ps: 38	Deut 6:10–25	Jer 17:5–14
				Acts 22:22 – 23:11	Act 16:6–34
R: Ps II		Mass	*Gl; Cr; Sunday Pref (PROPER 5)*		
			CW: Hos 5:15 – 6:6; Ps 50:7–15; Rom 4:13–25; Mt 9:9–13 & 18–26		
			R: Hos 6:3–6; Ps 50:7–15; Rom 4:18–25; Mt 9:9–13		
			(The Lord Demands Love And Mercy, Not Sacrifice)		
		2 EP		I Sam 18:1–16	I Kgs 10:1–13
			Ps: 39, 41	Lk 8:41–56	Jn 14:1–14
MONDAY			Feria *(S Ephraem, Dcn, Dr; S Columba, IRELAND*		
			Festum; SCOTLAND Memorial)		
9	G	MP	Ps: 71	Judg 8:22–end	II Sam 7
	(or W)			Lk 15:1–10	I Jn 3:1–12
		Mass	*of Sunday; no Gl or Cr; Common Pref (**Our Lady of Grace**)*		
			I Kgs 17:1–6; Ps 121; Mt 5:1–12		
		EP		Job 27	II Sam 9
			Ps: 72, 75	Rom 11:25–end	Mk 11:27 – 12:12
TUESDAY			Feria		
10	G	MP	Ps: 73	Judg 9:1–21	II Sam 11
				Lk 15:11–end	I Jn 3:13 – 4:6
		Mass	*as Monday*		
			I Kgs 17:7–16; Ps 4; Mt 5:13–16		
		EP		Job 28	II Sam 12:1–23
			Ps: 74	Rom 12:1–8	Mk 12:13–34
WEDNESDAY			**S Barnabas, Ap** *(R: Memorial)*		
11	R	MP	Ps: 100, 101, 117	Jer 9:23–24	◁
				Acts 4:32–37	◁
		Mass	*(Gl); R: Pref of Apostles, CW, of Saints*		
			CW: Job 29:11–16; Ps 112; Acts 11:19–30; Jn 15:12–17		
			R: Acts 11:21–26 & 13:1–3; Ps 98; Mt 10:7–13		
		EP		Eccles 12:9–14 or Tobit 4:5–11	◁
			Ps: 147	Acts 9:26–31	◁
THURSDAY			Feria		
12	G	MP	Ps: 78:1–39	Judg 11:1–11	II Sam 15:13–end
				Lk 16:19–end	I Jn 5
		Mass	*as Monday*		
			I Kgs 18:41–end; Ps 65:8–end; Mt 5:20–26		
		EP		Job 30	II Sam 16:1–19
			Ps: 78:40–end	Rom 13:1–7	Mk 13:14–end
FRIDAY			□ **S Anthony of Padua, Pr, Dr**		
13	W	MP	Ps: 55	Judg 11:29–end	II Sam 17:1–23
				Lk 17:1–10	II Jn
		Mass	*of the Saint*		
			I Kgs 19:9 & 11–16; Ps 27:8–16; Mt 5:27–32		
		EP		Job 31	II Sam 17:24 – 18:18
			Ps: 69	Rom 13:8–end	Mk 14:1–26
SATURDAY			Our Lady on Saturday or the Feria		
14	W	MP	Ps: 76, 79	Judg 12:1–7	II Sam 18:19–end
	(or G)			Lk 17:11–19	III Jn
		Mass	*Introduction Paragraph 26(b) (**Richard Baxter**)*		
			I Kgs 19:19–end; Ps 16:1–7; Mt 5:33–37		
	G	1 EP of foll (S Richard)		Job 32	II Sam 19:1–23
			Ps: 81, 84	Rom 14:1–12	Mk 14:27–52

✠ SUNDAY
15   G

R: Ps III

		11th SUNDAY and WEEK of YEAR	TRINITY 4
MP	Ps: 45	Deut 10:12 – 11:1	Jer 18:1–7
		Acts 23:12–35	Acts 17:16–end
Mass	*Gl; Cr; Sunday Pref (PROPER 6)*		
	CW: Exod 19:2–8a; Ps 100; Rom 5:1–8; Mt 9:35 – 10:8		
	R: Exod 19:2–6a; Ps 100; Rom 5:6–11; Mt 9:36 – 10:8 (The Lord's Call)		
2 EP		I Sam 21:1–15	I Kgs 12:1–20
	Ps: 42, 43	Lk 11:14–28	Jn 14:15–end

MONDAY
16   G
(or W)

Feria (S Richard, B: CHICHESTER, Solemnity of the Co-Principal Patron)

MP	Ps: 80, 82	Judg 13:1–24	II Sam 19:24–end
		Lk 17:20–end	Rom 1
Mass	*of Sunday; no Gl or Cr; Common Pref (**Joseph Butler, B**)*		
	I Kgs 21:1–16; Ps 5:1–5; Mt 5:38–42		
EP		Job 33	II Sam 23:1–17
	Ps: 85, 86	Rom 14:13–end	Mk 14:53–end

TUESDAY
17   G

Feria

MP	Ps: 87, 89:1–18	Judg 14	II Sam 24
		Lk 18:1–14	Rom 2:1–16
Mass	*as Monday (**Samuel and Henrietta Barnett**)*		
	I Kgs 21:17–end; Ps 51:1–9; Mt 5:43–end		
EP		Job 38	I Kgs 1:5–31
	Ps: 89:19–end	Rom 15:1–13	Mk 15:1–41

WEDNESDAY
18   G

Feria

MP	Ps: 119:105–128	Judg 15:1 – 16:3	I Kgs 1:32–end
		Lk 18:15–30	Rom 2:17–end
Mass	*as Monday (**Bernard Mizeki, M**)*		
	II Kgs 2:1 & 6–14; Ps 31:21–end; Mt 6:1–6 & 16–18		
EP		Job 39	I Chron 22:2–end
	Ps: 91, 93	Rom 15:14–21	Mk 15:42–16 end

THURSDAY
19   G
(or W)

Feria (☐ S Romuald, Ab)

MP	Ps: 90, 92	Judg 16:4–end	I Chron 28:1–10
		Lk 18:31–end	Rom 3
Mass	*as Monday (or of the Saint) (**Sundar Singh, Rel**)*		
	Ecclus 48:1–14; Ps 97:1–8; Mt 6:7–15		
EP		Job 40	I Chron 28:20 – 29:9
	Ps: 94	Rom 15:22–end	Lk 1:1–23

FRIDAY
20   R

S Alban, M*

MP	Ps: 88, 95	Judg 17	I Chron 29:10–end
		Lk 19:1–10	Rom 4
Mass	*of the Saint (**Our Lady Mother of Consolation**)*		
	II Kgs 11:1–4 & 9–18 & 20; Ps 132:1–5 & 11–13; Mt 6:19–23		
EP		Job 41	I Kgs 3
	Ps: 102	Rom 16:1–16	Lk 1:24–56

SATURDAY
21   W

☐ S Aloysius Gonzaga, Rel

MP	Ps: 96, 97, 100	Judg 18:1–20, 27–end	I Kgs 4:21–end
		Lk 19:11–27	Rom 5
Mass	*of the Saint (**Our Lady Mother of Mercy**)*		
	II Chron 24:17–25; Ps 89:25–33; Mt 6:24–end		
G 1 EP of foll		Job 42	1 Kgs 5
	Ps: 104	Rom 16:17–end	Lk 1:57–end

* The Roman date. This year, Sundays displace his CW date, and both dates for Ss Thomas More and John Fisher.

✠ SUNDAY			**12th SUNDAY and WEEK of YEAR**		**TRINITY 5**
22	G	MP	Ps: 49	Deut 11:1–15	Jer 26:1–16
				Acts 27:1–12	Acts 19:21–end
R: Ps IV		Mass	Gl; Cr; Sunday Pref (PROPER 7)		
			CW: Jer 20:7–13; Ps 69:8–11 (12–17) 18–20; Rom 6:1b–11; Mt 10:24–39		
			R: Jer 20:10–13; Ps 69:7–10 & 16–18; Rom 5:12–15; Mt 10:26–33		
			(He protects us from our attackers)		
		2 EP		I Sam 24:1–17	I Kgs 18:17–39
			Ps: 46, 48	Lk 14:12–24	Jn 15:1–16

MONDAY			**Feria (S Etheldreda, Ab)**		
23	G	MP	Ps: 98, 99, 101	I Sam 1:1–20	I Kgs 6:1–14
	(or W)			Lk 19:28–40	Rom 6
		Mass	of Sunday; no Gl or Cr; Common Pref (or of the Saint)		
			II Kgs 17:5–8 & 13–15 & 18; Ps 60:1–5 & 11–end; Mt 7:1–5		
			BIRTH OF S JOHN BAPTIST		
			R: Vigil Mass: Jer 1:4–10; Ps 71; I Pet 1:8–12; Lk 1:5–17 (Vigil Collect; Gl; Cr)		
	W	1 EP	H: 223 (NEH 168)	Judg 13:2–7 & 24–25	Mal 3:1–6
			Ps: 71	Lk 1:5–25 (Vigil Collect)	Lk 3:1–20

TUESDAY					
24	W	MP	H: 224	Mal 3:1–6 or Ecclus 48:1–10	Judg 13:1–7
			Ps: 50, 149	Lk 3:1–17	Lk 1:5–25
		Mass	Gl; Cr; R; Proper Pref; CW, of Saints		
			CW: Isa 40:1–11; Ps 85:7–13; Acts 13:14b–26; Lk 1:57–66 & 80		
			R: Isa 49:1–6; Ps 139; Acts 13:22–26; Lk 1:57–66 & 80		
		2 EP	H: 223 (NEH 168	Mal 4 (R: Jer 1:4–10 & 17–19)	Mal 4
			Ps: 80, 82	Mt 11:2–19	Mt 11:2–19

WEDNESDAY			**Feria**		
25	G	MP	Ps: 110, 111, 112	I Sam 2:12–26	I Kgs 10
				Lk 20:1–8	Rom 8:1–17
		Mass	as Monday		
			II Kgs 22:8–13 & 23:1–3; Ps 119:33–40; Mt 7:15–20		
		EP		Ezek 2:3 – 3:11	I Kgs 11:1–13
			Ps: 119:129–152	II Cor 2:5–end	Lk 3:1–22

THURSDAY			**Feria**		
26	G	MP	Ps: 113, 115	I Sam 2:27–end	I Kgs 11:26–end
				Lk 20:9–19	Rom 8:18–end
		Mass	as Monday (**Our Lady of Tichwin**)		
			II Kgs 24:8–17; Ps 79:1–9 & 12; Mt 7:21–end		
		EP	see p. 42	Ezek 3:12–end	I Kgs 12:1–24
			Ps: 114, 116, 117	II Cor 3	Lk 4:1–30

FRIDAY			**Feria (S Cyril of Alexandria, B, Dr)**		
27	G	MP	Ps: 139	I Sam 3:1–4.1a	I Kgs 12:25 – 13:10
	(or W)			Lk 20:20–26	Rom 9
		Mass	as Monday (or of the Saint) (**Our Lady of Perpetual Succour**)		
			II kgs 25:1–12; Ps 137:1–6; Mt 8:1–4		
		EP	see p. 42	Ezek 8	I Kgs 13:11–end
			Ps: 130, 131, 137	II Cor 4	Lk 4:31–end

SATURDAY			**S Irenaeus, B, M**		
28	R	MP	Ps: 120, 121, 122	I Sam 4:1b–end	I Kgs 14:1–20
				Lk 20:27–40	Rom 10
		Mass	of the Saint		
			Lam 2:2 & 10–14 & 18–19; Ps 74:1–3 & 21–22; Mt 8:5–17		
✠			**SS PETER & PAUL, APOSTLES**		
	R	1 EP of foll; H: 226 (NEH 171)		Ezek 3:4–11	◁
			Ps: 66, 67	Gal 1:13 – 2:8 (=R:) (Vigil Collect)	◁
			R: Vigil Mass; Acts 3:1–10; Ps 19; Gal 1:11–20; Jn 21:15–19 (Vigil Collect; Gl; Cr)		

✠ *SUNDAY*   **SS PETER & PAUL, APOSTLES**
29   R   MP   Ps: 71, 113   Isa 49:1–6   ◁
                                         Acts 11:1–18   ◁
R: Ps I   Mass   *Gl; Cr; R: Pref of Ss Peter and Paul; CW, of Saints*
                 CW: = R: Acts 12:1–11; Ps 125 (R: 34:2–9); II Tim 4:6–8 & 17–18; Mt 16:13–19
          2 EP   H: 226 (NEH 171)   Ezek 34:11–16   ◁
                 Ps: 124, 138   Jn 21:15–22   ◁

MONDAY   *Feria (☐ Holy Protomartyrs of the Holy Roman Church)*
30   G   MP   Ps: 123, 124, 125, 126   I Sam 5   II Chron 13
      (or R)   Lk 20:41 – 21:4   Rom 11:1–24
          Mass   *of Sunday the 13th week of the Year or Trinity 6; no Gl or Cr; Common Pref (or of the Saints)*
                 Amos 2:6–10 & 13–end; Ps 50:16–23; Mt 8:18–22
          EP   Ezek 10:1–19   II Chron 14
                 Ps: 127, 128, 129   II Cor 6:1 – 7:1   Lk 5:17–end

J U L Y †
TUESDAY   *Feria (☐ S Oliver Plunket: FESTUM IN IRELAND)*
1   G   MP   Ps: 132, 133   I Sam 6:1–16   II Chron 15
      (or R)   Lk 21:5–19   Rom 11:25–end
          Mass   *as Monday (or of the Saint)* (***John & Henry Venn, Prs***)
                 Amos 3:1–8 & 4:11–12; Ps 5:8–end; Mt 8:23–27
          EP   Ezek 11:14–end   II Chron 16
                 Ps: 134, 135   II Cor 7:2–end   Lk 6:1–9

WEDNESDAY   *Feria**
2   G   MP   Ps: 119:153–end   I Sam 7   I Kgs 16:15–end
                                          Lk 21:20–28   Rom 12
          Mass   *as Monday*
                 Amos 5:14–15 & 21–24; Ps 50:7–14; Mt 8:28–end
          EP   Ezek 12:1–16   I Kgs 17
                 Ps: 136   II Cor 8:1–15   Lk 6:20–38

THURSDAY   **S Thomas, Apostle**
3   R   MP   Ps: 92, 146   II Sam 15:17–21 or Ecclus 2   II Sam 15:17–21
                                          Jn 11:1–16   Jn 11:1–16
          Mass   *Gl; R: Pref of the Apostles; CW, of the Saint*
                 CW: Hab 2:1–4; Ps 31:1–6; Eph 2:19–22; Jn 20:24–29
                 R: Eph 2:19–22; Ps 117; Jn 20:24–29
          EP   Job 42:1–6   Gen 12:1–5a
                 Ps: 139   I Pet 1:3–12   I Pet 1:3–9

FRIDAY   *Feria (☐ S Elizabeth of Portugal)*
4   G   MP   Ps: 142, 144   I Sam 9:1–14   I Kgs 19
      (or W)   Lk 22:1–13   Rom 14
          Mass   *as Monday (or of the Saints) (First Friday: Sacred Heart, see p. 38)*
                 Amos 8:4–6 & 9–12; Ps 119:1–8; Mt 9:9–13
          EP   Ezek 13:1–16   I Kgs 21
                 Ps: 145   II Cor 9:6–end   Lk 7:11–35

SATURDAY   *Our Lady on Saturday or the Feria (☐ S Antony Mary Zaccaria, Pr)*
5   W   MP   Ps: 147   I Sam 9:15 – 10:1   I Kgs 22:1–40
      (or G)   Lk 22:14–23   Rom 15:1–13
          Mass   *Introduction Paragraph 26(b) (or of the Saint) (First Saturday: Immaculate Heart, see p. 38)*
                 Amos 9:11–end; Ps 85:8–13; Mt 9:14–17
         G   1 EP of foll   Ezek 14:1–11   II Chron 20:1–30
                 Ps: 148, 149, 150   II Cor 10   Lk 7:36–end

---

* July 2, the Deposition of the Robe of Our Lady at Constantinople, was until recently her Visitation in the West – see BCP.
† A Votive of the Most Precious Blood is traditional on the first free day.

✠ SUNDAY			**14th SUNDAY and WEEK of YEAR**		**TRINITY 7**
6	G	MP	Ps: 55:1–15 & 18–22	Deut 24:10–22	Jer 31:27–34
				Acts 28:1–16	Acts 21:15–36
R: Ps II		Mass	Gl; Cr; Sunday Pref (PROPER 9)		
			CW: Zech 9:9–12; Ps 145:8–15; Rom 7:15–25a; Mt 11:16–19 & 25–30		
			R: Zech 9:9–10; Ps 145:8–14; Rom 8:9 & 11–13; Mt 11:25–30 (He Comes in Humility)		
		2 EP		II Sam 2:1–11 & 3:1	I Kgs 21:1–23 (24–end)
			Ps: 56; 57	Lk 18:31 – 19:10	Jn 16:1–15
MONDAY			Feria		
7	G	MP	Ps: 1, 2, 3	I Sam 10:1–16	II Kgs 1
				Lk 22:24–30	Rom 15:14–end
		Mass	of Sunday; no Gl or Cr; Common Pref		
			Hos 2:16–18 & 21–22; Ps 145:2–9; Mt 9:18–26		
		EP		Ezek 14:12–end	II Kgs 2:1–22
			Ps: 4, 7	II Cor 11:1–15	Lk 8:1–21
TUESDAY			Feria		
8	G	MP	Ps: 5, 6, 8	I Sam 10:17–end	II Kgs 4:1–37
				Lk 22:31–38	Rom 16
		Mass	as Monday (**Our Lady of Kazan**)		
			Hos 8:4–7 & 11–13; Ps 103:8–12; Mt 9:32–end		
		EP		Ezek 18:1–20	II Kgs 5
			Ps: 9, 10	II Cor 11:16–end	Lk 8:22–end
WEDNESDAY			Feria (☐ Ss Augustine Zhao Rong, Pr, Comp, Ms)		
9	G	MP	Ps: 119:1–32	I Sam 11	II Kgs 6:1–23
	(or R)			Lk 22:39–46	I Cor 1:1–25
		Mass	as Monday (or of the Saints) (**Our Lady Mother of Divine Hope**)		
			Hos 10:1–3 & 7–8 & 12; Ps 115:3–10; Mt 10:1–7		
		EP		Ezek 18:21–32	II Kgs 6:24 – 7:2
			Ps: 11, 12, 13	II Cor 12	Lk 9:1–17
THURSDAY			Feria		
10	G	MP	Ps: 14, 15, 16	I Sam 12	II Kgs 7:3–end
				Lk 22:47–62	I Cor 1:26–2 end
		Mass	as Monday (**Our Lady of Koniev**)		
			Hos 11:1 & 3–4 & 8–9; Ps 105:1–7; Mt 10:7–15		
		EP		Ezek 20:1–20	II Kgs 8:1–15
			Ps: 18	II Cor 13	Lk 9:18–50
FRIDAY			**S Benedict, Abbot, Patron of Europe**		
11	W	MP	Ps: [17, 19]	[I Sam 13:5–18]	[II Kgs 9]
				[Lk 22:63–end]	[I Cor 3]
		Mass	Office Readings from Appendix 3: Religious		
			of the Saint; Gl; no Cr; Pref (R:) of Patrons, (CW) of Saints		
			R: Prov 2:1–9; Ps 34:1–10; Mt 19:27–29		
			CW: I Cor 3:10–11; Ps 34:1–8; Mt 19:23–30		
		EP		[Ezek 20:21–38]	[II Kgs 11:1–20]
			Ps: [22]	[James 1:1–11]	[Lk 9:51–end]
SATURDAY			Our Lady on Saturday of the Feria		
12	W	MP	Ps: 20, 21, 23	I Sam 13:19 – 14:15	II Kgs 11:21–12 end
	(or G)			Lk 23:1–12	I Cor 4:1–17
		Mass	Introduction Paragraph 26(b)		
			Isa 6:1–8; Ps 51:1–7; Mt 10:24–33		
	G	1 EP of foll		Ezek 24:15–end	II Kgs 13
			Ps: 24, 25	James 1:12–end	Lk 10:1–24

✠ SUNDAY

13   G   MP

R: Ps III   Mass

2 EP

		15th SUNDAY and WEEK of YEAR.	**TRINITY 8**
MP	Ps: 64, 65	Deut 28:1–14	Jer 36:1–26
		Acts 28:17–31	Acts 25:1–12 (13 end)

Mass: *Gl; Cr; Sunday Pref (PROPER 10)*
CW: Isa 55:10–13; Ps 65:(1–7) 8–13; Rom 8:1–11; Mt 13:1–9 & 18–23
R: Isa 55:10–11; Ps 65:(1–8) 9–13; Rom 8:18–23; Mt 13:1–9 (10–23)
(The fruitful Word goes forth)

2 EP		II Sam 7:18–29	I Kgs 22:1–38
	Ps: 60, 63	Lk 19:41 – 20:8	Jn 16:16–22

MONDAY   Feria (☐ S Camillus de Lelli, Pr)

14   G (or W)

MP	Ps: 27, 30	I Sam 14:24–46	II Kgs 14
		Lk 23:13–25	I Cor 4:18–5 end

Mass: *of Sunday; no Gl or Cr; Common Pref (or of the Saint)* (**John Keble, Pr**)
Isa 1:11–17; Ps 50:7–15; Mt 10:34 – 11:1

EP		Ezek 28:1–19	II Chron 26
	Ps: 26, 28, 29	James 2:1–13	Lk 10:25–end

TUESDAY   S Bonaventura, B and Dr

15   W

MP	Ps: 32, 36	I Sam 15:1–23	II Kgs 15:17–end
		Lk 23:26–43	I Cor 6

Mass: *of the Saint* (**S Swithun, B**)
Isa 7:1–9; Ps 48:1–7; Mt 11:20–24

EP		Ezek 33:1–20	II Kgs 16
	Ps: 33	James 2:14–end	Lk 11:1–28

WEDNESDAY   Feria (☐ Our Lady of Mount Carmel; S Osmund, B;
                          EAD: Solemnity in Salisbury)

16   G (or W)

MP	Ps: 34	I Sam 16	Isa 7:1–17
		Lk 23:44–56a	I Cor 7

Mass: *as Monday (or of Our Lady: Zec 2:14–17; Ps = Lk 1:46–55; Mt 12:46–50) or of the Saint*
Isa 10:5–7 & 13–16; Ps 94:5–11; Mt 11:25–27

EP		Ezek 33:21–end	Isa 8:1–18
	Ps: 119:33–56	James 3	Lk 11:29–end

THURSDAY   Feria

17   G

MP	Ps: 37	I Sam 17:1–30	II Kgs 17:1–23
		Lk 23:56b – 24:12	I Cor 8

Mass: *as Monday* (**The Humility of Our Lady**)
Isa 26:7–9 & 16–19; Ps 102:14–21; Mt 11:28–end

EP		Ezek 34:1–16	II Kgs 17:24–end
	Ps: 39, 40	James 4:1–12	Lk 12:1–34

FRIDAY   Feria

18   G

MP	Ps: 31	I Sam 17:31–54	II Kgs 18:1–8
		Lk 24:13–35	I Cor 9

Mass: *as Monday* (**Elizabeth Ferard**)
Isa 38:1–6 & 21–22 & 7–8; Isa 38:10–16; Mt 12:1–8

EP		Ezek 34:17–end	II Chron 30
	Ps: 35	James 4:13 – 5:6	Lk 12:35–53

SATURDAY   Our Lady on Saturday or the Feria (S Gregory of Nyssa, B, Dr, and
                          his sister S Macrina*)

19   W (or G)

MP	Ps: 41, 42, 43	I Sam 17:55 – 18:16	II Kgs 18:13–end
		Lk 24:36–end	I Cor 10:1 – 11:1

Mass: *Introduction Paragraph 26(b) or of the Saints* (**Bartolomé de las Casas**) (**Our Lady of the Don**)
Micah 2:1–5; Ps 10:1–5a & 12; Mt 12:14–21

G	1 EP of foll	Ezek 36:16–36	II Kgs 19
	Ps: 45, 46	James 5:7–end	Lk 12:54 – 13:9

* Byzantium observes her today and CW decided to unite her brother with her.

✠ *SUNDAY*   **16th SUNDAY and WEEK of YEAR**   **TRINITY 9**

20	G	MP	Ps: 71	Deut 30:1–10	Jer 38:1–13
				I Pet 3:8–18	Acts 27
R: Ps IV		Mass	*Gl; Cr; Sunday Pref (PROPER 11)*		
			CW: Wisd 12:13 & 16–19; Ps 86:11–17; Rom 8:12–25; Mt 13:24–30 & 36–43		
			R: Wisd 12:13 & 16–19; Ps 86:11–17; Rom 8:26–27; Mt 13:24–30 (31–43) (The Judge)		
		2 EP		I Kgs 2:10–12 & 3:16–28	II Kgs 4:8–37
			Ps: 67, 70	Acts 4:1–22	Jn 16:23–end

MONDAY   **Feria (☐ S Laurence of Brindisi, Pr, Dr**

21	G (or W)	MP	Ps: 44	I Sam 19:1–8	II Kgs 20
				Acts 1:1–14	I Cor 11:2–end
		Mass	*of Sunday; no Gl or Cr; Common Pref (or of the Saint)*		
			Micah 6:1–4 & 6–8; Ps 50:3–7 & 14; Mt 12:38–42		
		EP		Ezek 37:1–14	II Chron 33
			Ps: 47, 49	Mk 1:1–13	Lk 13:10–end

TUESDAY   **S Mary Magdalene***

22	W	MP	H: 231 (NEH 174)*	I Sam 16:14–23	◁
			Ps: 30, 32, 150	Lk 8:1–3	◁
		Mass	*(Gl); no Cr; Pref of Saints*		
			CW = R: Song S 3:1–4; Ps 42:1–10 (R: 63); II Cor 5:14–17; Jn 20:1–2 & 11–18		
		EP		Zeph 3:14–20	Isa 25:1–9
			Ps: 63	Mk 15:40 – 16:7	◁

WEDNESDAY   **S Bridget, Religious, Patron of Europe**

23	W	MP	Ps: [119:57–80]	[I Sam 20:18–end]	[II Kgs 23:21–35]
				[Acts 2:1–21]	[I Cor 12:27–13 end]
		Mass	*Office Reading from Appendix 3: Religious*		
			of the Saint; Gl; no Cr: Pref (R:) of Patrons; (CW) of Saints		
			R: Judith 8:2–8 or I Tim 5:3–10; Ps 10:1–2 & 10–15; Lk 2:36–38 or Mt 5:13–16		
		EP		[Ezek 39:21–end]	[II Kgs 23:36 – 24:17]
			Ps: [59, 60, 67]	[Mk 1:21–28]	[Lk 14:25 – 15:10]

THURSDAY   **Feria (☐ S Sharbel Makhluf, Pr)**

24	G (or W)	MP	Ps: 56, 57, 63	I Sam 21:1 – 22:5	II Kgs 24:18 – 25:7
				Acts 2:22–36	I Cor 14:1–19
		Mass	*as Monday (or of the Saint)*		
			Jer 2:1–3 & 7–8 & 12–13; Ps 36:5–10; Mt 13:10–17		
		EP		Ezek 43:1–12	II Kgs 25:8–end
			Ps: 61, 62, 64	Mk 1:29–end	Lk 15:11–end

FRIDAY   **S James Apostle**

25	R	MP	Ps: 7, 29, 117	II Kgs 1:9–15	Jer 26:1–15
				Lk 9:46–56	Lk 9:46–56
		Mass	*Gl; R: Pref of Apostles; CW, of Saints*		
			CW: Jer 45:1–5 or Acts 11:27 – 12:2; II Cor 4:7–15; Ps 126; Mt 20:20–28		
			R: II Cor 4:7–15; Ps 126; Mt 20:20–28		
		EP		Jer 26:1–15	Jer 45
			Ps: 94	Mk 1:14–20	Mk 14:32–42

SATURDAY   **Ss Joachim and Anne, Parents of the BVM**

26	W	MP	Ps: 68	I Sam 23	Jer 22:20 – 23:8
				Acts 3:1–10	I Cor 15:1–34
		Mass	*of the Saints*		
			CW: Zeph 3:14–17; Ps 127; Rom 8:28–30; Mt 13:16–17		
			R: Ecclus 44:1 & 10–15; Mt 13:16–17		
			[Jer 7:1–11; Ps 84:1–6; Mt 13:24–30]		
	G	1 EP of foll		Ezek 47:1–12	Jer 24
			Ps: 65, 66	Mk 2:13–22	Lk 17:1–19

* Like Byzantium, Rome, CW now disentangles S Mary M from Mary of Bethany and the Sinful Woman. In the Hymn, verse 5, correct 'feet' to 'limbs'. (In R: she is only a Memorial; no Gl.)

✠ SUNDAY **27** G	MP	**17th SUNDAY and WEEK of YEAR**	**TRINITY 10**
		Ps: 77	I Macc 2:(1–14) 15–22	Jer 52:1–11
			I Pet 4:7–14	Acts 28:11–end
R: Ps I	Mass	*Gl; Cr; Sunday Pref (PROPER 12)*	
		CW: I Kgs 3:5–12; Ps 119:129–136; Rom 8:26–39; Mt 13:31 & 44–52	
		R: I Kgs 3:5 & 7–12; Ps 119:129–136; Rom 8:28–30; Mt 13:44–52 (or 44–46)	
		(Seeking God's Treasure)	
	2 EP	I Kgs 6:11–14 & 23–38	II Kgs 5:1–19 (20–end)
		Ps: 75, 76	Acts 12:1–17	Jn 17

MONDAY **28** G	MP	*Feria*	
		Ps: 71	I Sam 24	Jer 25:1–14
			Acts 3:11–end	I Cor 15:35–end
	Mass	*of Sunday; no Gl or Cr; Common Pref (**Our Lady of Smolensk**)*	
		Jer 13:1–11; Ps 82 or Deut 32:18–21; Mt 13:31–35	
	EP	Prov 1:1–19	Jer 27:2–end
		Ps: 72, 75	Mk 2:23 – 3:6	Lk 17:20–end

TUESDAY **29** W	MP	*S Martha (CW adds: Mary and Lazarus)*	
		Ps: 73	I Sam 26	Jer 28
			Acts 4:1–12	I Cor 16
	Mass	*of the Saint(s)*	
		CW: Isa 25:6–9; Ps 49:5–10 & 16; Heb 2:10–15; Jn 12:1–8	
		R: I Jn 4:7–16; Jn 11:19–27 or Lk 10:38–42	
		Jer 14:17–end; Ps 79:8–end; Mt 13:36–43	
	EP	Prov 1:20–end	Jer 29:1–20
		Ps: 74	Mk 3:7–19a	Lk 18:1–30

WEDNESDAY **30** G (or W)	MP	*Feria (☐ S Peter Chrysologus, B, Dr)*	
		Ps: 77	I Sam 28:3–end	Jer 32:1–25
			Acts 4:13–31	II Cor 1:1–22
	Mass	*as Monday (or of the Saint) (**William Wilberforce**)*	
		Jer 15:10 & 16–end; Ps 59:1–4 & 18–end; Mt 13:44–46	
	EP	Prov 2	Jer 32:26–end
		Ps: 119:81–104	Mk 3:19b–end	Lk 18:31 – 19:10

THURSDAY **31** W	MP	*S Ignatius of Loyola, Pr*	
		Ps: 78:1–39	I Sam 31	Jer 33
			Acts 4:32 – 5:11	II Cor 1:23–2 end
	Mass	*of the Saint*	
		Jer 18:1–6; Ps 146:1–5; Mt 13:47–53	
	EP	Prov 3:1–26	Jer 34:8–end
		Ps: 78:40–end	Mk 4:1–20	Lk 19:11–28

A U G U S T

FRIDAY **1** W	MP	☐ *S Alfonso Maria de'Liguori, B, Dr*	
		Ps: 55	II Sam 1	Jer 37
			Acts 5:12–26	II Cor 3
	Mass	*of the Saint (First Friday: Sacred Heart, see p. 38)*	
		Jer 26:1–9; Ps 69:4–10; Mt 13:54–end	
	EP	Prov 3:27 – 4:19	Jer 38:1–13
		Ps: 69	Mk 4:21–34	Lk 19:29–end

SATURDAY **2** W (or G)	MP	*Our Lady on Saturday or the Feria (☐ S Eusebius of Vercelli, B;* ☐ *S Peter Iuliani Eymard, Pr)*	
		Ps: 76, 79	II Sam 2:1–11	Jer 38:14–end
			Acts 5:27–end	II Cor 4
	Mass	*(First Saturday: Immaculate Heart, see p. 38)*	
		Jer 26:11–16 & 24; Ps 69:14–20; Mt 14:1–12	
	G	1 EP of foll	Prov 6:1–19	Jer 39
			Ps: 81, 84	Mk 4:35–end	Lk 20:1–26

✠ SUNDAY
3   G   MP   **18th SUNDAY and WEEK of YEAR**   **TRINITY 11**

✠ SUNDAY	G	MP	Ps: 85	I Macc 3:1–12	Ezek 11:14–20
3				II Pet 1:1–15	Lk 4:1–15
R: Ps II		Mass	*Gl; Cr; Sunday Pref (PROPER 13) (TRANSFIGURATION? Int P.5A)*		
			CW: Isa 55:1–5; Ps 145:8–9 & 15–22; Rom 9:1–5; Mt 14:13–21		
			R: Isa 55:1–3; Ps 145; Rom 8:35 & 37–39; Mt 14:13–21 (Rich Food, Freely Given)		
		2 EP		I Kgs 10:1–13	II Kgs 17:1–23
			Ps: 80	Acts 13:1–13	Gal 1
MONDAY	W	MP	Ps: 80, 82	II Sam 3:12–end	Jer 40
4				Acts 6	II Cor 5:1–19
		Mass	*of the Saint*		
			Jer 28; Ps 119:89–96; Mt 14:22–end		
		EP		Prov 8:1–21	Jer 41
			Ps: 85, 86	Mark 5:1–20	Lk 20:27 – 21:4

MONDAY
4   W   **S John Mary Vianney, Pr**

TUESDAY
5   G (or W or R)   **Feria ☐ Dedication of the Basilica of Great S Mary's;**
S Oswald, K and M (Assumption Novenas may start)

	MP	Ps: 87, 89:1–18	II Sam 5:1–12	Jer 42
			Acts 7:1–16	II Cor 5:20 – 7:1
	Mass	*of Sunday; no Gl or Cr; Common Pref (or of the Saint)*		
		Jer 30:1–2 & 12–15 & 18–22; Ps 102:16–21; Mt 14:22–36		
	EP		Prov 8:22–end	Jer 43
		Ps: 89:19–end	Mk 5:21–34	Lk 21:5–end

WEDNESDAY
6   W   **Transfiguration of the Lord**

	MP	H: 233 or 238:1, 2, 4, 7, 8	Ecclus 48:1–10	Exod 34:29–end
		Ps: 27, 150	I Jn 3:1–3	II Cor 3 (=R:)
	Mass	*Gl; R: Pref of Transfiguration; CW, Common Pref*		
		CW = R: Dan 7:9–10 & 13–14; Ps 97; II Pet 1:16–19; Lk 9:28–36 (R: Mt 17:1–9)		
	EP	H: 234 (NEH 176)	Exod 34:29–35	I Kgs 19:1–16
		Ps: 72	II Cor 3	II Pet 1:12–end

THURSDAY
7   G (or R or W)   **Feria (☐ S Xystus, Pp & Comp, Ms; ☐ S Cajetan, Pr;**
Holy Name of Jesus)

	MP	Ps: 90, 92	II Sam 7:1–17	Ezek 1:1–14
			Acts 7:44–53	II Cor 8
	Mass	*of the Saint (**John Mason Neale, Pr**)*		
		Jer 31:31–34; Ps 51:11–18; Mt 16:13–23		
	EP		Prov 10:1–12	Ezek 2:1 – 3:3
		Ps: 94	Mk 6:1–13	Lk 22:39–53

FRIDAY
8   W   **S Dominic, Pr**

	MP	Ps: 88, 95	II Sam 7:18–end	Ezek 3:4–end
			Acts 7:54 – 8:3	II Cor 9
	Mass	*of the Saint*		
		Nahum 2:1–3 & 3:1–3 & 6–7; Deut 32:35–36 & 39 & 41; Mt 16:24–end		
	EP		Prov 11:1–12	Ezek 8
		Ps: 102	Mk 6:14–29	Lk 22:54–end

SATURDAY
9   R   **S Teresa Benedicta of the Cross, V and M, Patron of Europe***

	MP	Ps: [96, 97, 100]	[II Sam 9]	[Ezek 11:14–end]
			[Acts 8:4–25]	[II Cor 10]
	Mass	*Office Readings from Appendix 3: Martyrs (**Mary Sumner**)*		
		of the Saint; Gl; no Cr; R: Pref of Ms; CW, of Saints		
		Hos 2:14b & 15b & 19–20; Ps 45; Mt 25:1–13		
		[Hab 1:12 – 2:4; Ps 9:7–11; Mt 17:14–20]		
G	1 EP of foll		Prov 12:10–end	Ezek 12:17–end
		Ps: 104	Mk 6:30–44	Lk 23:1–25

---

* Suggested Office Readings: MP Esther 3:1–8 & Rom 9:1–5.

ASSUMPTION OF THE BVM

1. August 15 was the Festival of Our Lady in Jerusalem by the fourth Century. (The word 'Assumption' in early Christian Latin antedates by many centuries the definition of 1950.) PPL: 'In many places the feast is synonymous with the person of our Lady. It is simply referred to as "Lady Day" or as "The Immacolada" in Spain and Latin America.' CW follows this Hispanic baroque instinct.

2. 'We affirm together the teaching that God has taken the Blessed Virgin Mary in the fullness of her person into his glory as consonant with Scripture, and only to be understood in the light of Scripture.' (ARCIC 2005).

3. The EVE: the Assumption has been called the Easter of the Mother of God (and preceded, in the Byzantine rite, by a Lent of fourteen days; in the west Novenas are kept). R: provides a separate collect for 1 EP and the Vigil mass. In some places the Eve is marked with some solemnity – texts from the compiler:–

- the lit Paschal Candle may be processed to our Lady's statue or icon, and incense offered to both;
- a form of *Exsultet;* then the Vigil mass *or* 1 EP *or* a Liturgy of the Word, including:
- Gospel (Ceremonies as at mass; Lk 10:38–42 & 11:27b–28 – cf Byzantium and Rome before 1950);
- Te Deum;
- Collect from the Vigil mass;
- Blessing or Benediction.

4. The *Office Hymns*, Eleventh Century and later, now used are not in EH or NEH but may be obtained from the Compiler. The Common Hymns are 213, 214, 215 (NEH 180, 181, 183). The Assumption is mentioned in EH215 and 217, and NEH 182, 183, 184, and 185. For the Akathist Hymn see p. xxvi.

    EH 218 (NEH 188) – Fr V.S.S. Coles' hymn *Ye Who Own The Faith Of Jesus* – contains verses omitted in the hymnbooks. Since the hymn thus (except as a Processional) becomes rather long, it could be divided and treated as two separate hymns: (A) 1, 2, 3, 4, 5, 7; (B) 1, 2a, 2b, 2c, 6, 7.

    2a Thus prepared, and thus exalted,
    Lowly still, and still unknown,
    Mary waited till the fullness
    Of her destiny was shown,
    Till the maid became God's Mother,
    And her nursing arms his throne: *Hail Mary . . .*

    2b For the King of men and angels
    Chose her out of all He made,
    And in robes of grace and glory
    Her humility arrayed,
    With the radiant sun He clothed her,
    At her feet the moon He laid: *Hail Mary . . .*

    2c As we sing, her prayer is rising,
    For her Heart with us is one;
    We with confidence will ask it
    That the Mother from her Son
    May obtain the full perfection
    Of His work in us begun: *Hail Mary . . .*

5. *Readings* prefixed * are those customarily offered in this ORDO, based upon Western Catholic tradition. Their use is covered by CLC p. 36 paragraph 6. Those prefixed † are now offered by CW.

6. August 22, Our Lady, Queen, is the old octave day.

✠ *SUNDAY*		**19th SUNDAY and WEEK of YEAR**		**TRINITY 12**	
10 G	MP	Ps: 88	I Macc 14:4–15	Ezek 18:1–4 & 19–end	
			II Pet 3:8–13	Lk 4:16–30	
R: Ps III	Mass	*Gl; Cr; Sunday Pref (PROPER 14)*			
		CW: I Kgs 19:9–18; Ps 85:8–13; Rom 10:5–15; Mt 14:22–33			
		R: I Kgs 19:9a & 11–13a; Ps 85; Rom 9:1–5; Mt 14:22–33 (His Voice Speaks of Peace)			
	2 EP	I Kgs 11:41 – 12:20		II Kgs 18:17–22 & 28 – 19:7	
		Ps: 86	Acts 14:8–20	Gal 6:1–10	

MONDAY   **S Clare, V**

11 W	MP	Ps: 98, 99, 101	II Sam 11	Ezek 13:1–16
			Acts 8:26–end	II Cor 11
	Mass	*of the Saint (**John Henry Newman, Pr**)*		
		Ezek 1:2–5 & 24–end; Ps 148:1–4 & 12–13a; Mt 17:22–end		
	EP		Prov 14:31 – 15:17	Ezek 14:1–11
		Ps: 103, 105	Mk 6:45–end	Lk 23:26–49

TUESDAY   **Feria (☐ S Jane Frances de Chantal, Rel)**

12 G (or W)	MP	Ps: 106	II Sam 12:1–25	Ezek 14:12–end
			Acts 9:1–19a	II Cor 12:1–13
	Mass	*as Wednesday (or of the Saint) (S Jane originally appeared on December 12)*		
		Ezek 2:8 – 3:4; Ps 119:65–72; Mt 18:1–5 & 10 & 12–14		
	EP		Prov 15:18–end	Ezek 20:12–20
		Ps: 107	Mk 7:1–13	Lk 23:50 – 24:12

WEDNESDAY   **Feria (☐ Ss Pontianus, Pp and Hippolytus, Pr, Ms)**

13 G (or R)	MP	Ps: 110, 111, 112	II Sam 15:1–12	Ezek 20:27–44
			Acts 9:19b–31	II Cor 12:14–13 end
	Mass	*of Sunday; no Gl or Cr; Common Pref (or of the Saints) (**Jeremy Taylor, B;***		
		***Florence Nightingale; Octavia Hill**) (**Our Lady Refuge of Sinners; of Paletz**)*		
		Ezek 9:1–7 & 10 & 18–22; Ps 113; Mt 18:15–20		
	EP		Prov 18:10–end	Ezek 33:21–end
		Ps: 119:129–152	Mk 7:14–23	Lk 24:13–end

THURSDAY   **S Maximilian Kolbe, Pr, M**

14 R	MP	Ps: 113, 115	II Sam 15:13–end	Ezek 34:1–16
			Acts 9:32–end	Gal 1
	Mass	*of the Saint*		
		Ezek 12:1–12; Ps 78:58–64; Mt 18:21 – 19:1		

ASSUMPTION OF THE BVM (see p. 49)
R: Vigil Mass: I Chron 15:3–4 & 15–16 & 16:1–2; I Cor 15:54–57
Lk 11:27–28 (Collect of Vigil; Gl; Cr)

W	1 EP of foll	* I Sam 26	} or from the	†Prov 8:22–31	
		Ps: 72	* Lk 1:26–38	Vigil Mass	†Jn 19:23–27

FRIDAY

15 W	MP	Ps: 98, 138, 147:1–12	*Gen 3:1–15	†Isa 7:10–15
			*Eph 1:16 – 2:10 (=R:)	†Lk 11:27–28
	Mass	*Gl; Cr; R: Proper Pref; CW, of the Annunciation; or ASB 6*		
		R: Rev 11:19a & 12:1–6a & 10ab; Ps 45; I Cor 15:20–26; Lk 1:39–56		
		CW: Rev 11:19 – 12:6 & 10; Ps 45:10–17; Gal 4:4–7; Lk 1:46–55		
	2 EP	*Song of S 6:3–10		†Song of S 2:1–7
		Ps: 132	* I Cor 15:37–44 & 49–54 (55–7)	†Acts 1:6–14

SATURDAY   **Our Lady on Saturday or the Feria (☐ S Stephen of Hungary)**

16 W (or G)	MP	Ps: 120, 121, 122	II Sam 17:1–23	Ezek 37:15–end
			Acts 10:17–33	Gal 3
	Mass	*Introduction Paragraph 26(b)*		
		Ezek 18:1–10 & 13 & 30 & 32; Ps 51:1–3 & 15–17; Mt 19:13–15		
	G 1 EP of foll	Prov 24:23–end		Ezek 47:1–12
		Ps: 118	Mk 8:1–10	Jn 2

* † See p. 49 note 5.

✠ **SUNDAY**			**20th SUNDAY and WEEK of YEAR**		**TRINITY 13**
17	G	MP	Ps: 92	Ecclus 3:1–15	Ezek 33:1–11
				II Pet 3:14–18	Lk 6:20–38
R: Ps IV		Mass	*Gl; Cr; Sunday Pref (PROPER 15)*		
			CW: Isa 56:1 & 6–8; Ps 67; Rom 11:1–2a & 29–32; Mt 15:21–28		
			R: Isa 56:1 & 6–7; Ps 67; Rom 11:13–15 & 29–32; Mt 15:21–28 (Foreigners, too!)		
		2 EP		II Kgs 4:1–37	II Kgs 19:8–35
			Ps: 90	Acts 16:1–15	I Cor 1:1–25

MONDAY			**Feria**		
18	G	MP	Ps: 123, 124, 125, 126	II Sam 18:1–18	Ezra 1
				Acts 10:34–end	Gal 4:1 – 5:1
		Mass	*of Sunday; no Gl or Cr; Common Pref*		
			Ezek 24:15–24; Ps 78:1–8; Mt 19:16–22		
		EP		Prov 25:1–14	Ezra 3
			Ps: 127, 128, 129	Mark 8:11–21	Jn 3:1–21

TUESDAY			**Feria (☐ S John Eudes, Pr)**		
19	G (or W)	MP	Ps: 132, 133	II Sam 18:19 – 19:8a	Ezra 4
				Acts 11:1–18	Gal 5:2–end
		Mass	*as Monday (or of the Saint)*		
			Ezek 28:1–10; Ps 107:1–3 & 40 & 43; Mt 19:23–end		
		EP		Prov 25:15–end	Hag 1:1 – 2:9
			Ps: 134, 135	Mk 8:22–26	Jn 3:22–end

WEDNESDAY			**S Bernard, Ab, Dr**		
20	W	MP	Ps: 119:153–end	II Sam 19:8b–23	Zech 1:1–17
				Acts 11:19–end	Gal 6
		Mass	*of the Saint (**William and Catherine Booth**)*		
			Ezek 34:1–11; Ps 23; Mt 20:1–16		
		EP		Prov 26:12–end	Zech 1:18 – 2–end
			Ps: 136	Mk 8:27 – 9:1	Jn 4:1–26

THURSDAY			**☐ S Pius X, Pp**		
21	W	MP	Ps: 143, 146	II Sam 19:24–end	Zech 3
				Acts 12:1–17	Eph 1:1–14
		Mass	*of the Saint*		
			Ezek 36:23–28; Ps 51:7–12; Mt 22:1–14		
		EP		Prov 27:1–22	Zech 4
			Ps: 138, 140, 141	Mk 9:2–13	Jn 4:27–end

FRIDAY			**Our Lady Queen (EXETER & TRURO FESTUM)**		
22	W	MP	Ps: 142, 144	II Sam 23:1–7	Zech 6:9–end
				Acts 12:18–end	Eph 1:15–end
		Mass	*of our Lady (Isa 9:1–6; Ps 113; Lk 1:26–38)*		
			[Ezek 37:1–14; Ps 107:1–8; Mt 22:34–40]		
		EP		Prov 30:1–9, 24–31	Hag 2:10–end
			Ps: 145	Mk 9:14–29	Jn 5:1–23

SATURDAY			**Our Lady on Saturday or the Feria (S Rose of Lima, V)**		
23	W (or G)	MP	Ps: 147	II Sam 24	Ezra 5
				Acts 13:1–12	Eph 2:1–10
		Mass	*Introduction Paragraph 26(b) (or of the Saint) (**John Grandisson**)*		
			Ezek 43:1–7; Ps 85:7–end; Mt 23:1–12		
	G	1 EP of foll		Prov 31:10–end	Ezra 6
			Ps: 148, 149, 150	Mk 9:30–37	Jn 5:24–end

✠ *SUNDAY*   **21st SUNDAY and WEEK of YEAR**   **TRINITY 14**

24 G   MP   Ps: 104:1–25   Ecclus 3:17–29   Ezek 33:21–end
                                         Rev 1   Lk 6:39–end

R: Ps I   Mass *Gl; Cr; Sunday Pref (PROPER 16)* **S BARTHOLOMEW?** *see p. ii*
                   CW: Isa 51:1–6; Ps 138; Rom 12:1–8; Mt 16:13–20
                   R: Isa 22:19–23; Ps 138:1–3 & 6 & 8bc; Rom 11:33–36; Mt 16:13–20 (Peter Bears the Keys)
             2 EP II Kgs 6:8–23   II Kgs 22
                   Ps: 95   Acts 17:15–34   I Cor 1:26 – 2:9 (10–end)

MONDAY   **Feria (☐ S Louis; ☐ S Joseph Calasanz, Pr)**

25 G   MP   Ps: 1, 2, 3   I Kgs 1:5–31   Zech 7
      (or W)   Acts 13:13–43   Eph 2:11–end

             Mass *of Sunday; no Gl or Cr; Common Pref (or of the Saint)*
                   II Thess 1:1–5 & 11–12; Ps 39:1–9; Mt 23:13–22
             EP   Wisd 1   Zech 8
                   Ps: 4, 7   Mark 9:38–end   Jn 6:1–21

TUESDAY   **Feria (?S Ninian?, see p. 53, note 7)**

26 G   MP   Ps: 5, 6, 8   I Kgs 1:32 – 2:4; 2:10–12   Ezra 7
                                         Acts 13:44 – 14:7   Eph 3

             Mass *as Monday*
                   II Thess 2:1–3a & 14–17; Ps 98; Mt 23:23–36
             EP   Wisd 2   Ezra 8:15 end
                   Ps: 9, 10   Mk 10:1–16   Jn 6:22–40

WEDNESDAY   **S Monica**

27 W   MP   Ps: 119:1–32   I Kgs 3   Ezra 9
                                         Acts 14:8–end   Eph 4:1–16

             Mass *of the Saint*
                   II Thess 3:6–10 & 16–end; Ps 128; Mt 23:27–32
             EP   Wisd 3:1–9   Ezra 10:1–19
                   Ps: 11, 12, 13   Mk 10:17–31   Jn 6:41–end

THURSDAY   **S Augustine, B and Dr**

28 W   MP   Ps: 14, 15, 16   I Kgs 4:29 – 5:12   Neh 1
                                         Acts 15:1–21   Eph 4:17–30

             Mass *of the Saint*
                   I Cor 1:1–9; Ps 145:1–7; Mt 24:42–end
             2 EP Wisd 4:7–end   Neh 2
                   Ps: 18   Mk 10:32–34   Jn 7:1–24

FRIDAY   **The Beheading of S John Baptist**

29 R   MP   Ps: 17, 19   I Kgs 6:1, 11–28   Neh 4
                                         Acts 15:22–35   Eph 4:31 – 5:21

             Mass *of the Saint*
                   CW: Jer 1:4–10; Ps 11; Heb 11:32 – 12:2; Mt 14:1–12
                   R: Jer 1:17–19; Ps 71; Mk 6:17–29
                   [I Cor 1:17–25; Ps 33:6–12; Mt 25:1–13]
             EP   Wisd 5:1–16   Neh 5
                   Ps: 22   Mk 10:35–45   Jn 7:25–end

SATURDAY   **Our Lady on Saturday or the Feria (Ss Margaret Clitherow,**
                   Anne Line, and Margaret Ward, Ms)

30 W   MP   Ps: 20, 21, 23   I Kgs 8:1–30   Neh 6:1 – 7:4
      (or G)   Acts 15:36 – 16:5   Eph 5:22–end
      (or R) Mass *Introduction Paragraph 26(b)* **(John Bunyan) (Our Lady Health of the Sick;**
                   of Consolation)
                   I Cor 1:26–end; Ps 33:12–15 & 20–end; Mt 25:14–30
        G   1 EP of foll   Wisd 5:17 – 6:11   Neh 8
                   Ps: 24, 25   Mk 10:46–end   Jn 8:1–30

SEPTEMBER FESTIVALS

1. On **September 3** the Ebbsfleet Apostolic District celebrates S Gregory, who sent S Augustine (Ebbsfleet his landing place), as its Patron with the rank of Solemnity. Gl and Cr at mass; 1 EP on Saturday; Office from the Commons (p. xxx; a R: reading is Titus 1:7–11 & 2:1–8). Ebbsfleet propers: *Ecclus 47:8–11; Ps 36:1–3 & 7–8 & 10; Response verse 3; I Thess 2:2–8; Alleluia, Alleluia! The Lord sent me to bring the good news to the poor, and liberty to captives. Alleluia! Mt 16:13–19.*

2. **September 8** began in Jerusalem as a festival of the (5th Century) Basilica of Holy Mary's Birthplace; such tend to be the origins of early feasts of those who left no bodily relics (cf. September 29 and November 21). **September 14** also began in Jerusalem when, on the day after the Dedication of the Basilica of the Resurrection, the Wood of the Holy Cross was exposed for veneration.

3. Since CW provides no Office for **September 8**, we offer: *middle column* the ASB provision; *right hand column* a typological provision based upon Orthodox provisions, which your Compiler owes to Bishop Wilkinson of the Canadian TAC.

4. In Churches where August 15 is not observed, CW suggests **September 8** as the principal solemnity of our Lady. In such churches it will have a 1 EP. The Propers of August 14–15 are used.

5. The memorial of the Holy Name of Mary, which originally occupied the Sunday after her Nativity, has now been restored, as an optional memorial, to **September 12**. The mass propers may be had from your Compiler (see *PRAENOTANDA*) and remind us that, as well, as *Mary*, the Lord's Mother is 'named' *Mother of God* and *Ever-Virgin*. Rome urges those compiling local calendars who need a place for 'Our Lady of N' to consider September 12.

6. The old Octave day of the Nativity, **September 15**, which is also the day after Holy Cross Day, is, very neatly, the memorial of our Lady *Perdolentis*. (It was David Silk who had the happy notion of Englishing this as *Mary at the Cross*.) [The Stabat Mater, EH 115 (NEH 97) is optionally used as a Sequence at Mass. Divided, it is used for the Office Hymn.] But when CW put S John Chrysostom back onto its R: date of September 13, S Cyprian was evicted onto September 15, leaving our Lady out in the cold. This ORDO lets her back in and follows the significant tradition of associating S Cyprian with S Cornelius on their R: date of the 16th.

7. **September 16.** S Ninian, observed on the 16th in CW and other Anglican Calendars, is on August 26 in Roman Calendars.

8. **September 24** Our Lady of Walsingham is observed at Walsingham as a Solemnity, and as a Festum in the Diocese. Outside England, it is 'Our Lady of Ransom'.

9. **September 29** (originally the Dedication of the Roman Basilica of S Michael) had 'and All Angels' added by Dr Cranmer; 'and Ss Gabriel and Raphael' by the Roman revisers of 1969.

OCTOBER has traditionally been marked by the saying of the Rosary, followed by the Litany of our Lady. October 1, among Byzantines, commemorates the Protecting Veil of the Mother of God – ie., Our Lady, Mother of Mercy.

10. **October 7**, originally the feast of Our Lady of Victories, commemorated the victory of Christian arms at the Battle of Lepanto.

✠ SUNDAY

31   G   **22nd SUNDAY and WEEK of YEAR**   **TRINITY 15**

	MP	Ps: 107:1–32	Ecclus 11:(7–18) 19–28	Ezek 34:1–16
			Rev 3:14–22	Lk 7:36 – 8:3
R: Ps II	Mass	*Gl; Cr; Sunday Pref (PROPER 17)*		
		CW: Jer 15:15–21; Ps 26:1–8; Rom 12:9–21; Mt 16:21–28		
		R: Jer 20:7–9; Ps 63:2–6 & 8–9; Rom 12:1–2; Mt 16:21–27 (Bearing The Cross)		
	2 EP		II Kgs 6:24–25 & 7:3–20	Ezra 1:1–8
		Ps: 105:1–5	Acts 18:1–16	I Cor 3

SEPTEMBER

MONDAY

1   G   (or W)   **Feria (S Giles, Hermit)**

	MP	Ps: 27, 30	I Kgs 8:31–62	Neh 9:1–23
			Acts 16:6–24	Eph 6:1–9
	Mass	*of Sunday; no Gl or Cr; Common Pref (or of the Saint)*		
		I Cor 2:1–5; Ps 33:12–21; Lk 4:16–30		
	EP		Wisd 6:12–23	Neh 9:24–end
		Ps: 26, 28, 29	Mk 11:1–11	Jn 8:31–end

TUESDAY

2   G   **Feria**

	MP	Ps: 32, 36	I Kgs 8:63 – 9:9	Neh 13
			Acts 16:25–end	Eph 6:10–end
	Mass	*as Monday (**The Martyrs of Papua New Guinea**)*		
		I Cor 2:10–end; Ps 145:10–17; Lk 4:31–37		
	EP		Wisd 7:1–14	Dan 1
		Ps: 33	Mk 11:12–26	Jn 9

WEDNESDAY

3   W   **S Gregory the Great, Pp and Dr (see p. 53)**

	MP	Ps: 34	I Kgs 10:1–25	Dan 2:1–24
			Acts 17:1–15	Phil 1:1–11
	Mass	*of the Saint (**Our Lady Mother of the Good Shepherd**)*		
		I Cor 3:1–9; Ps 62; Lk 4:38–end		
	EP		Wisd 7:15 – 8:4	Dan 2:25–end
		Ps: 119:33–56	Mk 11:27–end	Jn 10:1–21

THURSDAY

4   G   (or W)   **Feria (S Cuthbert, B; S Birinus, B)**

	MP	Ps: 37	I Kgs 11:1–13	Dan 4:1–18
			Acts 17:16–end	Phil 1:12–end
	Mass	*as Monday (or of the Saint)*		
		I Cor 3:18–end; Ps 24:1–6; Lk 5:1–11		
	EP		Wisd 8:5–18	Dan 4:19–end
		Ps: 39, 40	Mk 12:1–12	Jn 10:22–end

FRIDAY

5   G   (or W)   **Feria (☐ Bl Teresa of Calcutta, V)**

	MP	Ps: 31	I Kgs 11:26–end	Dan 7:9–end
			Acts 18:1–21	Phil 2:1–11
	Mass	*as Monday (First Friday: Sacred Heart, see p. 38) (or of the Blessed)*		
		I Cor 4:1–5; Ps 37:3–8; Lk 5:33–end		
	EP		Wisd 8:21 – 9–end	Dan 9
		Ps: 35	Mk 12:13–17	Jn 11:1–44

SATURDAY

6   W   (or G)   **Our Lady on Saturday or the Feria**

	MP	Ps: 41, 42, 43	I Kgs 12:1–24	Dan 10
			Acts 18:22 – 19:7	Phil 2:12–end
	Mass	*(First Saturday: Immaculate Heart, see p. 38) (**Allen Gardiner**)*		
		I Cor 4:6–15; Ps 145:18–end; Lk 6:1–5		
	G 1 EP of foll		Wisd 10:15 – 11:10	Dan 12
		Ps: 45, 46	Mk 12:18–27	Jn 11:45–end

✠ SUNDAY
7 G   MP
R: Ps III   Mass

23rd SUNDAY and WEEK of YEAR		**TRINITY 16**
Ps: 119:17–32	Ecclus 27:30 – 28:9	Ezek 36:22–28 & 34–36
	Rev 8:1–5	Lk 9:46–end

Gl; Cr; Sunday Pref (PROPER 18)
CW: Ezek 33:7–11; Ps 119:33–40; Rom 13:8–14; Mt 18:15–20
R: Ezek 33:7–9; Ps 95; Rom 13:8–10; Mt 18:15–20 (Winning Back The Sinful Brother)

2 EP

	Ezek 12:21 – 13:16	Ezra 3
Ps: 108, 115	Acts 19:1–20	I Cor 13

MONDAY
8 W   MP

Birth of the BVM *(see p. 53)*

H: 214 or 215	Is 61:10 – 62:3 (R: Gen 3:9–20)	Gen 28:10–17
(NEH 181 or 183)		
Ps: 98, 138, 147:1–12	Jn 2:1–12	Rev 12:1–6

Mass

Gl; R: Pref of BVM; CW, of the Annunciation; or ASB 6
CW: Micah 5:1–4; Ps 45:10–17; Rom 8:18–30; Lk 1:39–47
R: Micah 5:1–4 or Rom 8:28–30; Mt 1: (1–16) 18–23

EP

H: 213 (NEH 180)	Prov 8:22–31	Ezek 44:1–4
Ps: 98, 138	Jn 19:23–27	Rev 7:9–12

TUESDAY
9 G   MP
(or W)

Feria (☐ S Peter Claver, Pr)

Ps: 48, 52	I Kgs 13:11–end	Esther 3
	Acts 19:21–end	Phil 4

Mass

of Sunday; no Gl or Cr; Common Pref (or of the Saint)
(Charles Fuge Lowder, Pr, Founder of SSC)
I Cor 6:1–11; Ps 149:1–5; Lk 6:12–19

EP

	Wisd 12:12–21	Esther 4
Ps: 50	Mk 12:35–end	Jn 12:20–end

WEDNESDAY
10 G   MP

Feria

Ps: 119:57–80	I Kgs 17	Esther 5
	Acts 20:1–16	Col 1:1–20

Mass

as Tuesday
I Cor 7:25–31; Ps 45:11–end; Lk 6:20–26

EP

	Wisd 13:1–9	Esther 6 & 7
Ps: 59, 60, 67	Mk 13:1–13	Jn 13

THURSDAY
11 G   MP

Feria

Ps: 56, 57, 63	I Kgs 18:1–20	I Macc 1:1–19
	Acts 20:17–end	Col 1:21 – 2:7

Mass

as Tuesday
I Cor 8:1–7 & 11–end; Ps 139:1–9; Lk 6:27–38

EP

	Wisd 16:15 – 17:1	I Macc 1:20–40
Ps: 61, 62, 64	Mk 13:14–23	Jn 14

FRIDAY
12 G   MP
(or W)

Feria (☐ The Most Holy Name of Mary)

Ps: 51, 54	I Kgs 18:21–end	I Macc 1:41–end
	Acts 21:1–16	Col 2:8–19

Mass

as Tuesday (or of our Lady) (Gal 4:4–7 or Eph 1:3–6 & 11–12; Magnificat; Lk 1:39–47)
I Cor 9:16–19 & 22–end; Ps 84:1–6; Lk 6:39–42

EP

	Wisd 18:6–19	I Macc 2:1–28
Ps: 38	Mk 13:24–31	Jn 15

SATURDAY
13 W   MP

S John Chrysostom, B, Dr

Ps: 68	I Kgs 19	I Macc 2:29–48
	Acts 21:17–36	Col 2:20 – 3:11

Mass

of the Saint
I Cor 10:14–22; Ps 116:10–end; Lk 6:43–end

R   1 EP of foll

	Isa 52:13 – 53:12	◁
Ps: 66	Eph 2:11–22	◁

✠ SUNDAY
14　R　MP　　The Exaltation of the Holy Cross (see p. 53)

✠ SUNDAY	R	MP	H: 96 (NEH 78)	Gen 3:1–15	◁
14			Ps: 2, 8, 146	Jn 12:27–36a	◁
R: Ps IV		Mass	*of the Feast; Gl; Cr; Pref of Cross (R:) or (CW) the Short Pref 'From the Fifth Sunday of Lent . . .'*		
			CW=R: Num 21:4–9; Ps 22:23–28 (R: 78); Phil 2:6–11; Jn 3:13–17		
		EP	H: 94 (NEH 79)	Isa 63:1–16	◁
			Ps: 110, 150	I Cor 1:18–25	◁

MONDAY
15　W

MONDAY			Our Lady at the Cross (see p. 53)		**(24th WEEK of YEAR)**
15	W	MP	Ps: 71	I Kgs 21	I Macc 3:1–26
				Acts 21:37 – 22:21	Col 3:12 – 4:1
		Mass	*of our Lady (Heb 5:7–9; Jn 19:25–7 or Lk 2:33–5)*		
			I Cor 11:17–26 & 33; Ps 40:7–11; Lk 7:1–10		
		EP		I Macc 1:1–19	I Macc 3:27–41
			Ps: 72, 75	Mk 14:1–11	Jn 17

TUESDAY
16　R

TUESDAY			Ss Cornelius, Pp and Cyprian, B, Ms (see p. 53)		
16	R	MP	Ps: 73	I Kgs 22:1–28	I Macc 3:42–end
				Acts 22:22 – 23:11	Col 4:2–end
		Mass	*of the Saints*		
			(*Edward Bouverie Pusey, Pr*)		
			I Cor 12:12–14 & 27–end; Ps 100; Lk 7:11–17		
		EP		I Macc 1:20–40	I Macc 4:1–25
			Ps: 74	Mk 14:12–25	Jn 18:1–27

WEDNESDAY
17　G (or W)

WEDNESDAY			Feria (□ S Robert Bellarmine, B and Dr; S Hildegard, Ab)*		
17	G (or W)	MP	Ps: 77	I Kgs 22:29–45	I Macc 4:26–35
				Acts 23:12–end	Philemon
		Mass	*of Sunday (24th; Trinity 17); no Gl or Cr; Common Pref (or of the Saint)*		
			I Cor 12:31b–13 end; Ps 33:1–12; Lk 7:31–35		
		EP		I Macc 1:41–end	I Macc 4:36–end
			Ps: 119:81–104	Mk 14:26–42	Jn 18:28–end

THURSDAY
18　G

THURSDAY			Feria		
18	G	MP	Ps: 78:1–39	II Kgs 1:2–17	I Macc 6:1–17
				Acts 24:1–23	I Thess 1
		Mass	*as Wednesday*		
			I Cor 15:1–11; Ps 118:1–2 & 17–20; Lk 7:36–end		
		EP		I Macc 2:1–28	I Macc 6:18–47
			Ps: 78:40–end	Mk 14:43–52	Jn 19:1–30

FRIDAY
19　G (or R) (or W)

FRIDAY			Feria (□ S Januarius, B & M; S Theodore, B, Rel)*		
19	G (or R)	MP	Ps: 55	II Kgs 2:1–18	I Macc 7:1–20
				Acts 24:24 – 25:12	I Thess 2:1–16
	(or W)	Mass	*as Wednesday (or of the Saint)*		
			I Cor 15:12–20; Ps 17:1–8; Lk 8:1–3		
		2 EP		I Macc 2:29–48	I Macc 7:21–end
			Ps: 69	Mk 14:53–65	Jn 19:31–end

SATURDAY
20　R

SATURDAY			S Andrew Kim Taegon, Pr, and all Martyrs of Korea and the Pacific†		
20	R	MP	Ps: 76, 79	II Kgs 4:1–37	I Macc 9:1–22
				Acts 25:13–end	I Thess 2:17 – 3 end
		Mass	*of the Saints*		
			I Cor 15:35–37 & 42–49; Ps 30:1–5; Lk 8:4–15		
	G	1 EP of foll		I Macc 2:49–end	I Macc 13:41–end & 14:4–15
			Ps: 81, 84	Mk 14:66–end	Jn 20

* Ember Days: see Introduction Paragraph 25.
† The R: memorial of S Andrew and the Korean Martyrs (Anglicans died as well as Roman Catholics) coincides with CW: John Coleridge Patteson, First Bishop of Melanesia and his Companions Martyrs. The Compiler suggests this convenient combination of today's commemorations.

✛ *SUNDAY*
21 G MP **25th SUNDAY and WEEK of YEAR**   **TRINITY 18**

✛ *SUNDAY*			**25th SUNDAY and WEEK of YEAR**	**TRINITY 18**
21	G	MP	Ps: 119:153–176 Isa 45:9–22	Dan 3
			Rev 14:1–5	Lk 11:37–end
R: Ps I		Mass	*Gl; Cr; Sunday Pref (PROPER 20)* **S MATTHEW?** *see p. ii*	
			CW: Jonah 3:10 – 4:11; Ps 145:1–8; Phil 1:21–30; Mt 20:1–16	
			R: Isa 55:6–9; Ps 145; Phil 1:20c–24 & 27; Mt 20:1–16 (God's More Generous Way)	
		2 EP	Ezek 33:23 & 30 – 34:10	Neh 2
			Ps: 119:113–136 Acts 26:1 & 9–25	Phil 2:1–18
MONDAY			*Feria*	
22	G	MP	Ps: 80, 82 II Kgs 5	Job 1
			Acts 26:1–23	I Thess 4:1–12
		Mass	*of Sunday; no Gl or Cr; Common Pref*	
			Prov 3:27–34; Ps 15; Lk 8:16–18	
		EP	I Macc 3:1–26	Job 2
			Ps: 85, 86 Mk 15:1–15	Jn 21
TUESDAY			☐ *S Pius of Pietrelcino, Pr*	
23	W	MP	Ps: 87, 89:1–18 II Kgs 6:1–23	Job 3
			Acts 26:24–end	I Thess 4:13 – 5:11
		Mass	*of the Saint, Padre Pio*	
			Prov 21:1–6 & 10–13; Ps 119:1–8; Lk 8:19–21	
		EP	I Macc 3:27–41	Job 4
			Ps: 89:19–end Mk 15:16–32	Heb 1
WEDNESDAY			☐ *Our Lady of Walsingham (outside England: of Ransom)*	
24	W	MP	Ps: 119:105–128 II Kgs 9:1–16	Job 5
			Acts 27:1–26	I Thess 5:12–end
		Mass	*of our Lady*	
			Prov 30:5–9; Ps 119:105–112; Lk 9:1–6	
		EP	I Macc 3:42–end	Job 6
			Ps: 91, 93 Mk 15:33–41	Heb 2
THURSDAY			*Feria* (S Sergius of Radonezh, Rel)*	
25	G (or W)	MP	Ps: 90, 92 II Kgs 9:17–end	Job 7
			Acts 27:27–end	II Thess 1
		Mass	*as Monday (or the Saint)* (**Lancelot Andrewes, B**)	
			Eccles 1:2–11; Ps 90:1–6; Lk 9:7–9	
		EP	I Macc 4:1–25	Job 8
			Ps: 94 Mk 15:42–end	Heb 3
FRIDAY			*Feria (☐ Ss Cosmas and Damian, Ms)*	
26	G (or R)	MP	Ps: 88, 95 II Kgs 12:1–19	Job 9
			Acts 28:1–16	II Thess 2
		Mass	*as Monday (or of the Saints)* (**Wilson Carlile**)	
			Eccles 3:1–11; Ps 144:1–4; Lk 9:18–22	
		EP	I Macc 4:26–35	Job 10
			Ps: 102 Mk 16:1–8	Heb 4:1–13
SATURDAY			*S Vincent de Paul, Pr*	
27	W	MP	Ps: 96, 97, 100 II Kgs 17:1–23	Job 11
			Acts 28:17–end	II Thess 3
		Mass	*of the Saint*	
			Eccles 11:9 – 12:8; Ps 90:1–2 & 12–17; Lk 9:43–45	
	G	1 EP of foll	I Macc 4:36–end	Job 12
			Ps: 104 Mk 16:9–end	Heb 4:14 – 5:10

---

* Anniversary of the Episcopal Ordination in 1996 of John, tenth Bishop of Fulham.

✠ *SUNDAY*   **26th SUNDAY and WEEK of YEAR**   **TRINITY 19 (see p. 53)**

28   G   MP   Ps: 125, 126, 127   Isa 48:12–21   Dan 5
                                      Lk 11:37–54   Lk 12:1–21

R: Ps II   Mass   *Gl; Cr; Common Pref (PROPER 21)*
                  CW: Ezek 18:1–4 & 25–32; Ps 25:1–8; Phil 2:1–13; Mt 21:23–32
                  R: Ezek 18:25–28; Ps 25; Phil 2:1–5 (6–11); Mt 21:28–32
                  (Who is Upright, Who The Sinner?)

           2 EP   Ezek 37:15–28   Ruth 1
                  Ps: 120, 123, 124   I Jn 2:22–29   Phil 3:1–16

MONDAY   **Michaelmas (see p. 53)**

29   W   MP   H: 241   Tobit 12:6–22 or Dan 12:1–4   II Kgs 6:8–17
                  Ps: 34, 150   Acts 12:1–11   Acts 12:1–11

           Mass   *Gl; R: Pref of Angels; ASB 21; CW Common Pref*
                  CW: Gen 28:10–17; Ps 103:19–22; Rev 12:7–12; Jn 1:47–51
                  R: Dan 7:7–9 & 13–14 or Rev 12:7–12; Ps 138; Jn 1:47–51

           EP   Dan 10:4–21   Dan 12:1–4
                  Ps: 138, 148   Rev 5   Rev 5

TUESDAY   **S Jerome, Pr, Dr**

30   W   MP   Ps: 103, 106   II Kgs 18:1–12   Job 15:1–16
                                     Phil 1:12–end   I Tim 1:18 – 2 end

           Mass   *of the Saint*
                  Job 3:1–3 & 11–17 & 20–23; Ps 88:14–19; Lk 9:51–56

           EP   I Macc 6:18–47   Job 16:1 – 17:2
                  Ps: 107   Jn 13:12–20   Heb 7

O C T O B E R   **MONTH OF THE ROSARY (see p. 53)**

WEDNESDAY   ☐ *S Teresa of the Child Jesus, V, Dr*

1   W   MP   Ps: 110, 111, 112   II Kgs 18:13–end   Job 17:3–end
                                     Phil 2:1–13   I Tim 3

          Mass   *of the Saint (**S Remigius, B; Anthony Ashley Cooper**)*
                 Job 9:1–12 & 14–16; Ps 88:1–6 & 11; Lk 9:57–end

          EP   I Macc 7:1–20   Job 18
                 Ps: 119:129–152   Jn 13:21–30   Heb 8

THURSDAY   ☐ *Holy Guardian Angels*

2   W   MP   Ps: 113, 115   II Kgs 19:1–19   Job 19
                                     Phil 2:14–end   I Tim 4

          Mass   *of the Angels (Exod 23:20–23; Ps 90; Mt 18:1–5 & 10)*
                 [Job 19:21–27a; Ps 27:13–16; Lk 10:1–12]

          EP   I Macc 7:21–end   Job 21
                 Ps: 114, 116, 117   Jn 13:31–end   Heb 9:1–14

FRIDAY   *Feria*

3   G   MP   Ps: 139   II Kgs 19:20–36   Job 22
                                     Phil 3:1 – 4:1   I Tim 5

          Mass   *of Sunday; no Gl or Cr; Common Pref (First Friday: Sacred Heart, see p. 38)*
                 Job 38:1 & 12–21 & 40:3–5; Ps 139:6–11; Lk 10:13–16

          EP   I Macc 9:1–22   Job 23
                 Ps: 130, 131, 137   Jn 14:1–14   Heb 9:15–end

SATURDAY   **S Francis of Assisi**

4   W   MP   Ps: 120, 121, 122   II Kgs 20   Job 24
                                     Phil 4:2–end   I Tim 6

          Mass   *of the Saint (First Saturday: Immaculate Heart, see p. 38)*
                 Job 42:1–3 & 6 & 12–end; Ps 119:169–176; Lk 10:17–24

        G   1 EP of foll   I Macc 13:41–end, 14:4–15   Job 25 & 26
                 Ps: 118   Jn 14:15–end   Heb 10:1–18

✠ *SUNDAY*			**27th SUNDAY and WEEK of YEAR**		**TRINITY 20***
5	G	MP	Ps: 128, 129, 134	Isa 49:13–23	Dan 6:1–23
				Lk 12:1–12	Lk 12:22–34
R: Ps III		Mass	*Gl; Cr; Sunday Pref (PROPER 22)*		
			CW: Isa 5:1–7; Ps 80:9–17; Phil 3:4b–14; Mt 21:33–46		
			R: Isa 5:1–7; Ps 80; Phil 4:6–9; Mt 21:33–44 (The Lord's Vineyard)		
		2 EP		Prov 2:1–11	Ruth 2:1–20a & 4:13–17
			Ps: 136	I Jn 2:1–17	Phil 4

MONDAY			**Feria (☐ S Bruno, Pr)**		
6	G	MP	Ps: 123, 124, 125, 126	II Kgs 21:1–18	Job 27
	(or W)			I Tim 1:1–17	Titus 1:1 – 2:8
		Mass	*of Sunday; no Gl or Cr; Common Pref (**William Tyndale Ref M**)*		
			Gal 1:6–12; Ps 111:1–6; Lk 10:25–37		
		EP		II Macc 4:7–17	Job 28
			Ps: 127, 128, 129	Jn 15:1–11	Heb 10:19–end

TUESDAY			**☐ Our Lady of the Rosary**		
7	W	MP	Ps: 132, 133	II Kgs 22:1 – 23:3	Job 29:1 – 30:1
				I Tim 1:18 – 2 end	Titus 2:9 – 3 end
		Mass	*of our Lady (R: Acts 1:12–14; Ps Mag; Lk 1:26–38)*		
			[Gal 1:13–end; Ps 139:1–9; Lk 10:38–end]		
		EP		II Macc 6:12–end	Job 31:13–end
			Ps: 134, 135	Jn 15:12–17	Heb 11:1–16

WEDNESDAY			**Feria**		
8	G	MP	Ps: 119:153–end	II Kgs 23:4–25	Job 32
				I Tim 3	II Tim 1
		Mass	*as Monday*		
			Gal 2:1–2 & 7–14; Ps 117; Lk 11:1–14		
		EP		II Macc 7:1–19	Job 33
			Ps: 136	Jn 15:18–end	Heb 11:17–end

THURSDAY			**Feria (Ss Denys, B, Comp, Ms; ☐ S John Leonardi, Pr)**		
9	G (or	MP	Ps: 143, 146	II Kgs 23:36 – 24:17	Job 38:1–21
	W or			I Tim 4	II Tim 2
	R)	Mass	*as Monday (or of the Saints) (**Robert Grosseteste, B**)*		
			Gal 3:1–5; Benedictus; Lk 11:5–13		
		EP		II Macc 7:20–41	Job 38:22–end
			Ps: 138, 140, 141	Jn 16:1–15	Heb 12:1–13

FRIDAY			**Feria (S Paulinus, B)**		
10	G	MP	Ps: 142, 144	II Kgs 24:18 – 25:12	Job 39
	(or W)			I Tim 5:1–16	II Tim 3
		Mass	*as Monday (or of the Saint) (**Thomas Traherne**)*		
			Gal 3:7–14; Ps 111:4–10; Lk 11:15–26		
		EP		Tobit 1	Job 40
			Ps: 145	Jn 16:16–22	Heb 12:14–end

SATURDAY			**Our Lady on Saturday of the Feria (S James, Dcn; S Ethelburga, Ab)**		
11	W	MP	Ps: 147	II Kgs 25:22–end	Job 41
	(or G)			I Tim 5:17–end	II Tim 4
		Mass	*Introduction Paragraph 26(b)† (or of the Saints)*		
			Gal 3:22–end; Ps 105:1–7; Lk 11:27–28		
	G	1 EP of foll		Tobit 2	Job 42
			Ps: 148, 149, 150	Jn 16:23–end	Heb 13

* See Introduction Appendix 2 for Dedication.

† Festival of our Lady Portaitissa, called the Iberian, on Mount Athos. A copy of this ikon is venerated in the shrine church at Walsingham. S Philip the Deacon enters the Church of Ireland as a Festum.

✠ *SUNDAY*   **28th SUNDAY and WEEK of YEAR**   **TRINITY 21**

12 G   MP   Ps: 138, 141   Isa 50:4–10   I Macc 2:1–22
                                          Lk 13:22–30   Lk 12:35–end
R: Ps IV   Mass   *Gl; Cr; Sunday Pref (PROPER 23)*
                     CW: Isa 25:1–9; Ps 23; Phil 4:1–9; Mt 22:1–14
                     R: Isa 25:6–10a; Ps 23; Phil 4:12–14 & 19–20; Mt 22:1–10 (11–14)
                     (The Lord's Great Banquet)
               2 EP   Prov 3:1–18   Ecclus 3:17–29
                     Ps: 139:1–18   I Jn 3:1–15   II Cor 1:1–22

MONDAY   **Feria (S Edward the Confessor)**

13 G   MP   Ps: 1, 2, 3   Judith 4   Prov 1:1–19
   (or W)   I Tim 6:1–10   Jas 1:1–11
               Mass   *of Sunday; no Gl or Cr; Common Pref (or of the Saint)* (**Our Lady of Iverskia**)
                     Gal 4:21–24 & 26–27 & 31 & 5:1; Ps 113; Lk 11:29–32
               EP   Tobit 3   Prov 1:20–end
                     Ps: 4, 7   Jn 17:1–5   Jas 1:12–end

TUESDAY   **Feria (☐ S Callistus I, Pp, M)**

14 G   MP   Ps: 5, 6, 8   Judith 5:1 – 6:4   Prov 2
   (or R)   I Tim 6:11–end   Jas 2:1–13
               Mass   *as Monday (or of the Saint)*
                     Gal 5:1–6; Ps 119:41–48; Lk 11:37–41
               EP   Tobit 4   Prov 3:1–26
                     Ps: 9, 10   Jn 17:6–19   Jas 2:14–end

WEDNESDAY   **S Teresa of Avila, V, Dr**

15 W   MP   Ps: 119:1–32   Judith 6:10 – 7:7   Prov 3:27 – 4:19
                                          II Tim 1:1–14   Jas 3
               Mass   *of the Saint*
                     Gal 5:18–end; Ps 1; Lk 11:42–46
               EP   Tobit 5:1 – 6:1a   Prov 4:20 – 5:14
                     Ps: 11, 12, 13   Jn 17:20–end   Jas 4

THURSDAY   **Feria (☐ S Hedwig, Rel; ☐ S Margaret Mary Alacoque)**

16 G   MP   Ps: 14, 15, 16   Judith 7:19–end   Prov 6:1–19
   (or W)   II Tim 1:15 – 2:13   Jas 5
               Mass   *as Monday (or of the Saint)* (**Nicolas Ridley, B, Ref M**) (**The Purity of Our Lady**)
                     Eph 1:1 & 3–10; Ps 98:1–4; Lk 11:47–end
               EP   Tobit 6:1b–end   Prov 8
                     Ps: 18   Jn 18:1–11   I Pet 1:1–12

FRIDAY   **S Ignatius of Antioch, B, M**

17 R   MP   Ps: 17, 19   Judith 8:9–end   Prov 9
                                          II Tim 2:14–end   I Pet 1:13–end
               Mass   *of the Saint*
                     Eph 1:11–14; Ps 33:1–6 & 12; Lk 12:1–7
               EP   Tobit 7   Prov 10:1–22
                     Ps: 22   Jn 18:12–27   I Pet 2:1–10

SATURDAY   **S Luke, Evangelist**

18 R   MP   Ps: 145, 146   Isa 55   Isa 61:1–6
                                          Lk 1:1–4   II Tim 3:10–end
               Mass   *Gl; R: Pref of the Apostles; CW, of Saints*
                     CW: Isa 35:3–6 or Acts 16:6–12a; Ps 147:1–7; II Tim 4:5–17; Lk 10:1–9
                     R: II Tim 4:10–17b; Ps 145; Lk 10:1–9
        G   1 EP of foll   Tobit 8   Prov 12:10–end
                     Ps: 24, 25   Jn 18:28–end   I Pet 3:8–end

✠ *SUNDAY*

19   G

R: Ps I

					TRINITY 22
		29th SUNDAY and WEEK of YEAR			
	MP	Ps: 145, 149	Isa 54:1–14		I Macc 2:49–69
			Lk 13:31–35		Lk 13:18–end
	Mass	*Gl; Cr; Sunday Pref (PROPER 24)*			
		CW: Isa 45:1–7; Ps 96:1–9 (10–13); I Thess 1:10; Mt 22:15–22			
		R: Isa 45:1 & 4–6; Ps 96; I Thess 1:1–5b; Mt 22:15–21 (God and Caesar)			
	2 EP		Prov 4:1–8		Ecclus 4:11–28
		Ps: 142; 143:1–11	I Jn 3:16 – 4:6		II Cor 4

MONDAY

20   G

		Feria		
	MP	Ps: 27, 30	Judith 10	Prov 14:9–27
			II Tim 4:1–8	I Pet 4:1–11
	Mass	*of Sunday; no Gl or Cr; Common Pref*		
		Eph 2:1–10; Ps 100; Lk 12:13–21		
	EP		Tobit 9	Prov 15:18–end
		Ps: 26, 28, 29	John 19:1–16	I Pet 4:12–end

TUESDAY

21   G

		Feria		
	MP	Ps: 32, 36	Judith 11	Prov 16:31 – 17:17
			II Tim 4:9–end	I Pet 5
	Mass	*as Monday*		
		Eph 2:12–end; Ps 85:7–end; Lk 12:35–38		
	EP		Tobit 10	Prov 18:10–end
		Ps: 33	Jn 19:17–30	I Jn 1:1 – 2:6

WEDNESDAY

22   G

		Feria		
	MP	Ps: 34	Judith 12	Prov 20:1–22
			Titus 1	I Jn 2:7–17
	Mass	*as Monday (**Our Lady of Kazan**)*		
		Eph 3:2–12; Ps 98; Lk 12:39–48		
	EP		Tobit 11	Prov 22:1–16
		Ps: 119:33–56	Jn 19:31–end	I Jn 2:18–end

THURSDAY

23   G
   (or W)

		Feria (☐ S John of Capestrano, Pr)		
	MP	Ps: 37	Judith 13	Prov 24:23–end
			Titus 2	I Jn 3:1–18
	Mass	*as Monday (or of the Saint)*		
		Eph 3:14–end; Ps 33:1–6; Lk 12:49–53		
	EP		Tobit 12	Prov 25
		Ps: 39, 40	Jn 20:1–10	I Jn 3:19 – 4:6

FRIDAY

24   G
   (or W)

		Feria (☐ S Antony Mary Claret, B)		
	MP	Ps: 31	Judith 15:1–13	Prov 26:12–end
			Titus 3	I Jn 4:7–end
	Mass	*as Monday (or of the Saint) (**Our Lady Joy of the Afflicted**)*		
		Eph 4:1–6; Ps 24:1–6; Lk 12:54–end		
	EP		Tobit 13:1 – 14:1	Prov 27:1–22
		Ps: 35	Jn 20:11–18	I Jn 5

SATURDAY

25   W
   (or G)
   (or R)

    G

		Our Lady on Saturday or the Feria (Ss Crispin and Crispinian, Ms)		
	MP	Ps: 41, 42, 43	Judith 15:14 – 16 end	Prov 30:1–16
			Philemon	II Jn
	Mass	*Introduction Paragraph 26(b) (or of the Saints)*		
		Eph 4:7–16; Ps 122; Lk 13:1–9		
	1 EP of foll		Tobit 14:2–end	Prov 31:10–end
		Ps: 45, 46	Jn 20:19–end	III Jn

NOVEMBER FESTIVALS

1. CW encourages All Saints on November 2, and the English RC makes this transference (see Introduction Paragraph 5A), so we follow the convergence. All Souls follows on the Monday.

2. **November 3**: ALL SOULS DAY. Rome retains the custom that arose (1915) during the carnage of the First World War, of allowing every priest to say three masses, for these intentions: (1) the priest's own; (2) for all the Departed; (3) to make up for testamentary masses neglected or forgotten, and for the souls of all, especially youth, who fall victim to the appalling carnage of war. The Missal provides three sets of texts; CW 'Pastoral Services' could be drawn upon. (The three masses should be said at different times.) PHG provides the Office.

3. **November 8**: the old Octave day of All Saints. Your Compiler suggests the traditional Western title 'All Saints of N' and continues to offer Office readings from PHG. Mass propers: National Appendix to Weekday Missal under November 6. The Collect, borrowed from Roman sources by 1928, is: We beseech thee/ask you, O Lord, to multiply thy/your grace upon us who commemorate the Saints of our nation; that, as we rejoice to be their fellow citizens on earth, so we may have fellowship also with them in heaven. (Between November 6 and 16, most religious orders have a festival of All their Saints.)

4. **November 9**: Dedication of the Lateran Basilica, the papal Cathedral in Rome, dedicated to Christ (replicated by S Augustine in the dedication of Canterbury Cathedral), is a Festum of the Lord. Office and Mass readings from Appendix 2. *Gl and Cr; Dedication Pref.* In creating a 'Little Rome' at Canterbury, the Augustinian Mission there also perpetuated the Roman dedications to Ss Peter and Paul and S Mary (see August 5). In R: this displaces the Sunday.

5. **November 11**: Where the great patriarch of Western Monasticism, S Martin of Tours, is Patron, PHG suggests:1EP Isa 58:6–12 & Acts 20:28–35 MP Ezek 34:11–16 & 11 Cor 4:1–10 2EP Mal 2:5–7 & Phil 4:4–9 (Psalms 1, 15, 112). Forward in Faith celebrates this day as its foundation day.

6. **November 17, 18, and 19**:

	R:	CW
November 17 18 19	Ss Hilda†, Hugh†, Elizabeth†, or BVM on Saturday Dedication of SS Peter and Paul†*	S Hugh† Elizabeth† S Hilda† or S Mechtild†

† Optional – all of them, in both Calendars.
* Mass: Acts 28:11–16 & 30–31; Ps 98; Mt 14:22–33. Propers of Apostles NOT of Dedication; the mass theme is Rome as the place of their linked martyrdoms.

7. **November 21**: Presentation of our Lady: *not* a mistaken duplication of February 2! Originally (543) the Dedication of New S Mary's By The Temple in Jerusalem, it is one of the year's Twelve Great Festivals among the Orthodox, from whom it reached Saxon England (it was not grudgingly accepted by Rome until 1585). FESTUM in Ebbsfleet.

Your Compiler tentatively suggests that those for whom their Cathedral is no longer their Mother Church because they doubt the orders of its Eucharistic celebrants might treat this as a substitute for the Solemnity of the Dedication of the Cathedral.

The *mythos* that, aged three, Mary was lodged as a contemplative in the Temple and fed by angels with fruit as from the Tree of Life in Eden highlights her immaculate sanctity and anticipates her bodily Assumption.

✠ *SUNDAY*   **30th SUNDAY and WEEK of YEAR; CW: LAST AFTER TRINITY**
BCP: TRINITY 23

26	G	MP	Ps: 119:137–152	Isa 59:9–20	I Macc 3:42–end
				Lk 14:1–14	Lk 14:15–end
R: Ps II		Mass	*Gl; Cr; Sunday Pref (PROPER 25)*		
			CW: Lev 19:1–2 & 15–18; Ps 1; I Thess 2:1–8; Mt 22:34–46		
			R: Exod 22:21–26; Ps 18; I Thess 1:5c–10; Mt 22:34–40 (The Commandment of Love)		
		2 EP		Eccles 11 & 12	Ecclus 4:29 – 6:1
			Ps: 119:89–104	II Tim 2:1–7	II Cor 5

MONDAY   **Feria**

27	G	MP	Ps: 44	Azariah and Song 1–27*	Ecclus 1:1–10
				Phil 1	Acts 1
		Mass	*of Sunday; no Gl or Cr; Common Pref*		
			Eph 4:32 – 5:8; Ps 1; Lk 13:10–17		
		EP		Joel 1:1–14	Ecclus 1:11–end
			Ps: 47, 49	Jn 13:1–11	Acts 2:1–21

TUESDAY   **Ss Simon & Jude, Apostles**

28	R	MP	Ps: 116, 117	Wisd 5:1–16 or Isa 45:18–26	Isa 45:18–end
				Lk 6:12–16	Lk 6:12–19
		Mass	*Gl; R: Pref of Apostles; CW, of Saints*		
			CW: Isa 28:14–16; Ps 119:89–96; Eph 2:19–22; Jn 15:17–27		
			R: Eph 2:19–22; Ps 19; Lk 6:12–16 (17–19)		
		EP		I Macc 2:42–66	Jer 3:11–18
			Ps: 119:1–16	or Jer 3:11–18	
				Jude 1–4 & 17–25	Eph 2:11–end

WEDNESDAY   **Feria**

29	G	MP	Ps: 119:57–80	Song 28–end	Ecclus 4:11–28
				Phil 2:1–13	Acts 4:5–31
		Mass	*as Monday (**James Hannington, B, M**)*		
			Eph 6:1–9; Ps 145:10–20; Lk 13:22–30		
		EP		Joel 1:15–end	Ecclus 4:29 – 6:1
			Ps: 59, 60, 67	Jn 13:12–20	Acts 4:32 – 5:11

THURSDAY   **Feria**

30	G	MP	Ps: 56, 57, 63	Susannah 1–27	Ecclus 6:14–31
				Phil 2:14–end	Acts 5:12–end
		Mass	*as Monday*		
			Eph 6:10–20; Ps 144:1–2 & 9–11; Lk 13:31–35		
		EP		Joel 2:1–17	Ecclus 7:27–end
			Ps: 61, 62, 64	Jn 13:21–30	Acts 6:1 – 7:16

FRIDAY   **Feria**

31	G	MP	Ps: 51, 54	Susannah 28–end	Ecclus 10:6–8 & 12–24
				Phil 3:1 – 4:1	Acts 7:17–34
		Mass	*as Monday (**Martin Luther, Pr, Rel**)*		
			Phil 1:1–11; Ps 111; Lk 14:1–6		
		EP		Joel 2:18–27	Ecclus 11:7–28
			Ps: 38	Jn 13:31–end	Acts 7:35 – 8:4

N O V E M B E R   **(ALL SAINTS: see p. 62)**

SATURDAY   *Our Lady on Saturday or the Feria*

1	W	MP	Ps: 68	Bel and the Dragon	Ecclus 14:20 – 15:10
				Phil 4:2–end	Acts 8:4–25
		Mass	*Introduction Paragraph 26(b) (First Saturday: Immaculate Heart, see p. 38)*		
			Phil 1:18–26; Ps 42:1–7; Lk 14:1 & 7–11		
			ALL SAINTS		
	W	1 EP of foll; H: 249 (NEH 196)		Ecclus 44:1–15 or Isa 40:27–31	Isa 65:17–end
			Ps: 1, 5	Rev 19:6–10 (R: 5:1–14)	Heb 11:32 – 12:2

* Ferial CW Office Readings this week: see PRAENOTANDA.

✠ *SUNDAY*			**ALL SAINTS**		
2	W	MP	Ps: 15, 84, 149	Isa 35:1–9	Wisd 3:1–9
				Lk 9:18–27	Rev 19:6–10
R: Ps III		Mass	*Gl; Cr; R: and CW: Proper Pref*		
			CW: Rev 7:9–17; Ps 34:1–10; I Jn 3:1–3; Mt 5:1–12		
			R: Rev 7:2–4 & 9–14; Ps 24:1–6; I Jn 3:1–3; Mt 5:1–12		
		2 EP*	H: 249 (NEH 196)	Isa 65:17–25	Ecclus 44:1–15
			Ps: 148, 150	Heb 11:32 – 12:2	Heb 12:18–24

MONDAY			**ALL SOULS DAY (see p. 62)**		
3	B or P	MP	Ps: 90	Job 19:21–27a	◁
				II Cor 4:16 – 5:10	Jn 5:24–9
		Mass	*of the day; no Gl or Cr; Seq ad lib (EH 351 NEH 524); ASB Pref (16) is the traditional Pref for*		
			the Departed. R: additionally offers four more Prefaces of Christian Death.		
			CW: Lam 3:17–26 & 31–33 or Wisd 3:1–9; Ps 23 or 27:1–6 & 16–17; Rom 5:5–11 or		
			I Pet 1:3–9; Jn 5:19–25 or Jn 6:37–40		
			R: (others allowed) Isa 25:6–9; Rom 5:5–11; Jn 6:37–40 (three Masses may be said)		
		EP	H: 350 (NEH 327)	Dan 12:1–3	Isa 38:10–20
			Ps: 121, 130	I Thess 4:13–end	Rev 1:9–18

TUESDAY			☐ *S Charles Borromes, B*		
4	W	MP	Ps: 73	Dan 2:1–24	Ecclus 18:1–14
				Rev 2:1–11	Act 10:1–23
		Mass	*of the Saint*		
			Phil 2:5–11; Ps 22:22–27; Lk 14:15–24		
		EP		Isa 1:21–end	Ecclus 19:13–end
			Ps: 74	Mt 2:1–15	Act 10:24–end

WEDNESDAY			*Feria*		
5	G	MP	Ps: 77	Dan 2:25–end	Ecclus 21:1–17
				Rev 2:12–end	Acts 11:1–18
		Mass	*of Sunday; no Gl or Cr; Common Pref*		
			Phil 2:12–18; Ps 27:1–5; Lk 14:25–33		
		EP		Isa 2:1–11	Ecclus 22:6–22
			Ps: 119:81–104	Mt 2:16–end	Acts 11:19–end

THURSDAY			*Feria (S Leonard, Hermit)*		
6	G	MP	Ps: 78:1–39	Dan 3:1–18	Ecclus 22:27 – 23:15
	(or W)			Rev 3:1–13	Acts 12:1–24
		Mass	*as Wednesday (or of the Saint)* (**William Temple, B**)		
			Phil 3:3–8; Ps 105:1–7; Lk 15:1–10		
		EP		Isa 2:12–end	Ecclus 24:1–22
			Ps: 78:40–end	Mt 3	Acts 12:25 – 13:12

FRIDAY			*Feria (S Willibrord, B)*		
7	G	MP	Ps: 55	Dan 3:19–end	Ecclus 24:23–end
	(or W)			Rev 3:14–end	Acts 13:13–43
		Mass	*as Wednesday (or of the Saint) (First Friday: Sacred Heart, see p. 38)*		
			Phil 3:17 – 4:1; Ps 122; Lk 16:1–8		
		EP		Isa 3:1–15	Ecclus 27:30 – 28:9
			Ps: 69	Mt 4:1–11	Acts 13:44 – 14:7

SATURDAY			**All Saints of England (see p. 62)**		
8	W	MP	Ps: 1, 34	Isa 61:4–9	◁
			H: 253: 1, 3, 7–13	II Cor 4:5–15	◁
		Mass	*of the Saints. Gl. R: Pref of All Saints Missal, National Appendix, November 6*		
			CW: Ecclus 44:1–15; Ps 15; Rev 19:5–10; Jn 17:18–23		
			PHG = R: Ecclus 44:1–15; Ps 15; Lk 6:17–23		
	G	1 EP of foll		Isa 4:2 – 5:7	Ecclus 34:9–end
			Ps: 81, 84	Mt 4:12–22	Acts 15:1–21

* May be followed by an EP for the Departed.

✠ *SUNDAY*

32nd SUNDAY and WEEK of YEAR; CW: 3rd BEFORE ADVENT
(BCP see PRAENOTANDA). REMEMBRANCE SUNDAY (see p. 62)*

9	G	MP	Ps: 91	Deut 17:14–20	Ecclus 15:11–end
				I Tim 2:1–7	Lk 17:1–10
R: Ps IV		Mass	*Gl; Cr; Sunday Pref*		
			CW: Wisd 6:12–16; Ps Wisd 6:17–20; I Thess 4:13–18; Mt 25:1–13		
			R: Wisd 6:12–16; Ps 63; I Thess 4:13–14 (15–18); (Mt 25:1–13 (Be awake)		
		2 EP		Judg 7:2–22	Ecclus 27:30 – 28:9
			Ps: 20, 82	Jn 15:9–17	I Tim 6:1–16 (17–end)

MONDAY   **S Leo the Great, Pp**

10	W	MP	Ps: 80, 82	Dan 4:19–end	Ecclus 35
				Rev 5	Acts 15:22–35
		Mass	*of the Saint*		
			Titus 1:1–9; Ps 24:1–6; Lk 17:1–6		
		EP		Isa 5:8–24	Ecclus 37:7–15
			Ps: 85, 86	Mt 4:23 – 5:12	Acts 15:36 – 16:5

TUESDAY   **S Martin of Tours, B**

11	W	MP	Ps: 87, 89:1–18	Dan 5:1–12	Ecclus 38:1–14
				Rev 6	Acts 16:6–end
		Mass	*of the Saint*		
			Titus 2:1–8 & 11–14; Ps 37:3–5 & 30–32; Lk 17:7–10		
		EP	H:188	Isa 5:25–end	Ecclus 38:24–end
			Ps: 89:19–end	Mt 5:13–20	Acts 17:1–15

WEDNESDAY   ☐ **S Josaphat, B, M**

12	R	MP	Ps: 119:105–128	Dan 5:13–end	Ecclus 39:1–11
				Rev 7:1–4, 9–end	Acts 17:16–end
		Mass	*of the Saint*		
			Titus 3:1–7; Ps 23; Lk 17:11–19		
		EP		Isa 6	Ecclus 39:13–end
			Ps: 91, 93	Mt 5:21–37	Acts 18:1–23

THURSDAY   **Feria**

13	G	MP	Ps: 90, 92	Dan 6	Ecclus 42:15–end
				Rev 8	Acts 18:24 – 19:7
		Mass	*of Sunday; no Gl or Cr; Common Pref (**Charles Simeon, Pr**)*		
			Phil 7–20; Ps 146:4–end; Lk 17:20–25		
		EP		Isa 7:1–17	Ecclus 43:1–12
			Ps: 94	Mt 5:38–end	Acts 19:8–20

FRIDAY   **Feria (☐ The Reading Martyrs, Festum in the Reading area)**

14	G (or R)	MP	Ps: 88, 95	Dan 7:1–14	Ecclus 43:13–end
				Rev 9:1–12	Acts 19:21–end
		Mass	*as Thursday (or of the Saints) (**Samuel Seabury, B**)*		
			II Jn 4–9; Ps 119:1–8; Lk 17:26–end		
		EP		Isa 8:1–15	Ecclus 50:1–24
			Ps: 102	Mt 6:1–18	Acts 20:1–16

SATURDAY   **Our Lady on Saturday or the Feria (☐ S Albert the Great, B, Dr)**

15	W (or G)	MP	Ps: 96, 97, 100	Dan 7:15–end	Ecclus 51:1–12
				Rev 9:13–end	Acts 20:17–end
		Mass	*Introduction Paragraph 26(b) (or of the Saint)*		
			*(**Our Lady Mother of Divine Providence**)*		
			III Jn 5:8; Ps 112; Lk 18:1–8		
	G	1 EP of foll		Isa 8:16 – 9:7	Ecclus 51:13–end
			Ps: 104	Mt 6:19–end	Acts 21:1–16

* In R: the Dedication of the Luteran Basilica, as a Festival of the Lord, displaces the Sunday Mass and Office. See p. 62, note 4.

✠ *SUNDAY*   **33rd SUNDAY and WEEK of YEAR; CW: 2nd BEFORE ADVENT**
                               (BCP see PRAENOTANDA)

16   G   MP   Ps: 98   Dan 10:19–21   Ecclus 42:15–end
                                            Rev 4   Lk 20:1–19
R: Ps I   Mass   *Gl; Cr; Sunday Pref*
                        CW: Zeph 1:7 & 12–18; Ps 90:1–8 (9–11) 12; I Thess 5:1–11; Mt 25:14–30
                        R: Prov 31:10–13 & 19–20 & 30–31; Ps 128; I Thess 5:1–6;
                        Mt 25:14–15 (16–18) 19–20 (21–30) (The Profitable Servant)
                 2 EP   I Kgs 1: (1–14) 15–40   Ecclus 43:13–26
                        Ps: 89:19–37   Rev 1:4–18   II Tim 1:1–14 (15–2:7)

MONDAY   *See p. 62*
17   G   MP   Ps: 98, 99, 101   Dan 8:1–14   Eccles 1
         (or W)   Rev 10   Acts 21:17–36
                 Mass   *Rev 1:1–4 & 2:1–5; Ps 1; Lk 18:35–end*
                 EP   Isa 9:8 – 10:4   Eccles 2:1–23
                        Ps: 103, 105   Mt 7:1–12   Acts 21:37 – 22:22

TUESDAY   *See p. 62*
18   G   MP   Ps: 106   Dan 8:15–end   Eccles 3:1–15
         (or W)   Rev 11:1–14   Acts 22:23 – 23:11
                 Mass   *Rev 3:1–6 & 14–end; Ps 15; Lk 19:1–10*
                 EP   Isa 10:5–19   Eccles 3:16 – 4:6
                        Ps: 107   Mt 7:13–end   Acts 23:12–end

WEDNESDAY   *See p. 62*
19   G   MP   Ps: 110, 111, 112   Dan 9:1–19   Eccles 4:7–end
         (or W)   Rev 11:15–end   Acts 24:1–23
                 Mass
                        Rev 4; Ps 150; Lk 19:11–28
                 EP   Isa 10:20–32   Eccles 5
                        Ps: 119:129–152   Mt 8:1–13   Acts 24:24 – 25:12

THURSDAY   *Feria (S Edmund, KM)*
20   G   MP   Ps: 113, 115   Dan 9:20–end   Eccles 6
         (or R)   Rev 12   Acts 25:13–end
                 Mass   *of Sunday; no Gl or Cr; Common Pref (or of the Saint)* (**Priscilla Lydia Sellon, Rel**)
                        Rev 5:1–10; Ps 149:1–5; Lk 19:41–44
                 EP   Isa 10:33 – 11:9   Eccles 7:1–14
                        Ps: 114, 116, 117   Mt 8:14–22   Acts 26

FRIDAY   ☐ *The Presentation of the BVM (EAD FESTUM)*
21   W   MP   Ps: 139   Dan 10:1 – 11:1   Eccles 7:15–end
                                            Rev 13:1–10   Acts 27:1–26
                 Mass   *of our Lady*
                        R: Zech 2:14–17; Ps Mag; Mt 12:46–50
                        [Rev 10:8–11; Ps 119:65–72; Lk 19:45–end]
                 EP   Isa 11:10–12 end   Eccles 8
                        Ps: 130, 131, 137   Mt 8:23–end   Acts 27:27–end

SATURDAY   *S Cecilia, V, M*
22   R   MP   Ps: 120, 121, 122   Dan 12   Eccles 9
                                            Rev 13:11–end   Acts 28:1–15 (16–end)
                 Mass   *of the Saint*
                        Rev 11:4–12; Ps 144:1–9; Lk 20:27–40
         W   1 EP of foll   Isa 10:33 – 11:9   ◁ [Eccles 10:5–18]
                        Ps: 99, 100   I Tim 6:11–16   ◁ [Acts 28:16–end]

✠ SUNDAY   **SOLEMNITY OF CHRIST THE KING (BCP: PRAENOTANDA)**

23   W

MP	H: 142 (NEH 129)	Isa 4:2 – 5:7	◁ [Eccles 11 & 12]
	Ps: 29, 110	Lk 19:29–38	◁ [Heb 11:1–16]
Mass	*Gl; Cr; Proper Pref (CW page 327 = R:)*		
	CW: Ezek 34:11–16 & 20–24; Ps 95:1–7a; Eph 1:15–23; Mt 25:31–46		
	R: Ezek 34:11–12 & 15–17; Ps 23; I Cor 15:20–26 & 28; Mt 25:31–46		
2 EP	H: 419 pt 2 (NEH 386)	I Macc 2:15–29	◁ [Mal 3:1–6 & 4]
	Ps: 93, 97	Mt 28:16–20	◁ [Heb 11:17 – 12:2]

MONDAY   □ **S Andrew Dung Lac, Pr, Comp, Ms**   **34th WEEK of YEAR**

24   R

R: Ps II

MP	Ps: 123, 124, 125, 126	Isa 40:1–11	Wisd 1
		Rev 14:1–13	Mt 5:1–16
Mass	*of the Saints*		
	Rev 14:1–5; Ps 24:1–6; Lk 21:1–4		
EP		Isa 14:3–20	Wisd 2
	Ps: 127, 128, 129	Mt 9:18–34	Rev 1

TUESDAY   *Feria (S Catherine of Alexandria)*

25   G
(or R)

MP	Ps: 132, 133	Isa 40:12–26	Wisd 3:1–9
		Rev 14:14–15 end	Mt 5:17–end
Mass	*of Sunday; no Gl or Cr; Common Pref (or of the Saint)* (**Isaac Watts**)		
	Rev 14:14–19; Ps 96; Lk 21:5–11		
EP		Isa 17	Wisd 4:7–end
	Ps: 134, 135	Mt 9:35 – 10:15	Rev 2:1–17

WEDNESDAY   *Feria*

26   G

MP	Ps: 119:153–end	Isa 40:27 – 41:7	Wisd 5:1–16
		Rev 16:1–11	Mt 6:1–18
Mass	*as Tuesday*		
	Rev 15:1–4; Ps 98; Lk 21:12–19		
EP		Isa 19	Wisd 6:1–21
	Ps: 136	Mt 10:16–33	Rev 2:18 – 3:6

THURSDAY   *Feria*

27   G

MP	Ps: 143, 146	Isa 41:8–20	Wisd 7:15 – 8:4
		Rev 16:12–end	Mt 6:19–end
Mass	*as Tuesday* (**Our Lady of the Miraculous Medal; of Novgorod**)		
	Rev 18:1–2 & 21–23 & 19:1–3 & 9; Ps 100; Lk 21:20–28		
EP		Isa 21:1–12	Wisd 8:5–18
	Ps: 138, 140, 141	Mt 10:34 – 11:1	Rev 3:7–end

FRIDAY   *Feria*

28   G

MP	Ps: 142, 144	Isa 41:21 – 42:9	Wisd 8:21–9 end
		Rev 17	Mt 7:1–14
Mass	*as Tuesday*		
	Rev 20:1–4 & 11 – 21:2; Ps 84:1–6; Lk 21:29–33		
EP		Isa 22:1–14	Wisd 10:15 – 11:10
	Ps: 145	Mt 11:2–19	Rev 4

SATURDAY   *Our Lady on Saturday or the Feria*

29   W

MP	Ps: 147	Isa 42:10–17	Wisd 11:21 – 12:2
		Rev 18	Mt 7:15–end
Mass	*Introduction Paragraph 26(b)* (**Day of Prayer for Missionaries**)		
	Rev 22:1–7; Ps 95:1–7; Lk 21:34–36		
P 1 EP of foll		Isa 24	Wisd 12:12–21
	Ps: 148, 149, 150	Mt 11:20–end	Rev 5

---

* Ferial Office Hymns, as before: BUT, optionally Dies Irae: EH 351 (NEH 524). MP vv 1–8; EP vv 9–18.

2008			
NOV:	30	SUNDAY	ADVENT 1
DEC:	1	Monday	Feria
	2	Tuesday	Feria
	3	Wednesday	S Francis
	4	Thursday	(S John)
	5	Friday	Feria
	6	Saturday	(S Nicolas)
	7	SUNDAY	ADVENT 2
	8	Monday	MARY
	9	Tuesday	(S John)
	10	Wednesday	Feria
	11	Thursday	(S Damasus)
	12	Friday	Our Lady
	13	Saturday	S Lucy
	14	SUNDAY	ADVENT 3
	15	Monday	Feria
	16	Tuesday	Feria
	17	Wednesday	[O Sapientia]
	18	Thursday	Feria
	19	Friday	Feria
	20	Saturday	Feria
	21	SUNDAY	ADVENT 4

2008			
DEC:	22	Monday	Feria
	23	Tuesday	Feria
	24	Wednesday	Christmas Eve
	25	Thursday	CHRISTMAS
	26	Friday	S Stephen
	27	Saturday	S John
	28	SUNDAY	HOLY FAMILY
	29	Monday	In the Octave
	30	Tuesday	In the Octave
	31	Wednesday	In the Octave
2009			
JAN:	1	Thursday	MARY
	2	Friday	Ss Basil and Gregory
	3	Saturday	(Name of Jesus)
	4	SUNDAY	EPIPHANY transferred
	5	Monday	Feria
	6	Tuesday	[EPIPHANY]
	7	Wednesday	(S Raymund)
	8	Thursday	Feria
	9	Friday	Feria
	10	Saturday	Feria
	11	SUNDAY	BAPTISM

ET CUM SPIRITU TUO

Older generations of clergy will not need to be reminded of this anecdote; but it may not be as familiar to a more recent generation. Mervyn Stockwood, bishop of Southwark, found himself exasperated by the PA system of a south London church. "There's something wrong with this bloody microphone", he growled to his chaplain. He was right; the congregation heard only a distorted rumble; but they decided to do their best: **"And also with you"**, they neatly replied.

But Rome has now decided to shred that response. So **"And with your spirit"** is now prescribed. It will take some getting used to; as the Roman cardinal responsible observed, the change will "no doubt occasion some temporary discomfort". He went on to explain why it was necessary. "The literal translation in its historical context has always been understood in relation to the crucial distinction of liturgical roles between their priest and the people".

Since the 1960s liturgical and biblical scholars have been pointing out that *Et cum spiritu tuo* is not an old-fashioned semitic way of saying *And with you too*. It refers to the particular endowment of the Spirit which the priestly celebrant possesses. As Greek and Syrian patristic sources make clear, God's holy people are praying that their priest, endowed with the Spirit in his ordination, may have the Lord's help to perform his sacramental role. (We could adduce here *Addai and Mari* among liturgical evidence; Theodoret and John Chrysostom among the Fathers; W.C. Van Unnik among biblical scholars; Dom Bernard Botte and Fr Robert Taft among – respectively – Western and Eastern liturgical experts.)

There is another joke here, of course. Modern Anglican translators slavishly followed the corrupt and horrible English translation of the Roman Liturgy which followed Vatican II, and so we are saddled with a mistake which Rome itself is now abandoning. Why didn't we think for ourselves? Why didn't we preserve the sacral dialect of the BCP tradition?

J.W.H.

2009 (B1)

JANUARY

	E	B	2	3
Sun	**4**	11	18	25
Mon	5	12	19	26
Tue	6	13	20	27
Wed	7	14	21	28
Thu	1	8	15	22	29
Fri	2	9	16	23	30
Sat	3	10	17	24	31

FEBRUARY

	4	5	6	7
Sun	1	8	15	22
Mon	2	9	16	23
Tue	3	10	17	24
Wed	4	11	18	**25**
Thu	5	12	19	26
Fri	6	13	20	27
Sat	7	14	21	28

MARCH

	1	2	3	4	5
Sun	1	8	15	22	29
Mon	2	9	16	23	30
Tue	3	10	17	24	31
Wed	4	11	18	25	
Thu	5	12	19	26	
Fri	6	13	20	27	
Sat	7	14	21	28	

APRIL

	P	E	2	3
Sun		5	**12**	19	26
Mon		6	13	20	27
Tue		7	14	21	28
Wed	1	8	15	22	29
Thu	2	9	16	23	30
Fri	3	10	17	24	
Sat	4	11	18	25	

MAY

	4	5	6	7	P
Sun	3	10	17	24	**31**
Mon	4	11	18	25	
Tue	5	12	19	26	
Wed	6	13	20	27	
Thu	7	14	**21**	28	
Fri	1	8	15	22	29	
Sat	2	9	16	23	30	

JUNE

	T	11	12	PP
Sun		7	14	21	**28**
Mon	1	8	15	22	29
Tue	2	9	16	23	30
Wed	3	10	17	24	
Thu	4	**11**	18	25	
Fri	5	12	19	26	
Sat	6	13	20	27	

JULY

	14	15	16	17
Sun	5	12	19	26
Mon	6	13	20	27
Tue	7	14	21	28
Wed	1	8	15	22	29
Thu	2	9	16	23	30
Fri	3	10	17	24	31
Sat	4	11	18	25	

AUGUST

	18	19	A	21	22
Sun	2	9	**16**	23	30
Mon	3	10	17	24	31
Tue	4	11	18	25	
Wed	5	12	19	26	
Thu	6	13	20	27	
Fri	7	14	21	28	
Sat	1	8	15	22	29	

SEPTEMBER

	23	24	25	26
Sun	6	13	20	27
Mon	7	14	21	28
Tue	1	8	15	22	29
Wed	2	9	16	23	30
Thu	3	10	17	24	
Fri	4	11	18	25	
Sat	5	12	19	26	

OCTOBER

	27	28	29	30
Sun	4	11	18	25
Mon	5	12	19	26
Tue	6	13	20	27
Wed	7	14	21	28
Thu	1	8	15	22	29
Fri	2	9	16	23	30
Sat	3	10	17	24	31

NOVEMBER

	AS	32	33	CK	1
Sun	1	8	15	22	29
Mon	2	9	16	23	30
Tue	3	10	17	24	
Wed	4	11	18	25	
Thu	5	12	19	26	
Fri	6	13	20	27	
Sat	7	14	21	28	

DECEMBER

	2	3	4	HF
Sun		6	13	20	27
Mon		7	14	21	28
Tue	1	8	15	22	29
Wed	2	9	16	23	30
Thu	3	10	17	24	31
Fri	4	11	18	**25**	
Sat	5	12	19	26	

Sundays are numbered 'of the Year' or 'of Lent' or 'of Easter' or 'of Advent.'

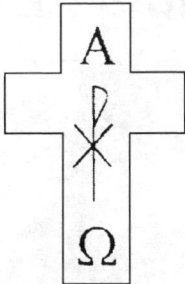

CHASTE

Churches Alert to Sex Trafficking Across Europe

Helping traumatised survivors find hope and a new future

- Developing Safe Housing capacity
- Creating resources for churches
- Addressing demand
- Training chaplaincy
- Educational intervention
- Influencing Government
- Working with the UKHTC
- Facilitating research
- *NOT FOR SALE SUNDAY* - Raising awareness

Click www.chaste.org.uk

Call 0845 456 9335

Text CHASTE to **82540** to donate **£1.50**
Or **NOT4SALE** to donate **£5.00**
CHASTE receives 92% after fees - Standard network charges apply

Post to CHASTE, P.O. Box 983, Cambridge, CB23 4WY

Company Limited by Guarantee no.4862586 Charity Registration No. 1106353

**ROYAL ARMY
CHAPLAINS' DEPARTMENT**

Take a leap of faith

Not all Chaplains jump out of aircraft but if you'd
like to take your ministry to new heights why not
become an Army Chaplain?
Working side by side with the world's youngest
and most dynamic workforce, you'll become a
valued member of our team.
For further information contact,
MOD Chaplains (A) Trenchard Lines,
Upavon, Pewsey, Wiltshire SN9 6BE
www.armychaplains.mod.uk
or call 08457 300 111 and quote ref: ORDO

ARMY

BE THE BEST

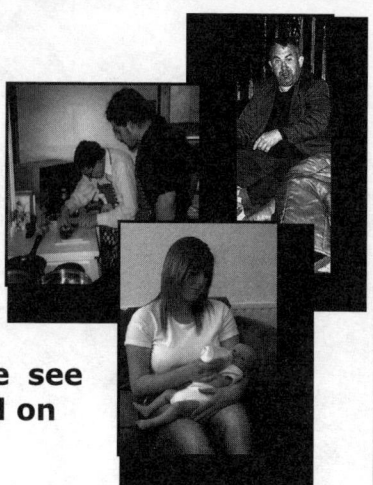
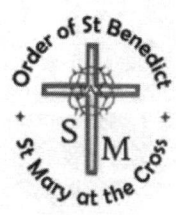